FIRST GRADE TEACHER'S MONTH-BY-MONTH ACTIVITIES PROGRAM

Elizabeth Crosby Stull

THE CENTER FOR APPLIED
RESEARCH IN EDUCATION
West Nyack, New York 10995

© 1990 by
THE CENTER FOR APPLIED
RESEARCH IN EDUCATION
West Nyack, NY

10 9 8 7 6 5 4 3

Library of Congress Cataloging-in-Publication Data

Stull, Elizabeth Crosby.
    First grade teacher's month-by-month activities program/
Elizabeth Crosby Stull.
        p.   cm.
    Includes bibliographical references.
    ISBN 0–87628–314–8
    1. Education, Primary—United States—Activity programs. 2. First
grade (Education—United States. I. Title. II. Title: 1st grade
teacher's month-by-month activities program.
LB1537.S84   1990
372.19—dc20   90–38396
                                                                        CIP

C3148-8
0-87628-314-8

 **THE CENTER FOR APPLIED
RESEARCH IN EDUCATION
BUSINESS & PROFESSIONAL DIVISION**
A division of Simon & Schuster
West Nyack, New York 10995

Printed in the United States of America

"The curriculum is so much necessary raw material but warmth is the vital element for the growing plant and for the soul of the child."

Carl G. Jung

This book is for those teachers who provide a warm, secure environment for young children so that the seeds of learning can take root. Under their care, we all flourish.

Many thanks to Diane Turso, Developmental Editor at The Center, who added her special touch to this manuscript, and also printed the names of the months.

And my thanks to Win Huppuch, Vice President at The Center, for continued support. We meet him in October as Winfield the Fire Fighting Bear.

E.C.S.

ABOUT THE AUTHOR

Elizabeth Crosby Stull, Ph.D. (The Ohio State University), has over 20 years of experience in education as a primary teacher and teacher educator. She began her career as a teacher of grades 1, 2, and 4 in the public schools of Greece Central, Camillus, and Pittsford in upstate New York, and is currently an assistant professor of education at Otterbein College in a suburb of Columbus, Ohio.

Dr. Stull has published many articles in professional journals such as *Instructor* and *Early Years* and is coauthor, with Carol Lewis Price, of *Science and Math Enrichment Activities for the Primary Grades* (The Center, 1987) and *Kindergarten Teacher's Month-by-Month Activities Program* (The Center, 1987). In addition, she has written *Children's Book Activities Kit* (The Center, 1988), which pertains to integrating children's literature into the classroom, and is a contributing author to *The Primary Teacher's Ready-to-Use Activities Program,* a monthly program also published by The Center.

Dr. Stull is a member of the National Association for the Education of Young Children and the International Reading Association.

ABOUT THIS BOOK

The *First Grade Teacher's Month-by-Month Activities Program* offers over 400 activities and over 100 full-page activity sheets to help you create an effective first grade environment. When planning for first grade, there are several important points to keep in mind:

- *Philosophy*—What do we know about child development and how does it relate to primary education? In what ways do children learn best?

- *Goals*—What are the educational goals of the school district, the faculty, the parents, and the children? What concepts need to be developed and learned?

- *Curriculum and Instruction*—How can we provide an attractive and inviting classroom that conveys the message that there is learning in progress, and that the curriculum is being implemented? How much flexibility does the teacher have in setting up a schedule? Does the classroom meet the needs of all types of learners?

- *Evaluation*—Is each child making progress? Are there opportunities for activities that offer reinforcement, skill building, and enrichment according to the specific needs of the students?

The activities in this book address these four areas. Divided into sections for each month of the school year, the book includes the following skill areas:

1. *Recommended Books*—Each month's listing of recommended books gives a brief description of the books. Read these books to your students during the particular month. The stories relate to the skill areas you will cover.

2. *Reading Skills Activities*—These activities help to teach and reinforce basic reading skills such as letter-sound relationships, and provide opportunities for language development. Storybook characters, such as Alligator, Ogre, and Love Bug, are developed throughout the months to help with long and short vowel sounds, and the structure of language. Integrating children's literature into the curriculum is encouraged, and, later in the year, a whole language approach is addressed.

3. *Math Skills Activities*—These activities lend themselves to manipulatives and a "hands on" approach to introduce and reinforce the concept

that math is a tool that helps us with counting, the calendar, money, addition and subtraction, fractions, estimation, prediction, and graphing.

4. *Science Skills Activities*—These activities include collecting and classifying rocks, setting up a science tools center, learning about ecology, and growing plants from seeds.

5. *Other Skill Areas Activities*—These activities relate to the particular month of the year. For example, your students will learn about pets in September, animal hibernation in January, and National Library Week in May.

6. *Reproducible Activity Pages*—At the end of each month are at least ten ready-to-use, full-page activity sheets that relate to some of the activities in that particular month. These activity pages can be reproduced as many times as needed for use with your students.

The *First Grade Teacher's Month-by-Month Activities Program* will give you an opportunity to work with enthusiastic and curious youngsters in setting the foundation for their learning during this cornerstone year.

Elizabeth Crosby Stull

SOME CHARACTERISTICS OF SIX-YEAR-OLDS

The average six-year-old looks forward to first grade with great anticipation and high expectations. Many have already been exposed to a wide variety of pre-reading and pre-math experiences, and are ready to get down to business. It is not unusual, however, to have tears the first day because of the increased expectations placed upon the child to perform. Tears are infectious, and make the others uneasy. What will you do? You need to allay these fears and to reassure all children that they've come to the right place—because in first grade, they will learn to do many wonderful things, even if they don't know how to do them right now.

EMOTIONALLY, the average six-year-old is:

- eager, exuberant, active, and wants to please
- restless and tires easily
- aggressive and less cooperative than the five-year-old
- highly imaginative and enjoys creative expression
- in need of encouragement, warmth, and an abundance of patience from you

PHYSICALLY, the average six-year-old is:

- losing baby teeth and getting permanent teeth
- developing large muscle coordination more rapidly than small muscle control
- at a high activity level and cannot stay still for long
- in need of at least ten hours of sleep per night

SOCIALLY, the average six-year-old is:

- friendly and wants to be first
- inconsistent in level of maturity—can be babyish and yet wise
- likes to have and be "best friends"
- in need of help in developing manners
- energetically involved in dramatic play and can problem-solve through play situations
- in need of supervision from a caring teacher

INTELLECTUALLY, the six-year-old learns best by direct experience, and by concrete manipulation of objects. They are, most likely, in the Piagetian Stage of Pre-operations. They are beginning to understand the cause-and-effect relationship of actions, although still centered on their own perspective. They begin to organize their world in an increasingly orderly and systematic manner.

The six-year-old is, usually, in the Preschematic Stage of Art Development (*Creative and Mental Growth*, Lowenfeld and Brittain). As first graders, they are developing associations between their own drawings/paintings and the world around them. The more detailed the drawings, the more awareness the child is showing toward the outside world. Exaggeration of body parts is common. The drawing is a record of concepts, feelings, and perceptions. The drawing *is* the child.

Finally, the six-year-old is a potential work of art, ready to be molded, and the first grade teacher has the awesome responsibility of being a sculptor!

SPECIFIC FORMS
TO USE IN FIRST GRADE

HOP-TO-IT ATTITUDE
ASSESSMENT FORMS

The Hop-to-It Reading Attitude Assessment and the Hop-to-It Math Attitude Assessment forms are designed to help you determine where the student is in relation to attitudes and feelings about the subject matter. Since the student's attitude toward a subject helps to determine the level of success with the subject, this is invaluable information. The student can fill out the form as you read each sentence. Directions are on the forms. Also, be sure to use math and reading flash cards daily.

OUR WEEKLY SCHEDULE

This form is useful for reading group plans, and can be kept in each teacher's edition. It is also useful for more specific plans in math, or any other subject area. In addition, later in the year, it can be used in individual student folders with the students who are reading independently, writing, working at learning centers, or on projects.

The Weekly Schedule can also be sent home to parents with arrival and departure times, lunch time, special class periods (art, music, physical education, library, and so on). It can be used during American Education Week, and during any other special event weeks. It is helpful for parents to have this information.

BUS LIST FOR ROOM NUMBER ____

In each square at the top, put a bus number and the names of students riding that bus. Make as many spaces as needed for the bottom. Post this by the door. At the end of the day, the bus list is a helpful aid. For the substitute teacher it is invaluable.

LITTLE RED HEN NOTES

This note paper is designed to be sent home to parents to tell them what you are "hatching" in first grade. The note paper can be used for individual notes, or it can be enlarged and used for a class newsletter that goes home monthly (or more often). Keeping parents informed of special projects, special events, and what's going on in general is helpful for busy parents. Keep it short.

PARENT CONFERENCE GUIDE

Duplicate one sheet per student and keep them in your student file folders. When it comes time for parent conferencing, you can use this guide for jotting down notes. During and after the conference, you can record information on the reverse side. This record will help when it comes time to formally write the conferences for school records.

CUT LETTER ALPHABET

This serves as a guide for folding paper and cutting letters. The sheet is self-explanatory. Use 9″ × 12″ paper when you want giant letters. Keep all of the letters that you cut and use them again on bulletin boards and charts, even if the colors vary. Also, they can be laminated and sorted by students for skill building.

HOP-TO-IT READING ATTITUDE ASSESSMENT

How does the rabbit FEEL about Reading? Read each statement to the student. The student can draw the rabbit where (s)he feels it will jump. (Or put an X on the line.) BIG JUMP—lots of excitement. LITTLE JUMP—not much enthusiasm.

PRACTICE MAKING THE RABBIT:

1. It's story time.

2. I'm going to show you the ABCs. You tell me what sound they make.

3. Today we're going to go on a "reading walk" outside.

4. Today we're going to learn three new words.

5. I'll put the words on the chalkboard. You tell me what they are.

6. Time to get out your reading workbook and turn to page six.

7. I'll go through the flashcards. You tell me what the words are.

8. Copy this story from the chalkboard.

9. I'd like you to write your own story.

10. I'll read you your favorite story. You have to pick it out.

11. Today we're going to work with beginning and ending sounds.

HOP-TO-IT MATH ATTITUDE ASSESSMENT

How does the rabbit FEEL about Mathematics? Read each statement to the student. The student can draw the rabbit where (s)he feels it will jump. (Or put an X on the line.) BIG JUMP—lots of excitement. LITTLE JUMP—not much enthusiasm.

PRACTICE MAKING THE RABBIT:

1   We're going to play a math game now.

2.   Practice your number facts. Print carefully.

3   Today we're going to measure with the BIG yardstick.

4.   Work with a partner and practice your number facts.

5.   Write your numerals from 1–100.

6.   Everybody take off your shoes. We're going to make a big graph.

7.   It's your turn at the computer.

8.   Your math papers have been corrected. We will now pass them out.

9.   Practice your math on the chalkboard during recess.

10.   Get out your math books and turn to page 43.

11.   Today we're going to go on a hunt for different shapes.

Our Weekly Schedule ✳

Date: _____

Time ↓	Mon.	Tues.	Wed.	Thurs.	Fri.	Notes

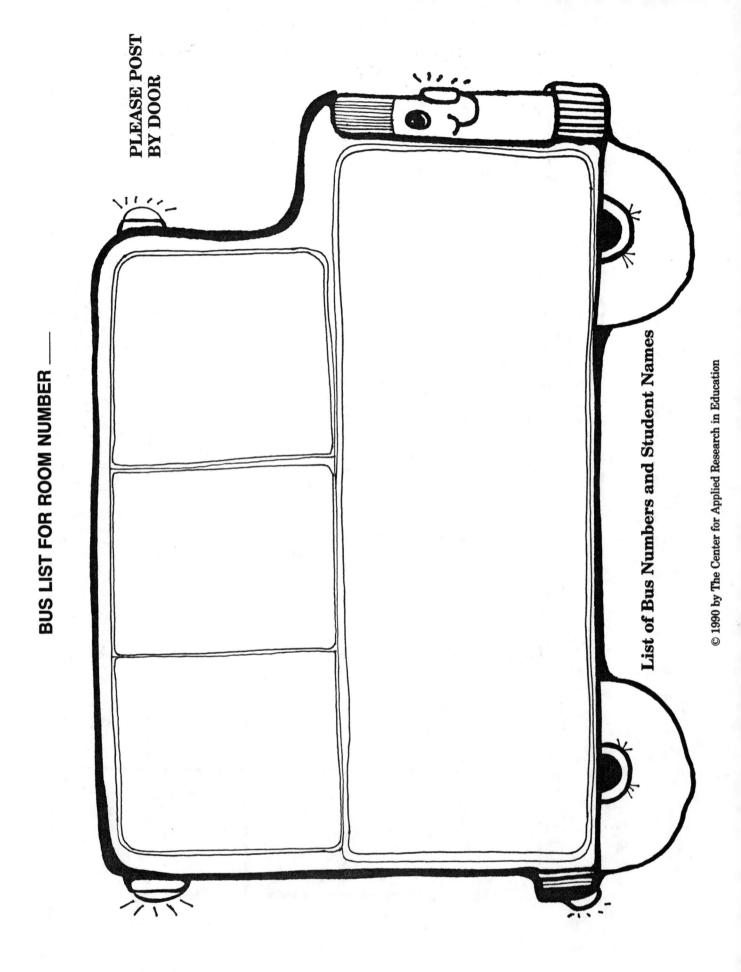

Little Red Hen Notes

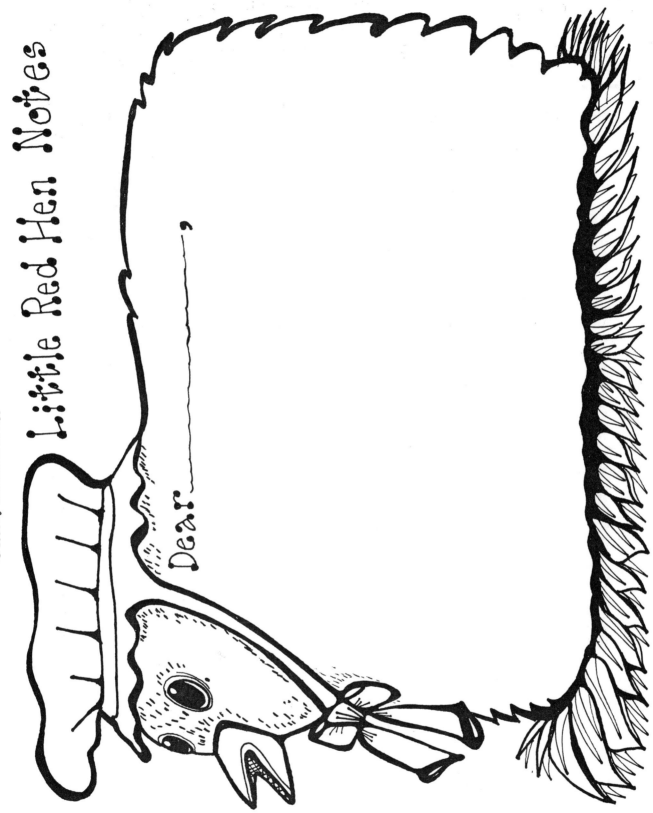

Dear

Parent Conference Guide

Student_____ Date:_____

Opening Positive Comments:

Academic Progress:
1. Reading-
2. Math-
3. Social St.-
4. Science-
5. Writing-
6.

Social Growth:
1. cooperation
2. sharing
3. listening
4.
5.
6.

Anecdotes:

Samples Attached

General Assessment and Suggestions:

CUT LETTER ALPHABET

This is an easy way to make letters for bulletin boards and charts. The size can vary.

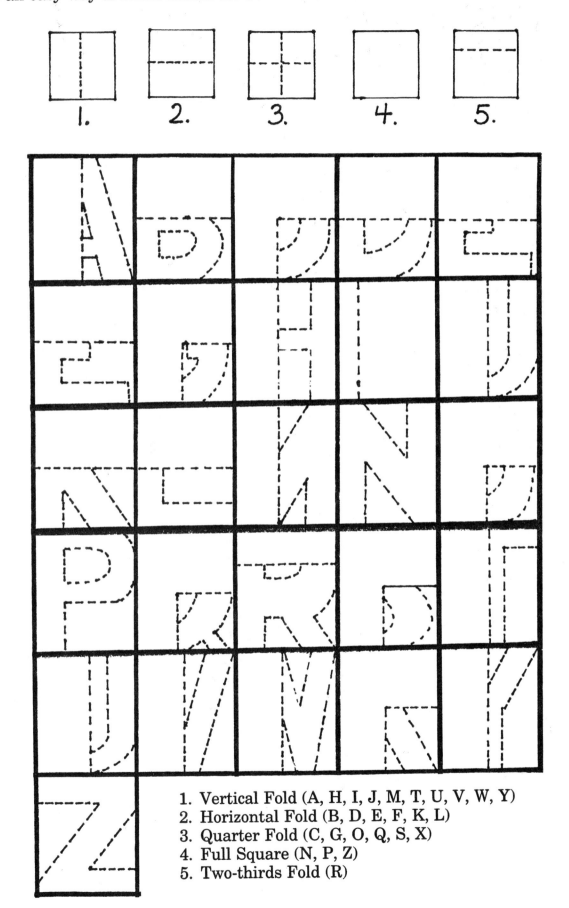

1. Vertical Fold (A, H, I, J, M, T, U, V, W, Y)
2. Horizontal Fold (B, D, E, F, K, L)
3. Quarter Fold (C, G, O, Q, S, X)
4. Full Square (N, P, Z)
5. Two-thirds Fold (R)

CONTENTS

OCTOBER ● 37

NOVEMBER ● 74

DECEMBER ● 111

JANUARY ● 147

FEBRUARY ● 182

MARCH • 216

APRIL • 251

MAY/JUNE ● 291

Author Checklist (five steps for writing) (318)
Cluster Bubbles (working with st, pl, sp, fl, cr) (319)
Let's Read Labels (using food cans and boxes for reading) (320)
Write a Want Ad for a Lost Pet (writing; critical thinking) (321)
Who's on the Farm? (reading and following directions) (322)
Walk a Shape (body movement; math) (323)
Merry, Merry Month of Math (calendar of activities) (324)
My Favorite Number (writing a story) (325)
Tens and Ones Grapes (working with tens and ones; odd and even) (326)
Read an Ice Cream Cone Graph (reading information) (327)
Plan Your Own Number Book (designing and making a book) (328)
Special Delivery from Duke the Dog (positive reinforcement) (330)
The Butterfly Story (stages of butterfly development) (331)
The Butterfly Story (butterfly shape) (332)
Red, White, and Bloom (Memorial Day flowers) (333)
Promise Coupons (Mother's Day; Father's Day) (334)
Bev's Blue Ribbon Winner (favorite book award) (335)
Ocean Pollution Patrol (ecology awareness) (336)
The July Activity Frog (25 activities for July) (337)
The August Busy Bear (25 activities for August) (338)

Labels on Tables

Make printed labels and place them on items in the room so that students will begin to associate the words with the print. Some examples include: table, clock, door, desk, sink, books, coats, cupboard, window, flag. Be sure to make an extra set of flashcards, too. Have students match the flashcards with the correct label on the items. Begin to build an awareness of the following:

- What is the beginning letter? What is the ending letter?
- Can we find something else in the room that begins with that very same sound?
- Does anyone's name begin with that letter?
- What other items do we need to make a label for in the room?

Here We Go 'Round the Alphabet Bush

ABC Bush

Make a set of ABC flashcards. Put them in a large cylindrical container that you have covered with bright green construction paper. Cut it so that it fans out like a bush at the top. Place the ABC bush on the floor. Students can join hands and make a circle around the bush. Sing "Here We Go 'Round the ABC Bush" to the tune of "Here We Go 'Round the Mulberry Bush." Stop, and then call upon one student to reach into the ABC bush, pull out a flashcard, and say the letter and something that begins with that sound. If unable to do so, the student may call upon another child to be a helper. Repeat the procedure.

Read Storybooks

Have an abundance of picture books in the classroom and read aloud to the students at least once in the morning and once in the afternoon. For children who have had limited experiences with books, this introduces them to a wealth of new characters, new stories, bright pictures, and the feeling that reading is pleasurable and something they want to learn to do for themselves. The books help to elicit stories that the children want to share, and this is good for their oral language development and for strengthening listening habits. However, the attention span of the group must be taken into consideration when determining how much time to spend on this activity. (See the October reading section for activities with ABC books.)

Begin the Day with Reading and Writing

On the chalkboard, have a formula such as:

Today is _____ (day of week)
It is _____ (month, date, year)
Today we will _____ (print something that you will
                         be doing in school today)

Do this as a total group activity. At first, you will fill in the "Today we will" sentence(s) to serve as a model. Later in the month, begin to ask students what they'd like to see printed there. Students will begin to make connections between speaking (oral language) and writing (written language).

Colorful Consonant Charts

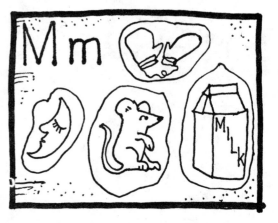

Paste a large cut-out of a letter in the upper left corner of a sheet of 12″ x 18″ construction paper. Then find large magazine pictures that begin with that sound and paste them to the construction paper. Display the chart and refer to it daily. Then begin with another color and another letter, using the same procedure until at least six colorful charts are on display. (Some good starter letters are S, T, R, B, M, and P.) Use the charts to play guessing games. First, model the game by saying, "I'm thinking of something that begins with T and it has a caboose." Have students raise their hands if they know, and call upon them for the answer. The student who gets it correct then comes to the chart and creates an "I'm thinking of . . ." story (perhaps with your help, if necessary).

When you have more than six charts, begin to replace them with new letters one by one. Make a book of the more familiar letters and have it available for students to use during their free-choice time or during playtime.

The ABC Animals

Encourage children to bring in stuffed animals and stuffed toys from home. Hopefully, you will get an assortment. Find out the name of each animal and toy, and line them up in alphabetical order. Which letter is represented the most? Are some letters not represented? What toy or animal *could* go in the unrepresented spots? Finding alphabet books in the library will be helpful to keep on hand for the students.

Also encourage the students to bring their stuffed animals or toys to story time. "Notice what excellent listeners those stuffed creatures are! That's wonderful. Maybe we can be just as quiet as they are when listening to the stories." (Perhaps you could have several stuffed animals available so that the shy child has something to cling to for comfort, and the fidgety child has something quiet to hold, and the boisterous child has to see if he or she can be just as quiet as the animal/toy being held.) Since the animals talk to you anyway, you can use the animals to tell the children that "the animals need to have it quiet," or "the pink horse can't hear what we just said and he's ready to cry, so let's settle down," and so on.

The Cow Wants to Jump over the Moon

If allowed by your school, hang a big yellow construction paper half-moon and two pieces of heavy string or colorful yarn all the way from a ceiling fixture to the floor. In ladder-style, staple flashcards with words printed on them. Have students take a pointer and see if they can say the words to help the cow jump over the moon. Keep track of those who succeed, and have a bright yellow "Man in the Moon" badge for them to wear. Let the students keep trying.

SPOTLIGHT ON MATH

September Bulletin Board Calendar

These activities are a natural lead-in to math skills:

A calendar is a *must* in a first-grade classroom. It can be a colorful focal point for teaching math concepts when it is used for number recognition, number recall, left-to-right progression, numbers that come *before* and *after* other numbers, math patterns, and so on.

For a striking September calendar, choose a red burlap background for the bulletin board covering. Staple white loopy yarn to form the grid and the outline of a school shape along with the letters S, M, T, W, TH, F, S. Use white

construction paper cut-outs in the shape of apples to pin to the grid. One a day can be added from the "apple basket." Students have to sort through to find the special apple number of the day. In this way, students watch the calendar fill in all month long. This apple-a-day calendar activity can be tied to the saying "An Apple a Day Keeps the Doctor Away." At the same time, promote Healthy Snack Time by recommending apples during calendar math time. ("How many brought an apple today for a snack?" Count and record the number. This is another way of using numbers to keep a record.)

My Favorite Storybook Calendar

Use the grid provided on the "Monthly Calendar" reproducible sheet and do a math lesson together by having the students slowly and carefully print the numerals from 1 through 30 (just as you are doing on the chalkboard) as they make their calendars. It is helpful if you have, in advance, placed the first numeral on each grid so that students have a starting point. IMPORTANT: When students get to the end of the very first line, have them put their pencils down and point with their finger to the square where they intend to print the next numeral. Give individual approval for them to begin on line 2. (This avoids the tendency to begin printing in the boxes on the first line, only to bump into the numerals they just finished making. It saves time and prevents frustration.)

When the numerals are completed, staple the calendar grid onto a sheet of colorful 12″ x 18″ construction paper. Students can print SEPTEMBER along the top, and use their crayons to show their favorite storybook character. Encourage students to use the calendar at home to help them keep track of when their library books are due, and so on.

Shapes of the Month

For some students, the circle, square, and triangle will be review from kindergarten, while for others it will be new. Here are some things you can do with shapes by concentrating on one shape per week:

- Use clay coils to roll out the three shapes so that students have a kinesthetic experience of grooving, rolling, and shaping the objects with their hands.

- Celebrate the basic shapes of a circle, square, and triangle. Dedicate several days to each shape. Make circle badges, square badges, and triangle badges to wear on the special days to reinforce the name and shape association.

- Have students sit in a circle, in a square, in a triangle. Then they can pretend to be a great big pencil as they line up and slowly move around the room in a circle shape, in a square shape, and in a triangle shape—Watch those sharp corners! How many corners were there on the square? the triangle? the circle?

- Go on a shape search. Wear a "Circle Detective" headband when on the lookout for circle shapes. Wear a "Triangle Trooper" headband when on the lookout for triangle shapes. Wear a magic "Square Squad" headband when hunting for square shapes. The headbands seem to help do the work! Make a giant shape chart so the shapes don't escape.

- Make shape bracelets. String cardboard cut-outs of triangles, circles, and squares on a colorful piece of yarn that can be tied gently around the wrist. Then play the Shape Game:
"Im thinking of a shape that has three sides. What is it?"
"I'm thinking of a shape that has **four** sides. What is it?"
"I'm thinking of a shape that looks like a ball. What is it?"
As the students point to the shape they're wearing, you can give and receive immediate feedback.

- Make shape birds. Use the flannelboard to create bird shapes using only squares, or only triangles, or only circles. Then have students cut a large shape (either circle, square, or triangle) from construction paper that they can use for the body. Use the other basic shapes to help complete the bird. There can be a Circle Bird, a Square Bird, a Triangle Bird, or a combination of all three.

- Make shape collections by cutting giant-sized circles, squares, and triangles from colorful posterboard. Prop them up in various locations around the room. Encourage students to bring in pictures that show these shapes, and also to search for them in magazines stored in the classroom. Cut them out and clip them onto the edge of the giant shapes using clip clothespins. Then, mix up some of the items and have students clip them back onto the correct shape.

- When finished with the shape areas, place the giant posterboard shapes on the floor. Make the triangle seating area into a quiet place for working with items from the counting box; make the circle seating area into a special place to curl up with a circular pillow and a good book; and make the square seating area into a place for searching through magazines and newspapers for square shapes and using a felt-tip pen to mark a square around them. Students could lean against square pillows as they do their work.

- Watch for the traffic signs! Have students be on the alert for basic shapes when it comes to signs around the school and around the community. Some signs to be on the lookout for are school crossing, slow, no pets, keep off the grass, and so on. Use the local automobile club and a travel agency as resources for traffic signs and have students get acquainted with the sign shapes and their meanings. Some students might even be ready for international signs. Classify the signs by shape: circle, square, triangle, other. Then find out what the "other" category contains in terms of more shapes to learn about.

The Counting Box

Many first graders will be able to do rote counting from 1 through 100. Let's work with counting from 1 through 25 with a variety of activities. First, get a large cardboard box and cover it with colorful self-stick vinyl. Begin to collect items for the box, such as large beads, blocks, acorns, assorted nuts, drinking straws, marbles, jacks, balls of yarn, empty containers, large colorful paper clips, and so on. (Write a letter to parents requesting certain items for the counting box.)

This box serves as a counting and classifying activity center. As students dive in and count, have them place the items in a row and say the numerals aloud (for example: 6 word processor ribbons, 1–2–3–4–5–6). Students can also write the numerals in order on a strip of paper placed underneath the items to show one-to-one correspondence.

- Keep a written record by attaching a sheet of paper to the outside of the box with a list of student names along the side. Place symbols at the top of the paper to represent objects in the box. Have students record on the sheet the total number of each item. This also helps to keep track of items as the number decreases or increases.

- As the number of items increases, begin to have students classify the items that are alike and place them in smaller containers with lids. This will help keep order inside the box. Small containers with lids can include shoeboxes, oatmeal containers, egg cartons, potato chip containers, plastic margarine tubs, and so on. Attach a colorful sticker to each container that has the number of items printed on it. In this way, students can gain practice working with boxes of 30 items, boxes of 10 items, boxes of 18 items, and so on.

More Counting Activities—Adding On

- Work with the total group. Use real items in a container and count them aloud as you remove them from the box. For example, ten blocks could be removed from a container and placed in a row along the chalkboard. Be sure to write the numerals from 1 to 10 above each item. Then, remove the first two items, erase the numerals 1 and 2, and start counting with 3 until you reach 10. When you reach 10, add on two more blocks to reach 12. Remove the blocks, erase the board, and begin again with numerals 1 to 10, remove the first four items and written numerals, and use the numeral 4 as a starting point to get to 10. Then, add on more blocks at the end.

- Count to 25 by starting with 6, or 8, or 10 so that students gain practice with counting by adding on. Do not always go back to 1 in order to count to 25. Later, add on to numerals beyond 25.

Number Sandwiches

- Write three numerals on the chalkboard to find out what numeral is in the middle. For example:

     4 ___ 6   10 ___ 12   2 ___ 4

     7 ___ 9   3 ___ 5   8 ___ 10

  Have students fill in the numeral in the middle. Some students may need to go back to the counting box for the concrete items in order to be successful with this activity.

- Make "yummy number sandwiches." Make a set of number cards from 1 to 10 on construction paper bread shapes. Make a set of number cards from 2 to 9 on a variety of shapes and colors that represent the contents (middle) of a sandwich. For example:

2 – peanut butter   6 – tomato

3 – hot dog   7 – jelly

4 – hamburger   8 – bologna

5 – cheese   9 – tuna

Set up two bread shapes along one chalkboard and all of the middle shapes along another chalkboard. Call upon a student to select the correct sandwich filling for the two slices of bread. Repeat this with other students using different numbers.

- Make "super number ice cream sandwiches." Begin to work up to 25 sandwiches. Have unique middles (in terms of names and fancy colored paper). For example, the two outer layers of the ice cream sandwich could be numbers 3 and 7. That means there are three numbers in the middle, which could be named as follows: 4—chocolate fudge, 5—pistachio, 6—marshmallow delight. Students enjoy learning math concepts using this math game.

HANDS-ON SCIENCE

Rock Around the Block

Go on a rock walk around the school and playground area. Encourage each child to select one interesting rock or large pebble (interesting in terms of shape, coloration, texture). Bring the rocks back to the classroom and put the into a storage bucket.

Be sure to examine the rocks and classify them by color, size, shape, and texture. Are some smooth? Are some rough and jagged? Are some shiny? Are some dull? Do they crumble when we scrape them with our fingernails? These are all questions that you will want to explore. (See the "Hands on the Rocks" reproducible page.)

Have students find the largest rock and then one that is *smaller than* the largest. Then find the smallest rock. Now line them up from smallest to largest. (This is a math activity in seriation.)

Find library resource books on rocks that contain color pictures so that the children can see the wide variety of rocks. Is there a giant rock in the local community? Does it have a special name? Rocks have scientific names, and depending upon the ability level of the group, names can be introduced, mentioned, or even memorized and learned. These names include sedimentary, igneous, limestone, conglomerate, and so on.

Our First Grade Rocks

Encourage the students to use their fertile imaginations to speculate about these special rocks that are going to first grade with us. What are they learning? (This is a good reinforcement and review time, along with language development.) Pretend the rocks can talk:

"What are they learning about the ABCs?"

"Do they have a favorite story?"

"Do they have a favorite subject?"

"What are they learning about the calendar?"

What do the rocks do when everyone goes home each day? Let the children's imaginations go to work on this. Their responses may include such things as the rocks have a rock concert, they go to the kitchen for snacks, they play computer games, they go through the teacher's desk, and so on.

Rock-a-Bye Rocks

When it's time to dismantle the rock collection, have each child take a rock and tell it one thing (aloud) that was learned about rocks. Then have each child tell the class what the rocks learned about first grade. It's then time to return the rocks to the outdoors and to let them get back to their natural business of being rocks. (Many children will continue to "visit" the rocks daily for some time and will report their "conversations" with them. Some may want to bring them back inside—especially when they're wet with rain or when the rock feels cold as the autumn temperature begins to drop.)

Scientists at Work

Set up a small table in your classroom for science. It serves to strengthen the skills of observation and classification, and can open up a whole new world of investigation and questions for young children. Initially, you can place a magnifying glass on the table as one of the "science tools" that helps with our investigation. Later, more science tools can be added, such as a microscope, paper and pencils for recording observations and sketches, various containers of different sizes, science books, charts, and so on. This area can be changed monthly, or more often, and should be an area in the classroom that is alive with learning possibilities—students can go there when work is finished, during free-choice time, or during indoor recess. Limit the number of participants to two or three at a time.

OTHER AREAS OF INTEREST FOR SEPTEMBER

Pets Are Precious

"Salute to Dog Week" is celebrated during the last week in September, so this is a good month to get acquainted with the pets that children have at home. Keep a tally of how many students have a pet dog, cat, bird, fish, or a "wish list" pet. (This reinforces the concept of math as an "enabler"—it helps us to record information.)

Even the shy child likes to share information about a pet (name, color, size, favorite food or snack, habits, funniest pet story, and so on). Most students get excited and have an enjoyable time when talking about their pets or even animals in the neighborhood. (This is a good opportunity to develop oral communication skills.)

Get books from the library about animals and have a whole week of reading aloud about animal adventures. Some good suggestions are:

Angus & the Cat by Marjorie Flack (New York: Doubleday, 1971)

Millions of Cats by Wanda Gag (New York: Putnam, 1977, 1988)

Harry, the Dirty Dog by Gene Zion (New York: Harper & Row Junior, 1956, 1976)

More Pet Projects

- Each student can answer with a "woof" or a "meow" when asked, "Do you prefer dogs or cats?"

- Students can have an animal-shaped cookie snack while listening to a good animal story.

- Shape or mold a pet from plasticene or flour dough, and make a pet farm on the table. Will fences be needed? Add as many details as possible.

- Use wallpaper sample books to make a cut-out of a favorite pet (or a storybook pet). Then use black, red, or dark blue construction paper for features, such as eyes, eyelashes, nose, mouth, claws, long whiskers curled at the edges (roll the strips around a pencil), and tail fringes. These pets can be displayed on the door—and are they ever glad to see us every day! Sh! Sometimes they're taking their naps so we have to be very quiet when we enter and leave the room so as not to disturb them.

- At the easel, set up sponges and tempera paints so students can paint a giant dog for "Salute to Dog Week." Display them in the hall, or make a giant picture book. Put a story strip along the bottom, and students can print or dictate a sentence about each dog.

Dogs Go to School

Many dogs go to obedience school and are trained to do work. There are seeing-eye dogs, and police dogs that use their sense of smell to help find objects or illegal drugs, and there's usually a dog at the fire station, too. A barking dog quickly gets our attention and helps alert us to danger.

Print reading words on dog-bone shapes and keep them in a colorful plastic dog dish. "Chow time" means it's time to practice those words.

Update on Dog Tags

Maybe by the time you read this, dog tags will be a thing of the past. Work is currently being done to insert a microchip (the size of a grain of rice) under the skin on a dog's back. This microchip would contain the same information that a dog now has on its tags.

What about people? Microchips can be put on back teeth by dentists that contain identification information. What would you put on your ID? Let's make our own ID on a pet dog, cat, bird, turtle, or fish shape. Use a hole punch, and insert brightly colored yarn through it, and then tie it in a big bow at the back of the neck. Students can help each other tie the bow.

AUTUMN'S IN THE AIR

Goodbye Summer, Hello Autumn

September is a time for changes and we can be on the lookout for them. We can use our five senses to help learn about autumn—the sights, sounds, smells, tastes, and the things we touch.

Make an autumn photo montage in the shape of a giant colorful leaf. Cut pictures of autumn from magazines, and overlap them as they are pasted onto the leaf shape. It gives the effect of a kaleidoscope of autumn colors and activities.

Honey Bear's Autumn Accordion Book

- Use two bear shapes, one for the front and one for the back book cover. Then fold a sheet of 9″ x 12″ construction paper five times (fan-like) so that it opens and closes like an accordian. Students can color one object on each space to represent autumn, using their five senses.

- Students can open and close their accordion books and sing to the tune of "Mary Had a Little Lamb." Their "sense words" (taste, saw, felt, heard, touched) can help with the items they made. For example:

David felt a drop of rain   Pamela heard the birds go by
Drop of rain, drop of rain   Birds go by, birds go by
David felt a drop of rain.   Pamela heard the birds go by
It fell from the sky.   High up in the sky.

Carrie ate a juicy apple   Freddy kicked a big football
Juicy apple, juicy apple   Big football, big football
Carrie ate a juicy apple   Freddy kicked a big football
It slurped her in the eye.   Kicked it way up high.

Get Ready for Chilly Weather

Use the flannelboard to teach this concept. Make a honey bear cut-out and cut-outs of a hat, sweater, jacket, pants, boots, raincoat, scarf, umbrella, gloves, and so on.

Also make weather symbol cut-outs (yellow circle for sun, umbrella for rain, gray shape for clouds, leaning tree for wind). On the flannelboard, place the weather symbol along with the honey bear. Then have students dress the bear appropriately for the weather. Honey bear is ready, but are we? Let's make sure to listen to the weather report and be ready for tomorrow.

SEPTEMBER WRITING

Straight Lines, Curved Lines

Have students practice making straight and curved lines on the chalkboard. Have them trace over curved and straight lines on the chalkboard—no small feat for students this age (small-motor activity). Also, put a shape on the chalkboard of curved and straight lines and turn out the lights. Students can switch on a flashlight and follow along the lines using two hands, using one hand (large motor activity).

Use very large paper and felt pens to practice the lines. Also use washable wallpaper with lines for tracing. This strengthens small muscle development. Some students are ready for paper and pencil before others. Let the students keep practicing.

Left Hand/Right Hand

For left-handed children, it is more natural to make a circle going clockwise instead of counter-clockwise. Also remember that their paper placement is the opposite of right-handed students.

Printing Keepsakes

Distribute a sheet of writing paper to each child. Instruct them to print their name as best they can. Collect these and put them in a manila envelope on your desk, labeled "Name." Then, next month, distribute these writing papers and have the students print their name. Do this each month. The progress will be right before their eyes! Share this with parents during conferences. Towards the end of the year, send these papers home for a Mother's Day Keepsake Gift or a First Grade Spring Gift.

Chalk, Brush, and Water

During recess, designate a portion of the chalkboard for students to practice making lines and letters using easel brushes or watercolor brushes dipped in a pail of water. At the end, just sponge it off clean. There is no chalkdust.

ARTS AND CRAFTS

Artists at Work!

Introduce the easel about the third week of September, after you have a manageable classroom. The bright-colored paintings that emerge from the easel can help decorate the room and the door. Show students how to hold the brush, how to dip and not drip (dip brush into paint and wipe it off along the rim before lifting it up to the easel). Have old shirts and smocks available, and have students wear them backwards so that they're covered. Have a "sign-up sheet" so that everyone gets a turn to paint.

Large Loom in the Room

Use the side of an appliance box for a very large loom in your classroom that can be propped up against the wall. Print labels on it, such as "top" and "bottom," and "left" and "right." String the loom with regular string or twine. Weave with strips of material, bulky yarn, or strips of cellophane. This is excellent kinesthetic review for the concepts of top, bottom, over, under, left, right, middle. Also, you have a work of art for the room when you remove it (snip and tie from the back).

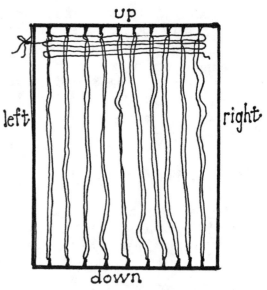

Good Color Sense

Set up a Color Table, and change the color twice per month. Start with bold red—use red material to cover the table. Set red items on the color table, and encourage students to bring in red items (bowls, plastic cups, clothing, and so on). Call attention to the different shades of red—even apples don't have a uniform red color. This area arouses a great deal of curiosity daily because it has such a variety of red items to smell, touch, hear, taste (apples, radishes, cherries, berries, tomatoes). What a feast for the senses! Read "What Is Red?" from *Hailstones and Halibut Bones* by Mary O'Neill. Ask, "What color shall we explore next on our Color Table?"

Pounding, Rolling, and Squashing

Obtain red, yellow, and blue plasticene for students to work and play with during recess, during free-choice time, or when work is finished. Keep the red in a red container, blue in a blue container, and yellow in a yellow container. Encourage students to make snake coils. Then they can roll out the alphabet letters, or their names, or their telephone numbers, and so on.

KEEP WORKING ON THE CLASSROOM RULES

Some classroom management can be related to traffic management and traffic patterns—when we can stop and go, when we have the right of way, when we have to slow down, when we can't honk the horn, when our muffler needs to be replaced because it's far too loud, when we need to speed up, when we need to put on the brakes, when we need to take a look in the rear-view mirror (reflect) so that we can settle our differences. The classroom can be likened to one big expressway—with rules and regulations for the good and safety of everyone. Many teachers have found hand signals are effective in helping to establish a smooth classroom routine that is buzzing with meaningful learning going on. Some use red, yellow, and green circle signals made from construction paper to resemble traffic lights to hold up as non-verbal messages. We want a pleasant trip along the first grade highway and we must convey to students that it is a team effort.

Reproducible Activity Pages for September

Bird Nest Alphabet (upper-case letters)
Frog Egg Alphabet (lower-case letters)
The Alligator Walk (alphabet)
The Story of "Silverlocks" (beginning sounds)
Buster Bear (beginning sounds)
Back-to-School Bear (addition facts)
Monthly Calendar (calendar)
Classroom Inventory (counting, recording)
Wild Goose Chase (shape identification)
Hands on the Rocks (science classification)
Getting Ready to Write (writing readiness)
Follow the Line (writing readiness)
X Marks the Spot (observation skills)
September Bookmarks (reading)
Show Me Your House (group sharing, oral expression)
Show Me Your Family (group sharing, oral expression)

BIRD NEST ALPHABET

This is Billy Bob Bird and he is in the first grade. He knows many of the big ABC letters. Can you help him trace the letters and fill in those that are missing?

Then color Billy Bob with the brightest crayons in your box!

Name ——————————————————   Date ——————————

FROG EGG ALPHABET

Francine the Frog has laid 26 eggs. Now she wants to put one letter of the alphabet on each egg. She wants to know if you can help. Sure you can! She likes it when you try. When finished, color her face a happy color.

Name ——————

THE ALLIGATOR WALK

Date ——————

This alligator swallowed a bird. The bird will be returned safely if we can help it identify the letters on the alligator. If you miss one, go back to the beginning and start again. Keep trying!

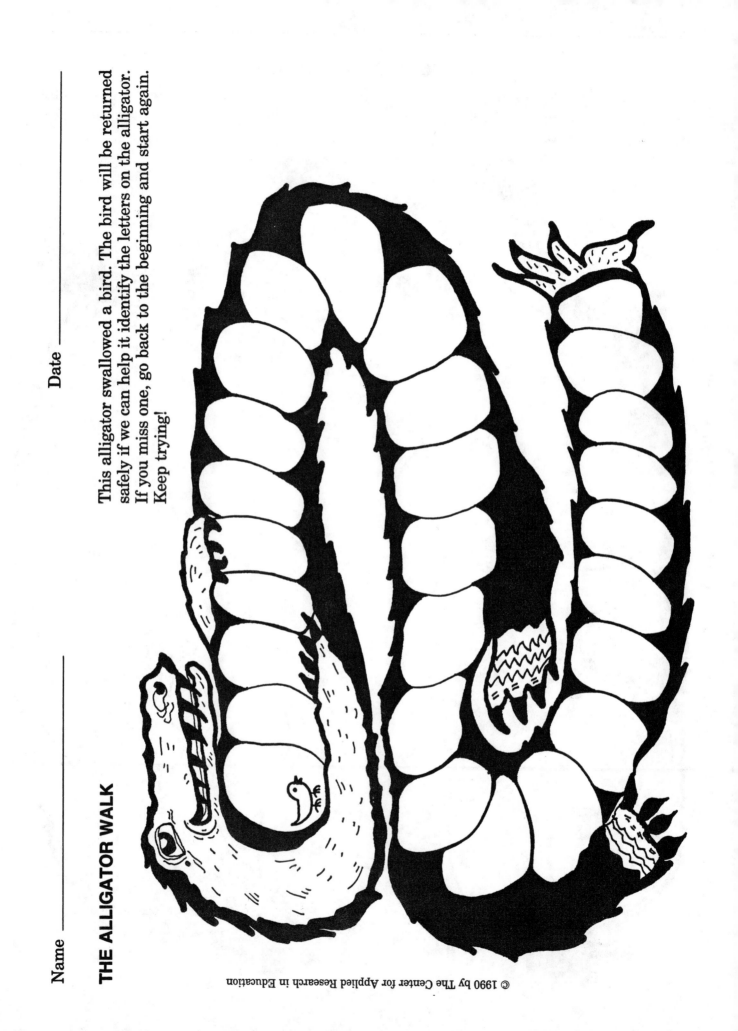

THE STORY OF "SILVERLOCKS"

Did you know that Goldilocks, from *Goldilocks and the Three Bears,* has a sister? Her name is Silverlocks! Silverlocks went into the woods and visited the home of the Three Slippery Snails. Instead of eating their porridge, she ate their salty soup.

You can tell the story of *Silverlocks and the Three Slippery Snails* because it is almost like her sister's story. How can you make Silverlocks's story different? Use lots of words that begin with the sound of "s."

salty soup

slippery snail

Silverlocks

As you color these pictures, tell the story of Silverlocks to yourself. Then tell your story out loud to some good listeners.

BUSTER BEAR

Let's make up a story. Tie these three items together in a creative way. Here's the problem: Buster Bear loves blueberries in a bucket. However, he can't move to get them! Can the butterfly help in some way? This is going to be a good story!

Don't forget to include words that begin with the letter "B." As you color the picture, think about how you are going to act out your nice story.

Buster Bear

blueberry bucket

butterfly

Name _____   Date _____

Ren Bear has new math patches on his pants. What is the total of each patch? Write the answers. Then color the new patches using this chart to help you:

2	green	4	red
6	blue	8	yellow
10	purple	12	orange

Color and cut out Ren Bear. Make a new hat for him, too.

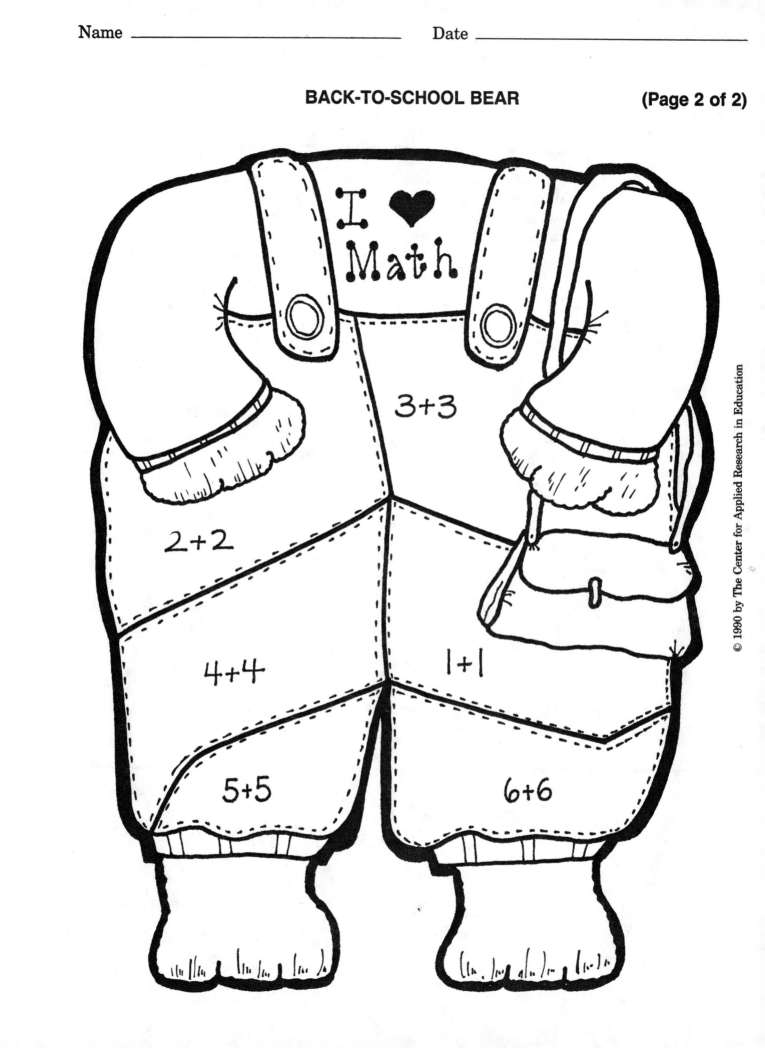

MONTHLY CALENDAR

Fill in the numerals for the month. Be sure to mark the special days. Cut out the calendar and paste it on a sheet of 12" x 18" colored paper. Print the name of the month at the top. Then make a beautiful picture for your calendar.

S	M	T	W	T	F	S

CLASSROOM INVENTORY

Let's count. How many of these items are in your classroom? Write the correct amount on the line. This is called a *record*. Use your new crayons to make all of the items look brand new, too!

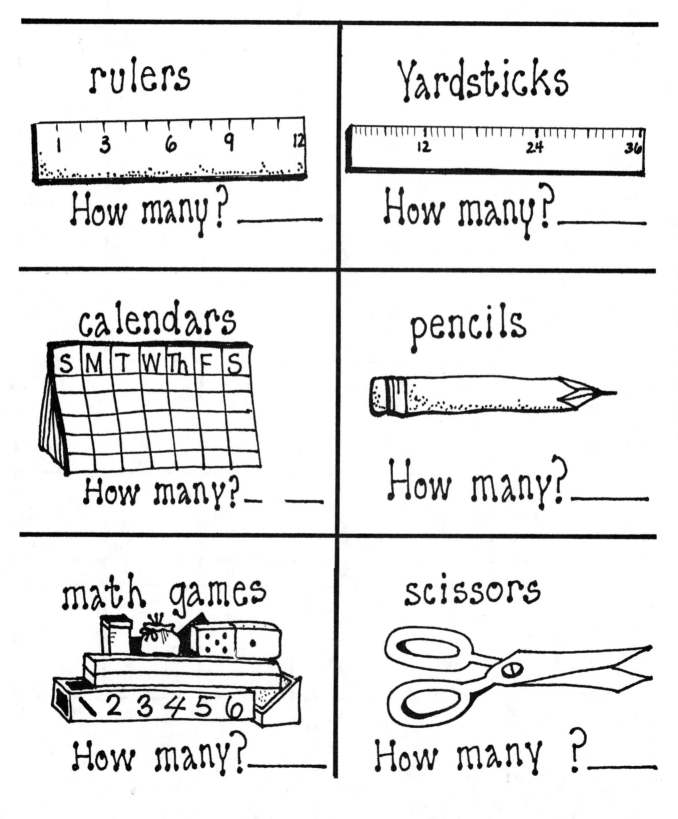

rulers

How many? _____

Yardsticks

How many? _____

calendars

How many? ___ ___

pencils

How many? _____

math games

How many? _____

scissors

How many ? _____

WILD GOOSE CHASE

These geese have been sent to look for triangles, circles, and squares. They don't know what the shapes look like. Can you help them?

Color all of the triangles RED.
Color all of the squares BLUE.
Color all of the circles ORANGE.

HANDS ON THE ROCKS

Start a classroom rock collection. Let's find out how many different ways we can sort, or classify, these rocks. Below are some ideas to get you started.

1. Classify all rocks by color.

Make a big colored rock chart for the room.

2. Classify all rocks by texture, such as:

smooth   rough

shiny   cracked

3. Classify your rocks by size from smallest to largest.

Rocks

GETTING READY TO WRITE

Follow the rounded and straight lines with a pencil. Then color the balloons.

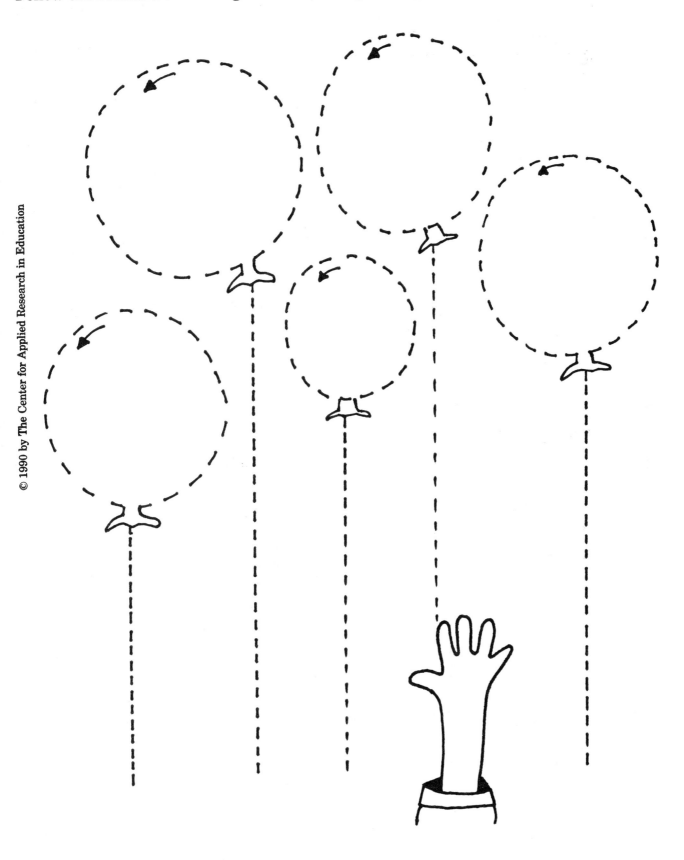

Name _____

FOLLOW THE LINE

Follow this line from the truck to the house. Use a crayon or large pencil.

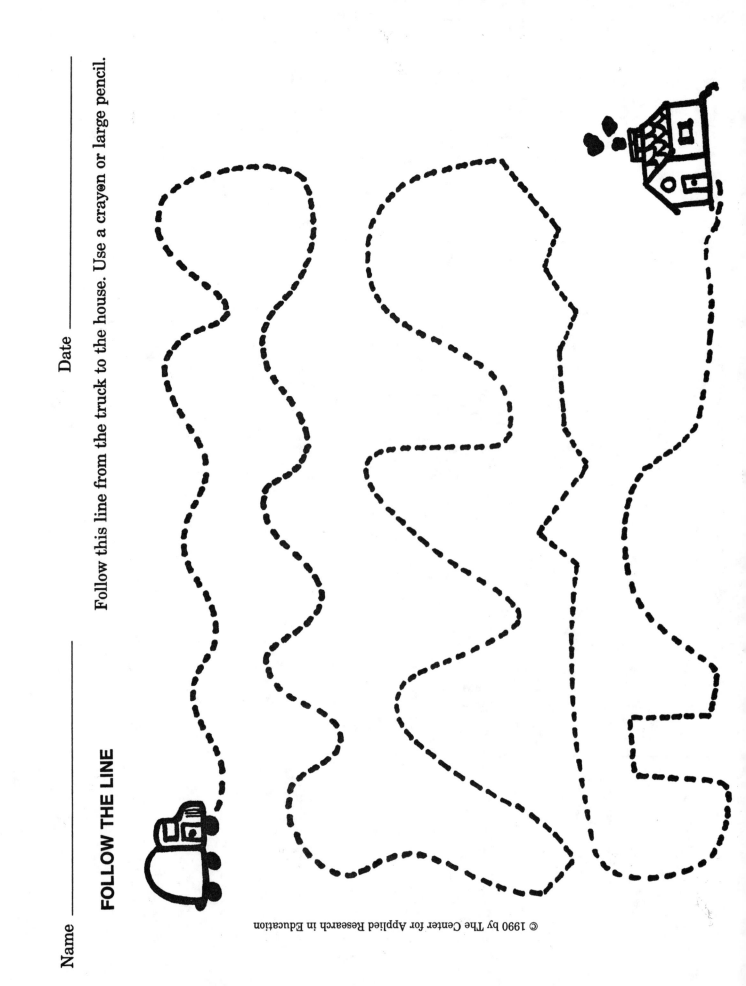

Name _____ Date _____

X MARKS THE SPOT

Put a great big letter X on the things that you do *not* find in your classroom. Color all of the things that you *do* find. Look carefully!

SEPTEMBER BOOKMARKS

Color each bookmark and then cut each one out. Use the bookmarks in your books.

Park me in a good book!

I ♥

Book Sitter

Name _____   Date _____

SHOW ME YOUR HOUSE

Buffy Bird is in her house today. She would like to see a picture of your house and your schoolhouse. Use your felt pen and crayons to make them look nice. She likes house pictures.

My House

My Schoolhouse

SHOW ME YOUR FAMILY

This bird family had their picture taken, but it came out black and white. They have bright colors. Can you use your crayons to help them out?

While you have your crayons out, the bird family would like to have you draw a picture of your family. Thank you.

My Family

October

BREWING UP A STORM OF LEARNING ACTIVITIES

October is an important month in first grade in terms of continuing to establish order and routines. Students are familiar with the environment by now and find security in knowing the daily and weekly schedules. They like to know what's coming next, and they'll quickly let you know when something is out of place. It is important to build trust and to make the environment a safe place in order that the seeds of learning can take root.

RECOMMENDED CHILDREN'S BOOKS FOR OCTOBER

- *Popcorn* by Frank Asch (New York: Parent's Magazine Press, 1979). When Mama and Papa Bear go to a Halloween party and leave Sam Bear home, he proceeds to call his friends and invite them to join him, to bring a costume, and something good to eat. They ALL bring popcorn and munch and crunch their way through the party until they could burst. When Mama and Papa return home from their party with a treat for Sam, it's something good to eat! Can you guess what they brought home? This is a good discussion book.

- *Ghost's Hour, Spook's Hour* by Eve Bunting, illustrations by Donald Carrick (New York: Clarion Books, 1987). When you awaken in the middle of the night, especially at midnight which is the ghost's hour and spook's hour, noises seem louder, shadows seem bigger, and a little boy's imagination grows wilder. All children can relate to this story. The book has a peaceful ending.

- *The Witch Who Lost Her Shadow* by Mary Calhoun, illustrations by Trina Hakes Noble (New York: Harper & Row, 1979). Falina the Witch has lost her shadow. No, not HER shadow, but her cat named "Shadow." Shadow has been faithful, and has followed Falina everywhere. Now, the witch is lonely. A striped cat comes to stay on her doorstep, but will this stay-at-home cat ever replace her wonderful Shadow?

- *Sir William and the Pumpkin Monster* by Margery Cuyler, pictures by Marsha Winborn (New York: Holt, Rinehart and Winston, 1984). Sir William is a proper ghost who does his job, which is haunting houses. However, when he meets the Neville family, they don't think he's scary; in fact, they think he's wonderful! He tries his best to scare them, but the children end up giving Sir William a fright!

- *Rickety Witch* by Maggie S. Davis, illustrations by Kay Chorao (New York: Holiday House, 1984). Meet the three prairie witches—two young ones as "sour as lemon seeds" and a rickety old one as "sweet as prairie roses." Even witches have problems getting along, but with a bit of magic anything can happen.

- *Things to Make and Do for Columbus Day* by Gail Gibbons (New York: Franklin Watts, 1977). This book is done with large pictures and cartoon bubbles that contain conversation. It begins with Columbus' voyage in 1492, and each page contains activities and information for the reader, such as how to make soap boats, sea mosters, a compass, and so on. It contains a tuna treat for Columbus Day and a Big Storm Game. This book teaches and entertains the reader.

- *Arthur's Halloween Costume* by Lillian Hoban (New York: Harper and Row, 1984). Arthur plans to be a ghost on Halloween until he learns that others have the very same idea. Now he won't be scary, he thinks, and sets out to create an unusual costume. The spirit of Halloween comes through in this "I-Can-Read" book.

- *The Dragon Nanny* by C. L. G. Martin, illustrations by Robert Rayersby (New York: Macmillan Publishing, 1988). Nanny Nell Hannah has been fired by the royal king and banished to the dragon's forest. The fierce dragon is ready to devour Nanny, but is sidetracked by Nanny's interaction with her two little dragons. Nanny charms the baby dragons, who save her life, but there's a lot of adventure when the king's men capture one of the baby dragons. Be ready for a ruckus—with Nanny in the middle.

- *The Beast of Monsieur Racine* by Tomi Ungerer (New York: Farrar, Straus and Giroux, 1975). Monsieur Racine, a retired tax collector, is quite a gardener. He's especially proud of his pears—but one day they're all gone! Under the tree he finds a beast, who he tames. Monsieur Racine has lost his pears, but he's gained a companion. The strange creature enriches his life in several ways, to the delight of the reader.

- *What the Moon Saw* by Brian Wildsmith (Toronto: Oxford University Press, 1978). This is an excellent review book for concepts such as many/few, outside/inside, front/back, and so on, as told from the point of view of the sun. At the end, the moon reveals something special that only it can see. The book contains colorful, exciting illustrations.

SPOTLIGHT ON READING

Reading on a Field Trip

During October, many teachers feel that the students are ready for a field trip. Wherever this outing takes you, you can get an abundance of reading material from it.

- Have students take a crayon and paper along on the bus, and keep a tally of how many STOP signs they see; how many traffic lights tell them to stop (red) and go (green); how many people are wearing hats; the tallest building they can see; and how many other signs they can "read" by the symbols. When you return to class, have them compare information. Make a "We Can Read Signs" chart.

- Have students draw a map of the route as they are taking it. Right turns, left turns, and landmarks can be sketched in. Compare visual representations when you return to class. "Read" a real map both before and after this experience.

- Give students a teacher-made worksheet that contains a drawing of the route, and have them follow it. They can put in landmarks (be sure to explain the meaning of that term) as the bus moves along, or later.

- Write an experience chart story about the wonderful visit when you return. The "experience" is still fresh in the mind of each child, and the words seem to come out effortlessly. Have students supply the art work for the large experience chart story, just like a big picture book page with colorful illustrations. You, an aide, an older student, or the students themselves can copy the story onto 9″ × 12″ paper. Duplicate a sufficient amount on the copy machine so that each child has one to illustrate and to "read" and to take home to share.

- Be sure to have the students compose and write a thank-you note to the proprietor of the apple farm, or the manager of the business, or the fire chief, or whomever is in charge of the special place you chose for the visit. Some of these letters with creative spellings and colorful illustrations have thrilled those who have received them. Sometimes they put them on display because adults enjoy the children's perceptions.

Book-Making Time

Children can make individual booklets. Use two sheets of 9″ × 12″ construction paper and fold them in half and staple. The front page is the title page, and can contain the title (dictated by the child and written by you or printed by the child), the author's name, and a colorful illustration. If you use both sides of the page, it becomes a six-page book; if you use one side of the page, it becomes a three-page book.

- Use orange and black paper for a Halloween theme. Students can write a story and illustrate it with crayons. Or, have one item per page with a title printed underneath.
- Use red and yellow paper for an autumn theme. Students can staple and label real tree leaves on the pages, or write a story about the season.

Whooooo! Blow Out the Candle

It's time to work with the letter/sound relationship for the letter "w." Have students put their hand up to their mouth and say the word "witch." They will feel the air being expelled from their lungs. Have students work up a "wh," "wh," "wh" practice session, as though they are about to blow out a candle. Settle back down and ask the students to repeat, after you, some words that the "Wonderful Witch" knows. If the word begins with a "w" and makes the "wh" sound, it can blow out a make-believe candle. Say the words one by one. If the candle goes out (if there is a "wh" sound), have students close their eyes; if the candle does not go out (if there is no "wh" sound), have students open their eyes wide. Here are some starter words for the witch.

windy	wobbly	wonderful
singing	whiskers	letters
wooly	buttons	whisper

Write the words on the chalkboard and have students notice that some are more "windy" than others. Show them that the "wh" words always seem to use a stronger windy sound than words that begin with the single "w."

Th-Th-Th—Thumbs Up!

Words that begin with "th" are difficult for students because many are sight words. To enable them to make a connection with the "th" sound, tell them that whenver they see "th" in a word, they have permission to stick out their tongue. Dramatically announce that AT NO OTHER TIME are they allowed to stick out their tongues in school, but the "th" sound makes it possible.

Have students say the word "this" and "that." Have them note that their tongue does indeed stick out, while it rests on the top teeth. Have them gently clamp their teeth together so that they can feel the "th" position. Have them turn to each other as they say the words so that they can see each other's tongue at work. After the giggles have subsided, let's put Mr. Tongue to work and say some "th" words that you have printed on the chalkboard. Some starter words are:

think   that   them   those   three

- To the tune of "Mary Had a Little Lamb," have students sing the following song as they hold up their thumbs and wiggle them for the "th" sound only:

  Mr. Thumb says, "th, th, th" (*wiggle thumbs*)

  "Th, th, th, th, th, th"

  Stick your tongue out, "Th, th, th"

  Thank you, Mr. Thumb. (*thumbs take a bow*)

- Now students are ready for the "thumbs up" sign. Say a word and if it begins with "th," students put their thumbs up. If it does not begin with "th," students put their thumbs down.

- On a large construction paper cut-out of a thumb, print some sight words that begin with "th." This visual cue may enable some students to learn the words with more ease.

Words, Phrases, and Sentences

Secure a variety of alphabet books from the library so that each child has one, or so that two students have one to share. When all of the books have been distributed, allow the children time to browse and enjoy the books. Then engage the children in some activities.

- Ask each student to turn to the "D" page. (Allow time and be prepared to help some children locate it.) Discuss the page by asking, "What's on your page, Chris?" (Dog) "Mike, what's on your page?" (Dish) "What does your book have for the letter D, Rebecca?" (Doll) As each student tells what is on his or her page, list the names on the chalkboard so that you have a variety of "D" words from which to work.

- Repeat this same technique for several letters. You can ask students to turn, for example, to the "S" page and then they can take turns telling what is on their "S" page. Again, list the words on the chalkboard or on experience chart paper. Students can draw their own illustrations for the words.

- If you use this directed browsing procedure for all of the letters A through Z, and you use experience chart paper and have the students illustrate the words, you will have your very own giant-sized ABC book for students to read. This will be a wonderful resource. Each child achieves success because each child has a word to contribute.

- Call attention to the size and shape of the letters, and where they are located on the page. Use directional terms such as upper, lower, right, left, middle, and corner.

- Ask children to examine their books to see if there are borders around the edge of any of the pages. Suggest that they could include a border around the big chart of letter pages. Is the border decorative, or does it contain hidden pictures that begin with the same sound as the big letter on the page? Have students examine carefully. Perhaps the class book can use a variety of borders.

- Collect the ABC books, or have students take them to the Reading Center, where they can go at their leisure and browse through the books again and again, making comparisons of the letter shapes and sizes, and the illustrations.

- Each time the books are distributed to the entire group, be certain that students get a book different from the one they worked with previously in order to maintain variety and interest.

- Some of the ABC books may have a phrase or a sentence rather than a single word. This helps the students to learn what a descriptive phrase is (and they can make up their own), and also see that a sentence begins with a capital letter and ends with a period and contains a complete thought (and they can make up their own).

- This is a way to utilize a genre of children's literature in the reading curriculum. The marvelous illustrations and bold print serve to stimulate the young learner, and provide an approach that is different from the basal text. It is also a springboard for making individual ABC books that are rich, varied, and colorful because of the input from the authors and illustrators of the wonderful books. Because there is an explosion in children's literature, and that includes ABC books, the school library or the public library should be a rich resource for your activities.

- Some ABC books to include in your collection are *The Farmer's Alphabet* by Mary Azarian (New York: David Godine Publisher, 1981); *We Read A to Z* by Donald Crews (New York: Greenwillow Press, 1984); *The Guinea Pig ABC* by Kate Duke (New York: Dutton, 1983); *Ed Emberly's ABC* by Ed Emberly (Boston: Little, Brown & Co., 1978); *A, B, See* by Tana Hoban (New York: Greenwillow, 1982); *Twenty-Six Letters and Ninety-Nine Cents* by Tana Hoban (New York: Greenwillow, 1987); *Animal Alphabet* by Bert Kitchen (New York: Dial Books, 1984); *The Old-Fashioned Raggedy Ann and Andy ABC Book* by Robert Kraus, et al (New York: Windmill Books, 1980); *On Market Street* by Arnold Lobel, illustrated by Anita Lobel (New York: Greenwillow, 1981); and *Curious George Learns the Alphabet* by H. A. Rey (Boston: Houghton-Mifflin, 1963).

We'll Take All of the "Junque" Mail You Can Deliver

Secure a country mailbox, a mail basket, or a bushel basket. Bring your own third or fourth class mail to school and drop it into the box. Encourage other teachers to save theirs for you, too. Write a note home for parents to send theirs. If it is unopened, students love to open the mail. After all, how many letters do they receive? If it is already opened, it is still valuable. Students can "read" some of the words used in advertisements with the aid of the visual cues. Students can select a letter of the alphabet and use a highlighter marking pen to circle the particular letter every time they find it on the page. This is a source of reading that remains fresh and constant. It gives us an appreciation of what is commonly called "junk" mail because of the exposure to words, phrases, and sentences.

SPOTLIGHT ON MATH

October Bulletin Board Calendar

Use a bulletin board to make a classroom calendar you can use for daily lessons. Have the children learn to say the month, and perhaps to write it. Also, have them repeat the days of the week (left-to-right progression) beginning with Sunday through Saturday. Point out that within each of the daily names is the ending word "day." In so doing, you can begin to plant the seed that there are sometimes "words within words."

- If you choose to have a blank grid, the children can take turns printing "today's date" on the calendar.

- If you choose to have all of the numerals already on the calendar, the children can designate "today's date" by circling it with yarn or a circular cut-out. Each day, they can put an X on the numeral that represents "yesterday." In so doing, they are being introduced, visually, to the concept of past, present, and future time.

- Work with the total calender for math review. Ask:
  Which day of the week has the most numbers?
  Does Tuesday have more numbers (days) than Saturday?
  Does Wednesday have more numbers (days) than Sunday?
  On which day does the month begin?
  On which day does the month end?
  How many days are there all together (total) for the month?
  Which day has the least number of days?
  Do any of the days have equal numbers of days?
  Can you find today's date? Which number comes before and which one comes after? Let's write it. (_____ 16 _____)

- Let's interview the month of October. Find out if any class member has an October birthday and be sure to have that child designate it on the calendar with a crayon. The child can print his or her name and make a yummy-looking birthday cake in that grid. Are there any special holidays in October? Let's find out and ask good workers to use their crayons to make a very colorful symbol that goes along with the date. (Columbus Day, Fire Prevention Week, and Halloween are several to get you started.) Consult a calender or book for other October days that you want to record, such as the harvest moon, area festivals, or special local events.

- Have each student make a calendar of his or her own. Use a reproducible grid and record the first and last numerals, or put an X on the appropriate grid so that the student can follow directions for completing the calendar. Every third or fourth numeral already printed on the grid by you can make the going much easier. If 9″ × 12″ ditto paper is used for the calendar, this can be pasted on the bottom half of a 12″ × 18″ sheet of colored construction paper. Each student can make his or her very own picture and decorative designs on the calendar. This treasure can be taken home for the child's own use in practicing number concepts at home. From the modeling that is used in school, children can begin to put an X on past days, circle present time, and see the stretch of time ahead for the month that we call "October"—our tenth month of the year, and our second (or third) month of the school year.

Shape of the Month

October's shape of the month is a sphere. Have a sample of a sphere (orange, baseball, globe, basketball, small pumpkin, large medicine ball, and so on) so that students can "get the feel" of this shape. Also, print the word "sphere" on the chalkboard.

- Encourage students to go on a sphere hunt at home (write a note to parents explaining that this is your shape of the month) and bring in an object in this shape to be set on the Math Table for further examination.

- Go on a sphere walk around the school building and on the playground. Look carefully to see if the sphere is a part of something else, such as a playground structure.

- Have a "Sphere-a-Thon" activity. Encourage parents to send in magazines and have students scour the magazines for pictures of spheres (semiconcrete learning) AFTER they have had the experience of handling spheres (concrete learning). Cut out the pictures and paste them in a sphere catalog.

- Make sphere mobiles and hang them from the ceiling. You will need strips of paper and paste to make the spheres.

- Integrate math with spelling and language development. Learn to spell "sphere" and point out that the "ph" is tricky because it takes on the sound of "f." Begin to list words that either begin with "ph" or have the "ph" letters with the "f" sound somewhere in the word (example: elephant).

- For further language development, have students use puppets for Interview-a-Shape time. Ask a representative sphere-shaped object what it likes and does not like about being sphere-shaped. Example: It likes to roll, it likes all of the food that choose to be its shape (list these), it likes to travel in space; it wishes it were not compared to the square because a square can only make sharp turns at corners. This exercise encourages listening, speaking, taking turns, creative thinking, and critical thinking.

Other-Side-of-the-Mountain Math

To review and reinforce verbal rote counting to 100 by one's, divide the class into two groups and have one group line up on one side of the room and the other group line up on the opposite side of the room. They can be called Team A and Team B. Ask the students to pretend that there is a big mountain in the middle of the room over which they cannot see, but they can hear. Have students cup their hands around their mouth. The first student in line on Team A begins the count by calling out "one"; the first person on Team B calls out "two"; the next person on Team A calls out "three"; and the next person on Team B calls out "four." The activity continues until 100 is reached. By having the students cup their hands around their mouth, they have a "hands off" policy when it comes to each other and the group is easier to control.

- *Variation:* Students can work with a partner and take turns counting aloud. They can sit cross-legged, if preferred, and face each other. They clap their hands on their knees for "one" and clap their hands together palm to palm with their partner for "two." (Later, they can count to 100 by two's by whispering the numbers when they touch their knees, and by saying aloud the numbers when they touch hands.)

- *Variation:* Two students can be paired to count pumpkin seeds, dried beans, dried peas, or dried lentils.

- *Variation:* Two students can take turns counting while skipping rope.

- *Variation:* Two students can bounce a ball back and forth between them, and take turns counting until they reach 100.

An Eye-Color Graph

You need kraft paper to make a giant grid. Label the categories at the bottom, and paste a colored circle above the word. Cut out circles in the colors of brown, blue, green, and light brown. You also need a mirror and glue.

Put the giant grid on the floor and explain that you are going to make a graph. Students will learn that a graph is a big picture that contains information. Individually, ask each student to name his or her eye color. If correct, they may take the construction paper cut-out of their eye color. If they don't know, have them check in the mirror and then take the color that closely approximates their eye color. When everyone has his or her eye color paper, have them come up individually and place the construction paper circle in the proper column. If it is correct, they can paste it on the grid.

When this procedure is completed, gently move the graph from the floor and place it in a vertical position on a bulletin board or on the chalkboard or wall. Students will be amazed to learn that by just looking at the graph, we get an instant picture of how many blue eyes, how many brown eyes, etc. Then ask, "Which eye color do most of us have? Which eye color do the least of us have?" Make up a catchy title for the graph, such as "Our Eye Colors at a Glance" or "The World as Seen from Our Eyes" or "The Eyes from Room _____."

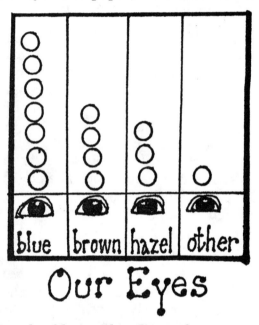

- Follow up this activity by doing a graph of hair color. In math, we can work with the concept of most, least, more than, less than, how many.

- If the eye color and hair color cut-outs are labeled with students' names, the graph can be worked into the day as an activity. For example, "How many brown eyes are here today?" Record the number. Repeat for other colors. Or, "How many people with red hair are here today?" Record the number. Repeat for other colors. This leads to more recordkeeping and graphing. By creating a number of graphs, the information has meaning for the students.

Let's Look at Thick and Thin

In the reading section, the children were told that the only time in school they are allowed to stick out their tongues is when they see the letters "th." Well, let's put that tongue to work on the math concepts of "thick" and "thin." First, take a look at the shoes everyone is wearing. Find some soles that are thick and some that are thin. Here are some other ways to work with the concept of thick and thin.

- Have students feel thick and thin pieces of material or paper. Then see if they can pick out the thick/thin one with their eyes closed, using only their sense of touch.

- Have students create thick and thin lines on paper using crayons. They can also cut thick and thin strips of paper to paste on a "thick/thin" worksheet.

- Look at wallpaper sample books to distinguish between the thick and thin lines, especially in plaids.

- Ask, "Who is wearing something with thin lines (or thick lines) on their clothing today?"

- Have students practice lacing and tying a bow using thick and thin materials such as rope, clothesline, string, ribbon, and shoelaces.

- To "spread it on thick" is a saying that means "to exaggerate." Perhaps some "Thick Halloween Ghost Stories" would be appropriate for party day.

- Discuss thick and thin foods and look for sample colorful pictures in magazines. A milkshake (thick) and a soft drink (thin) are examples; so, too, are pudding (thick) and soup (thin).

- For snack time, eat thick and thin by having crackers or bread topped with peanut butter (thick) along with milk (thin). (Be sure to check with parents for food allergies before serving any food to children.)

HANDS-ON SCIENCE

Pumpkins

Is the pumpkin a fruit? Arrange to have a large pumpkin brought into your classroom. After students have explored some activities (see the Reading and Math sections), find out about this enormous round, orange, gourd-like fruit (yes, fruit) with many seeds. This fruit grows on a vine. Look through seed catalogs or plant books to find other fruits that grow on vines. List them and draw pictures to illustrate them.

Bring in a collection of squash and gourds for students to examine and classify by color, size, shape, weight, and any other categories they can devise. There are many squash and gourds available at this time of year such as the acorn squash, the spaghetti squash, the Hubbard squash, yellow squash, and a variety of shapely, colorful gourds.

After the students have classified the objects, have them take their crayons and a sheet of paper and make a picture representation of their classification. Going from a concrete (actual item) activity to a semi-concrete (pictorial representation) activity is the way that children learn best, according to many child development theorists including John Dewey, Maria Montessori, and Jean Piaget.

Science Corner

If you have not already set up a science table in your classroom, now is the time to do so. If space is at a premium, then have a big science box (shallow boxes for under-the-bed storage work very well) that can be brought out and put in a section of the room and stored in the cupboard overnight, if necessary. Gradually equip your Science Corner with "tools" that scientists use. The very first tool can be the magnifying glass and/or the microscope for examination of pumpkin seeds, the stem, and the inside and the outside of the pumpkin itself.

Science on the Ground

Give each student a small plastic bag or a lunch bag and go on an "items from nature" science hunt outdoors for signs of autumn. Each student can put five items into his or her bag. When the items are brought into class, they can be carefully emptied onto the science table. The item will lead to an abundance of classification activities. Children will find objects such as various types of rocks, twigs of different colors and shapes, seeds (acorns, horsechestnuts, buckeyes), dried plants (thistles, teasels, milkweed pods), and leaves.

- Go on the science hunt, but this time focus upon living things (or things that were once living) such as dried weeds, pine needles, dried leaves, flower petals, bird feathers, and so on. It is amazing what students can find when they have a focus—even the remains of field mice. You may want to take along a toy shovel and adult garden gloves for some "finds" such as moss.

- Go on an "environmental squad hunt" with bags, focusing this time on things on the ground that are man-made and are cluttering up our environment. Students will find such items as bottle caps, paper, scraps of paper, boxes, soft drink cans, and bottles (but don't let the children pick up any glass). This can lead to an "Ecology Statement from Room ____" about the clutter, and can involve discussion (speaking and listening), listing of items (writing), and creating an awareness of the responsibility of people to preserve a safe, clean environment. This ecology statement can be included in the weekly newsletter (or bi-monthly newsletter) that is sent home to parents from your classroom. It may also be a statement that can be "broadcast" to each room at the same grade level.

SPOOKY HALLOWEEN

Orange and Black

Why orange and black for Halloween? Why not green and tan? Perhaps orange represents the "harvest moon" so prominent in October, and black represents the "night" as the days grow shorter and shorter. Ask the students why *they* think orange and black are used as traditional Halloween colors. Chances are they will say that orange is for the pumpkin and black is for the witch. Have them name all the things they can think of that are orange or black for Halloween (orange pumpkin, black spiders, and so on). HISTORICAL INFORMATION FOR THE TEACHER: The colors of Halloween are orange for the harvest and black for death. Halloween developed from a religious holiday when it was believed that the dead spirits came back on All Hallows Eve to roam the earth. People put out food on the doorstep to appease the spirits, which is how we have the custom of "trick or treat" as children go around asking for food. The custom of dressing up in costumes came from the idea that it was best to wear a disguise so that the spirits would not recognize you and would leave you alone.

For a multicultural aspect of Halloween, it is interesting to note that in many parts of Mexico, the people, to this day, set out delectable foods and treats on their doorsteps on All Hallows Eve in an effort to please the ancestral spirits who roam the area during the evening as they return for their annual visit.

Halloween Safety

This is a subject that should be reinforced in your classroom. Have a discussion of safe Halloween practices, and guide the children to make wise choices. This can be in the form of what "The Wise Old Owl Says. . ." (See the reproducible activity sheet.) Some ideas include the wearing of masks that have large holes so that vision is not impaired; avoiding long costumes that create a problem if feet become entangled in them; being accompanied by a parent if trick-or-treating in the neighborhood; having parents check the food bags upon returning home.

While we do not want to create a fearful experience, we do want to stress common-sense rules and adult supervision.

We've Got Our Very Own Ghost!

Bring in a large, white pillow case. Encourage the students to stuff it with paper, and then tie it with a piece of bulky white yarn. Use construction paper cut-outs for eyes. Put the ghost in a prominent area of the room and pretend that the ghost is afraid of not only Halloween, but also of many other things. (Elicit some ghost fears from the children, and recognize that some children contribute to the list from storybooks and some contribute because they are actually experiencing a particular fear.)

Say to the children, "Let's help the ghost to work out his fears by sharing a picture book with him, by sitting next to him during snacktime, by showing him how to play a boardgame, by instructing him to print or to use flashcards, and by having him whisper a fear to 'just me' and then sharing your own fear." Because of the fresh imagination that first graders bring to the setting, the sympathy and helpfulness that is directed toward the ghost is something pleasant to observe. Before long, the ghost isn't frightened by so many things because it has learned so many ways to cope. By now the ghost has usually been named by the children.

For the next step, bring in a colorful pillow case so that the ghost can be "transformed" into a colorful, splashy, "no longer afraid" ghost. Then, "someday" the ghost just disappears from the scene altogether and has left a goodbye note thanking the students for their help. Maybe it could reappear occasionally (as ghosts do) for special events or before or after an upsetting event.

Let's Go into the Garden and Pick a Pumpkin

To the tune of "Found a Peanut," teach the students "Pick a Pumpkin" with repetitive phrases and accompanying body/hand movements. The best way to teach it is for you to sing the entire song and demonstrate it, while the students listen and watch. Then, you can sing just the first phrase while the students listen and watch, and then the students can sing it along with you. Do it again, going phrase by phrase. You might also record it on a cassette tape so that the children can practice during recess. Here are the words and movements:

eyes wide open

> Saw a pumpkin, saw a pumpkin, saw a pumpkin on the vine;
> On the vine I saw a pumpkin, saw a pumpkin on the vine.

bend and pull with arms and hands

> Picked the pumpkin, picked the pumpkin, picked the pumpkin from the vine;
>
> From the vine I picked the pumpkin, picked the pumpkin from the vine.

use hands and arms to show big, bigger, biggest

> It's a big one, it's a huge one, it's a giant, and it's mine;
>
> It's a big one, it's a huge one, it's a giant, and it's mine.

point to eyes, nose, and smile broadly

> Put the eyes on, put the nose on, and put on a great big smile;
>
> Put the eyes on, put the nose on, and put on a great big smile.

extend arm with fist clasped around "latern handle" and sway arm back and forth

> Got a jack-o'-lantern, got a jack-o'-lantern, got a jack-o'-lantern now;
>
> Happy Halloween, Happy Halloween, I'm a jack-o'-lantern now!

A Witch's Snack

Make this "green with envy" witch's snack. Each child gets:

1 small chunk of green celery

7 (lucky number) green grapes

3 (magic number) scoops or cubes of lime gelatin

This tasty green snack is one of the witch's favorites because it's so nutritious and delicious. Eat it all and feel healthy. Smile a lot while you're eating, too. The witch gets "green with envy" when she sees people enjoying her favorite snack.

Let's Paint with Orange, Let's Paint with Black

After reading the poem "What Is Orange?" from *Hailstones and Hailibut Bones* by Mary O'Neill, set up the easel with three tones of orange tempera paint (bright red-orange, orange, and pastel orange). Students can paint a picture on 12″ × 18″ black construction paper. The painting can be inspired from the images in the poem, or it can be a Halloween painting. Also, after reading "What Is Black?" from Mary O'Neill's book, set up the easel with black, dark grey, and pastel grey tempera paints. Students can paint on a white or orange background. These delightful paintings are usually suitable for framing and displaying on the door, under the chalkboard, or in the hall.

CHRISTOPHER COLUMBUS, A SPACE PIONEER

Columbus Day is celebrated during October. The voyage of Christopher Columbus with his ships, the Nina, the Pinta, and the Santa Maria is similar to our present-day space explorations because they were/are both exploring unfamiliar and unknown territory. Make that connection for the young children. Explain that in the days of Columbus, most people believed that the world was flat, but that Columbus believed that it was round and set out to explore the earth. He proved that the earth was not flat, and is credited with "discovering" America. He was brave, just as our present-day space pioneers are brave.

On a large sheet of chart paper, conduct a class survey. First, to the entire group, read, "Would you want to explore outer space?" Give them time to think about it. Then, during work time, have students come to you individually to explain their "yes" or "no" reason. Print it as they dictate it, so that they can see the relationship between their words and the print that is being written. Some students begin to understand that they, too, can put their words into print.

Would You Want To Explore Outer ☺➤

YES	NO
I like rockets. (Pat)	I don't want to leave home. (Am)
I want to see the moon. (Alice)	My pet would miss me. (Joey)

FIRE PREVENTION WEEK

Each year at this time, we stress with students the importance of not playing with matches. Children need constant review of fire safety rules. These are some helpful activities.

- Smokey the Bear is the national symbol for preventing forest fires, but your class can adopt "Winfield Bear" as the class mascot. Winfield has the little word "win" in his name so we know that he will help us with fire safety. We can all "Win with Winfield Bear." (See the reproducible activity sheet.)

- Have a large stuffed bear represent Winfield in the classroom. Encourage all children to bring in their stuffed bears (or make paper ones) to hear the fire safety messages and to remind all of us that fire is dangerous.

- Winfield Bear asks that the class set aside one day during Fire Prevention Week to wear red clothing. Even the stuffed bears in the classroom can wear red ribbons. The message being sent is the same one that the traffic signal sends: RED MEANS STOP. Do not play with matches and do not go near fire. Perhaps the children could make small red badges for themselves and for their bears as well.

- Check with the students to see if they know the phone number of the local fire department. Practice dialing the number or touching the number squares on toy phones (or old phones that have been donated to the class).

- Practice making an emergency call to the fire department. Give the following information:
BEGIN: "I need help!"
TELL WHAT: _____
TELL WHERE: _____
GIVE YOUR NAME: _____

- Plan to have an extra classroom safety drill this week to teach the teddy bears the rules, such as walk quickly, no talking, eyes on the teacher (or leader) for directions, and so on. Caution children NEVER to run back into the building or a house to get something they have forgotten. It's not worth the risk.

- Practice the "stop, drop, roll" method that is effective in case clothing is on fire. Do not run.

- Plan a field trip to the fire station. The children learn valuable information from the firefighters. Seeing the trucks and equipment is also a good learning opportunity.

- If Winfield Bear cannot arrange it, you (or the principal) might call the local fire station to invite a fire truck visit to your school playground area. It is beneficial for all of the students to see the immense truck and to get a good look at fire safety equipment. It makes a lasting impression. In some cases, the children might even have the good fortune to get a ride in the "crow's nest"—that part of the truck that lifts to the upper floors of buildings.

- After a week with Winfield Bear, many students may decide to become firefighters when they grow up. Write letters to the local firefighters to thank them for helping to keep your area safe. Be sure to make illustrations on the letters.

INDIAN SUMMER

In some areas of the country, the temperatures get mild again AFTER the first frost. This return to a few days of warm weather is referred to as Indian Summer, and can happen twice. Early American Indians believed this Squaw Winter was a gift from the god of the southwest because the south winds bring the warm spell. It's a good time to look at some picture books under an autumn tree!

AUTUMN COLORS IN THE CLASSROOM

During this time of year, many parts of the country have a treat as the leaves on trees put on a dazzling display of color. To make colorful leaves for a classroom tree, use crayons and tempera paints.

You will need 9″ × 12″ manila paper, crayons, red and orange tempera paints, two large paintbrushes, paper towels, and scissors.

Give each student a 9″ × 12″ sheet of manila paper, and ask the students to outline a leaf shape (staying close to the edges of the paper). Next, they can use a variety of crayon colors to fill in the leaf space. Encourage students to press hard and fill in all of the spaces. Next, have the students brush over the brightly colored leaf using either red or orange tempera paint. Immediately rub off the paint with paper towels. The effect is a shiny leaf with colors showing through. Allow the leaves to dry, and then have the students cut out the shape. String them from a large, old tree branch that you have rescued from a park or woods, and potted in a can of plaster of Paris.

- Put the dazzling tree on the countertop and display seasonal books underneath.

- Put the spectacular tree on a tabletop, and sit under it while using headsets to listen to stories on tape. Or look at some picture books while sitting under the tree.

Reproducible Activity Pages for October

Mary's Magic Monday Mmmm Recipe (language experience)

Say-a-Story (creative thinking—letter C)

Play-a-Story (creative dramatics—letter F)

Frisky the Fox and Fall Fun (Halloween orange snack)

Flashcard Scatter (counting practice game)

Math Match Snack Time (counting; numeral recognition)

Hats, Pumpkins, and Brooms (counting; numerals; number words)

The Jack-o'-Lantern Witch (math)

Math Shapes: The Sphere (concept reinforcement)

Hands on the Pumpkin (science and math)

Daisy the Dragon (manuscript printing)

All Aboard the ABC Train (manuscript printing)

Ghost Story Writing and Rewriting (creative writing)

The Masked Owl Has a Halloween Message (Halloween safety)

Emily's Excellent Effort (rewarding desired behaviors)

Join the Firefighters! (fire safety)

MARY'S MAGIC MONDAY Mmmm RECIPE

Monday is a busy day for Mary. She has a quick and easy recipe to share with you. Mix it and taste it. Then say, "Mmmm!" It's so good, it even makes the cows say, "Mmmmoo-ooo!"

Name ———————————— Date ————————————

SAY-A-STORY

Let's make up a mystery story. Tie these three items together in a creative way. Who keeps eating the cake? Why does the candle keep going out? What else is happening in your story?

Today we are working with the letter C. In each case, the beginning letter sounds more like K.

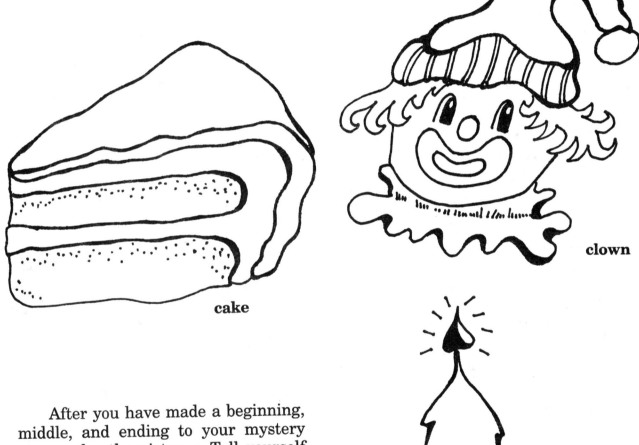

cake

clown

After you have made a beginning, middle, and ending to your mystery story, color the pictures. Tell yourself the story silently while you are working. Then tell your mystery story out loud (or in a whisper).

Later, print your story on paper (with the help of your teacher) and attach it to the back of this activity sheet.

candle

PLAY-A-STORY

Let's make up an adventure story. Link these three items together in a creative, unusual way. Pretend that the setting of the story is a hidden pond at the edge of the woods. Make up body movements for the fish, for the jumping frog, and for the flower as it sways in the breeze. The fish lives in the pond, the flower lives on land, but the frog can go back and forth between the two. This is going to be an exciting story!

Today we are working with the letter F.

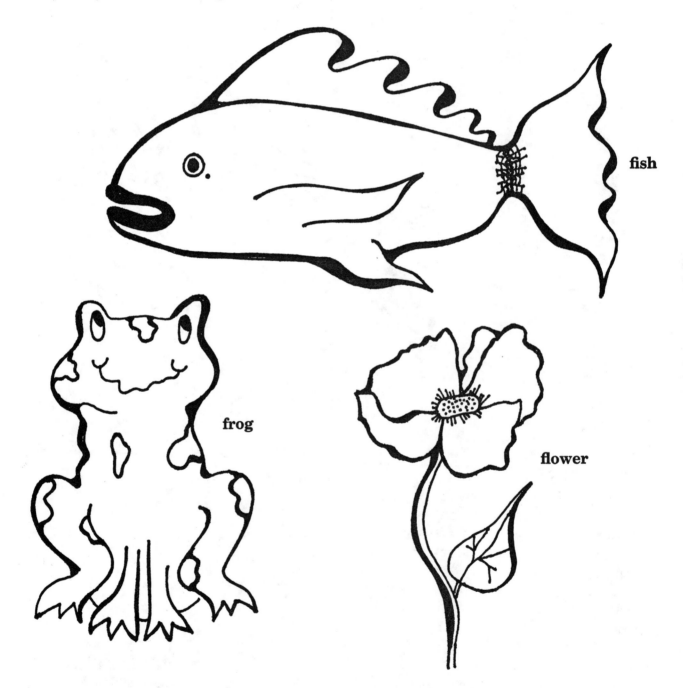

fish

frog

flower

Color the pictures. Tell yourself the beginning, middle, and ending of the story as you are thinking of a way to act out your story.

FRISKY THE FOX AND FALL FUN

Do you want to have some fun with Frisky? You will need an orange, and a black felt-tip pen. Using the felt-tip pen, make a jack-o'-lantern face on the orange. Then, peel and enjoy the orange for a snack.

Color Frisky the Fox and the orange jack-o'-lanterns below. Trace the letters on Frisky's dress, too.

FLASHCARD SCATTER

Cut the cards apart and keep them in an envelope. **FOR ONE PLAYER:** Match up the numeral card with the dot card. **FOR TWO PLAYERS:** Put the numeral cards in a pile, face down. Scatter the dot cards over the playing area. The first player turns over a numeral card and must point to the matching dot card *before* the other player does. The first one to find the match keeps the two cards. The second player now turns over a numeral card and must point to the matching dot card *before* the other player does. The player with the most matching cards at the end of the game wins. Shuffle, and play again. Keep score.

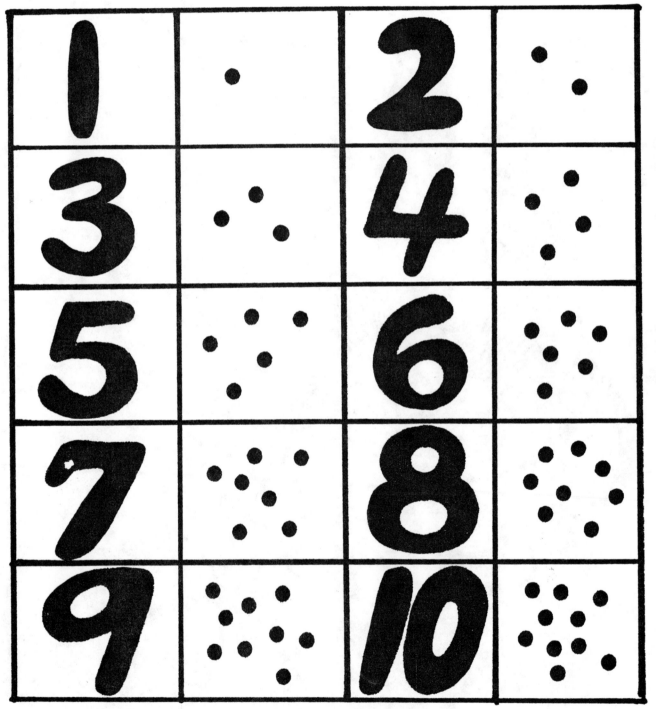

Name _____   Date _____

MATH MATCH SNACKTIME

It's time for some math snacks. Match the snack with the appropriate numeral. The first one has been done for you. Trace the numerals. Then use your crayons to make your snacks look yummy!

HATS, PUMPKINS, AND BROOMS

Each witch must find her own hat, pumpkin, and broom. First, count the stars on the hat and draw a line to the pumpkin that shows that numeral. Trace the numeral. Then match the pumpkin with the correct number word on the broom. BE CAREFUL! The witches are tricky. If information is missing, you can fill it in. The first one has been done to help you get started.

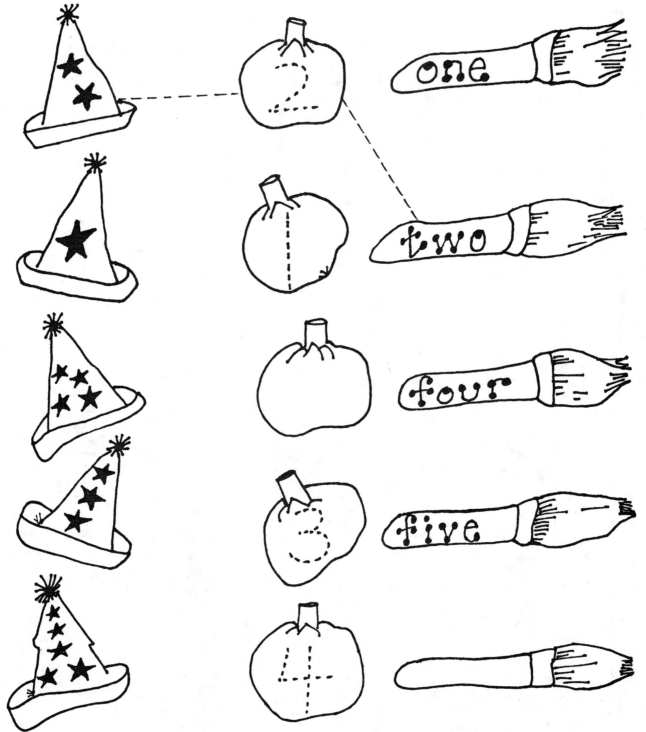

THE JACK-O'-LANTERN WITCH

This witch is making jack-o'-lantern deliveries. You can help her complete the orders. This is what you should do. Cut out small orange circles and paste the correct amount on each cat shape. Then, using your black crayon, make them into jack-o'-lanterns with different shapes for eyes, nose, and teeth. This busy witch says, "Thank you!"

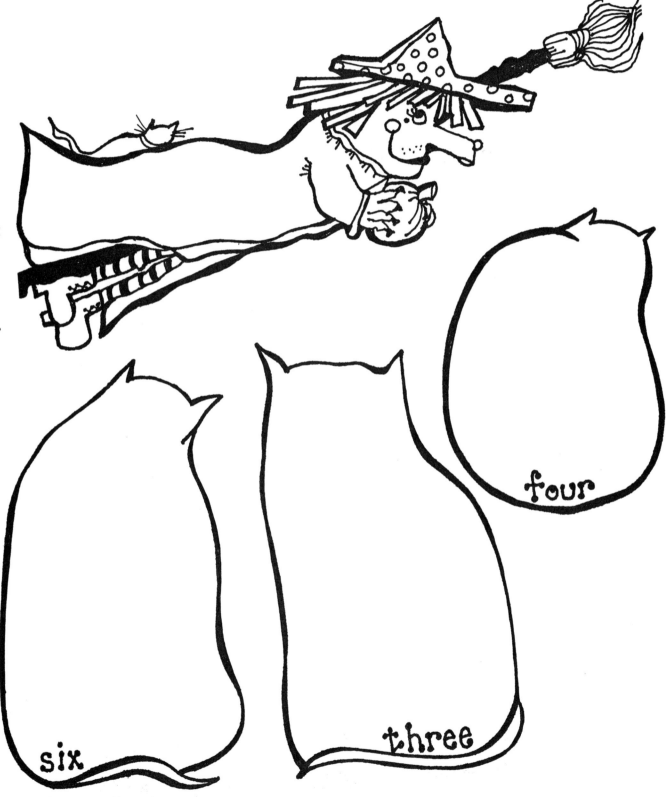

four

six

three

MATH SHAPES: THE SPHERE

There are five items on this page. Some of them are in the shape of a sphere. Find the sphere shapes and color the items. Put an X on the rest.

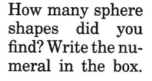 How many sphere shapes did you find? Write the numeral in the box.

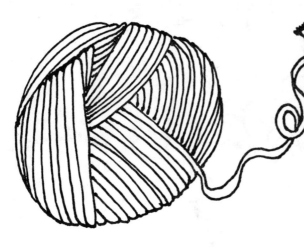

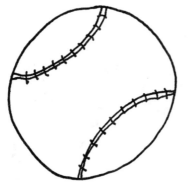

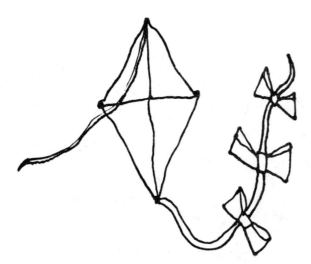

Cup your hands together as though you are holding a sphere-shaped object. Find an item in the room that is shaped like a sphere. Draw it on the back of this page.

HANDS ON THE PUMPKIN

   Let's do some exploring with our hands. We will need one giant-sized pumpkin, or several small pumpkins. We'll also need newspapers, a bowl, and water to wash the seeds. REMEMBER: Only your teacher is allowed to handle the knife.

1.

Feel the pumpkin before it is cut. Is it smooth, bumpy, or uneven? Is it heavy? Write a word or phrase to describe your pumpkin.

2.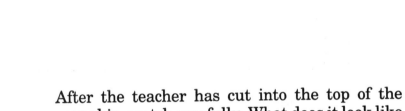

After the teacher has cut into the top of the pumpkin, watch carefully. What does it look like inside? Start dipping in with your hands to remove the insides. Write a word or phrase to describe this experience.

3.

Count by 1,2,3,4...

or by 5,10,15....

Put all of the seeds in a bowl. Wash them. Dry them.
ESTIMATE: How many seeds do you think there are?

_____

COUNT THEM: How many seeds are there?

_____

DAISY THE DRAGON

Daisy wants to help you with your printing. Do you have your pencil ready?

Daisy says you will need to make straight and curved lines when you print. You may copy hers. Then color Daisy.

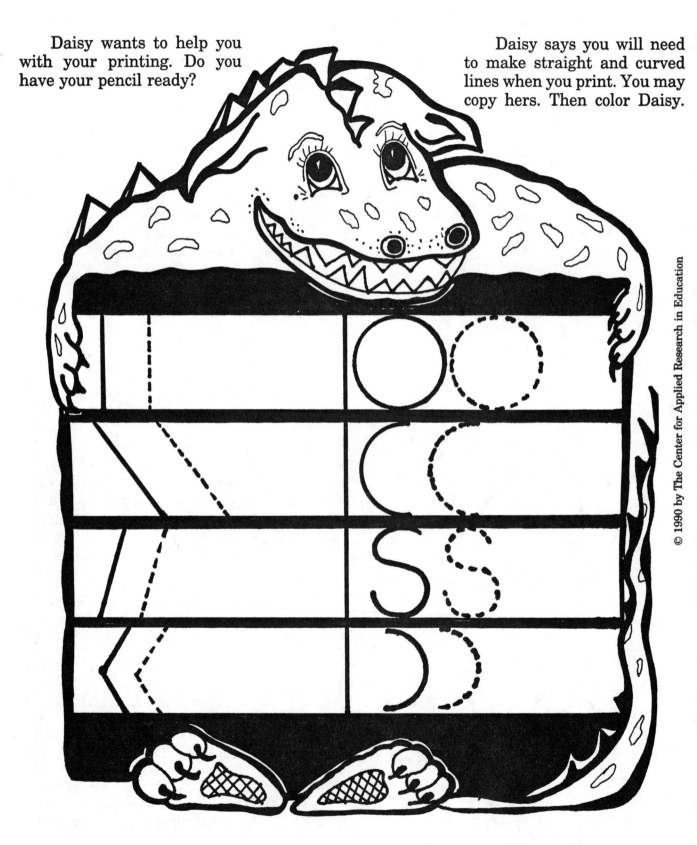

Name _____   Date _____

ALL ABOARD THE ABC TRAIN

Michael the Bear is ready to take a train ride. First, he must write his ABCs in the correct squares. Can you help him? Use your pencil and work slowly. When finished, color Michael to show what he looks like. "Thank you!" he says.

GHOST STORY WRITING AND REWRITING

The first time you write your scary Halloween story, this ghost will try to help you with some words. Write your story. Read it. Think about it. Get some suggestions for making it even more thrilling. Then rewrite your story. Now you are an author!

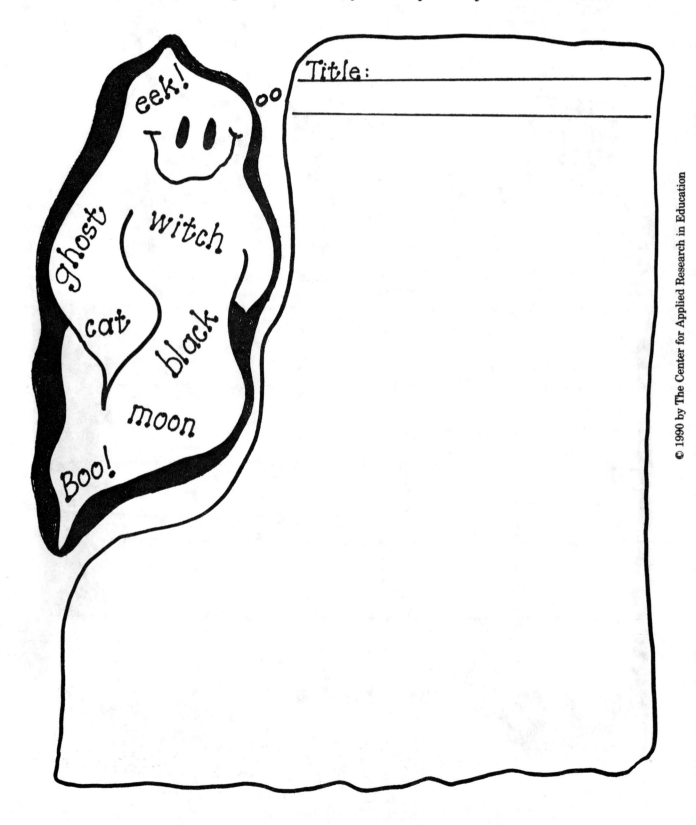

Title: _____
_____

THE MASKED OWL HAS A HALLOWEEN MESSAGE

List seven rules for a safe Halloween. Share the rules with classmates.

Seven Safe Halloween Rules
1.
2.
3.
4.
5.
6.
7.

EMILY'S EXCELLENT EFFORT

Emily the Moo has a message for you:

Try your best,
Aim to please.
Cover your nose
When you sneeze!
Don't forget to
   tie your shoe.
Act like yellow
   instead of blue.

Emily the Moo believes in you!

EMILY'S

EXCELLENT EFFORT BELL
GOES TO

_____

For _____

_____

_____

_____

_____

JOIN THE FIREFIGHTERS!

Fire Prevention Week is in October. Winfield Bear has a rhyme that he wants you to learn:

We play with leaves.
We play with snow.
When it comes to matches,
We JUST SAY NO!

Use your crayons to show Winfield's bright new firefighter's uniform

November

WE'RE NOT MIGRATING—WE'RE STAYING RIGHT HERE!

Here comes November, and with it comes a comfortable rhythm in the classroom as teacher and students work together in harmony. The youngsters are eager to come to school, and November seems to feed this eagerness with a variety of things to learn more about, such as the changing season, bird migration, and Thanksgiving. We also celebrate Children's Book Week and American Education Week this month. Because it's so busy, take time to rest and play and have quiet storytimes together.

RECOMMENDED CHILDREN'S BOOKS FOR NOVEMBER

- *Don't Eat Too Much Turkey!* by Miriam Cohen, pictures by Lillian Hoban (New York: Greenwillow Books, 1987). This is one in a series of books about Jim, Paul, and Anna Maria who are first graders. In this escapade, Anna Maria writes a play and gives everyone directions, but the cast of characters all have their own ideas about Thanksgiving. Under the teacher's direction, the children make a turkey project, a mural, and have their own feast for a happy Thanksgiving.

- *Cranberry Thanksgiving* by Wende and Harry Devlin (New York: Four Winds Press, 1971). What happens when Grandmother and Maggie, who have a famous secret cranberry bread recipe, invite Mr. Whiskers and Mr. Horace for Thanksgiving dinner? The secret recipe is stolen, that's what! The reader is in for a surprise when it comes to judging people by their looks and manners. As a special bonus, the cranberry recipe is printed at the end of this book. Enjoy!

- *A Three Hat Day* by Laura Geringer, illustrations by Arnold Lobel (New York: Harper and Row, 1985). R. R. Pottle the Third loves hats, and children will be introduced to many types—tam o'shanter, sombrero, beanie, and more. Although he has hats, R. R. has no one to share them with until he meets Isabel who has a "perfect" hat. In this fanciful tale, the two marry. When R. R. Pottle the Fourth is born, he doesn't like hats but he loves shoes. This book inspires dress-up play for children.

- *26 Letters and 99 Cents* by Tana Hoban (New York: Greenwillow Books, 1987). This is a combination alphabet book and number book. The ABC's are in bright, bold, glossy colors. But, what comes after the letter Z? Close the book, turn it over, and start from the other end for a number book! This is an excellet teaching tool, in which the children will delight!

- *One Fine Day* by Nonny Hogrogian (New York: Macmillan Publishing, 1971). This is a cumulative tale which sends the fox on a real fox chase so that he can give back to an old woman some milk that he took. If he can do that, she will sew his tail back on which she chopped off in anger. The fox must get his tail back; otherwise, all of his friends will laugh at him. This is a Caldecott Award winner.

- *Little Bear's Thanksgiving* by Janice, pictures by Mariana (New York: Lothrop, Lee and Shepard, 1967). Little Bear loves to eat but by the time Thanksgiving rolls around, he's fast asleep for the winter and it is very difficult to awaken him. He doesn't want to miss Thanksgiving this year, so how do the other animals help solve the problem?

- *The Quilt Story* by Tony Johnston, pictures by Tomie dePaola (New York: G. P. Putnam's Sons, 1985). This story centers around a child's quilt that serves to comfort Abigail, to be a companion to her, and to share her days. The beloved quilt eventually ends up in the attic, but continues to be the focal point of a story lovingly enhanced by charming illustrations.

- *Appelard and Liverwurst* by Mercer Mayer, pictures by Steven Kellogg (New York: Four Winds Press, 1978). This tale about Liverwurst the "rhinosterwurst," who livens things up on the farm after he arrives, takes place at harvest time in the autumn. Liverwurst is selected to pull the wagon, loaded with crops, to town. But, just dangle a delicious mushroom under Liverwurst's nose and he can't control himself. What happens when the mushroom farmers pull into town? Chaos! Children will howl with delight over this story, which is made all the more amusing with the illustrations.

- *In the Night Kitchen* by Maurice Sendak (New York: Harper and Row, 1970). Thanks to Mickey, we have cake every morning, and this picture book tells how we get the milk. The story is in rhyme, with Laurel and

Hardy type characters for cooks, and big writing in balloon captions done in cartoon style. Children enjoy this Caldecott Honor book.

- *Thanksgiving at the Tappletons'* by Eileen Spinelli, illustrated by Maryann Cocc-Leffler (New York: J. B. Lippincott, 1982). This hilarious story is about a Thanksgiving get-together where absolutely nothing goes right with the menu, but everything is right about the spirit at the end. Students like to hear this one again and again.

SPOTLIGHT ON READING

The Reading Backpackers

Line up 26 lunch bags on the counter, one for each letter of the alphabet. On each bag, paste a large cut-out of an alphabet letter, and arms, feet, head, and other features. Then have students collect real items or pictures of items that begin with the sound of the letter shown on the bag. Place the items and pictures inside the bag. Items can be brought in from home also (send a note to parents asking for assistance), and suitable items can be used from the playground, too.

Students can take a bag at a time, empty the contents, and make sure that the items are in the appropriate bag. Eventually, you might need to classify items within certain bags; such as, for the letter C: hard c sounds as in cake, cookie, calendar; and soft c sounds as in cent, celery, cement. Thus, some letter backpackers are more challenging than others.

One day, declare that the backpackers were rushing, causing their items to fall out and get mixed together. See if the students can restore order to the backpackers as they rework the letter/sound relationships. Then, one day, the backpackers just disappear. What happened? Well, the children had done such a nice job of helping to pack their bags, that the backpackers migrated to the south! (You can store the bags in a cupboard and return them to the counter in the spring as the backpackers migrate back to the room.)

Would You Rather Live in Pilgrim Days or Now?

In advance, have this question printed at the top of a large sheet of experience chart paper. As you proceed through November and read and talk about the days of Pilgrims and Indians and the customs of long ago, refer to the chart and have students think about their preference. Then, some day during a quiet working time or during an indoor recess period, call students to the chart on a one-to-one basis, and have them make their decision and give their reason. This can be printed on the chart by you or an aide. When finished, call upon students to decorate the chart with a colorful harvest border. The students will refer to this often and try to read the sentences.

Read Until You're Stuffed

The emphasis this month is upon children's literature, since Children's Book Week falls in the early part of November. Here's how to make a colorful book display area with a giant stuffed turkey.

Cut two oval shapes from butcher paper. Staple the edges, and stuff with newspaper. Then cut out a head, beak, wattle, and feet. Use a large easel brush with tempera paints to make feather strokes on the turkey body. The turkey can be surrounded by good storybooks, and can be propped up in a corner on a cozy rug for snuggling up to during a quiet reading time. (See the reproducible activity sheet section for a turkey to help keep track of this month's reading.)

The Long and Short of Vowels

It had to happen sometime! In the process of decoding words, students are stymied by those vowels. It helps to know that the vowels (a, e, i, o, u, and sometimes y) really have more than one sound. Basically, they have two sounds— one long (the letter says its name) and one short (ah, eh, ih, aah, uh—sounds made in the back of the throat). These are difficult to remember, and visual clues and stories are invaluable aids. Here's a tale that should help the students learn the sounds. (See the reproducible activity sheets for reinforcement.)

Meet the Alligator and the Ogre

Once upon a time, there lived an alligator, named Uncle Alligator, who gathered up all of the vowels (a, e, i, o, u) and took very good care of them. On the other side of the forest, there lived an ogre who also gathered up all of the vowels (a, e, i, o, u) and took very good care of them. Now, word got out to the ogre that the alligator had some vowels, and, of course, he was very greedy and wanted them. He sent word to the alligator that he was ready to fight for the vowels. The alligator would not give up his vowels without a fight, so he agreed. A date was set for the fight. But, the alligator had to send word that he could not be there, so they set a date for another fight.

This happened time after time after time. The truth was that every time the alligator thought about the fight, his elbows began to itch. He then spent all his time scratching. The note sent to the ogre always said the same thing:

Uncle Alligator has itch on elbows.

(TEACHER: Write phrase on the chalkboard and circle the words that begin with u, a, i, o, e. Then read it aloud, emphasizing the short vowel sounds. Place the cup shape ˘ above the vowels.)

Now, the ogre, who was not all bad, wanted Uncle Alligator to get better so that he could fight. He desperately wanted those vowels, so he decided to send Uncle Alligator his favorite treat—icy acorns:

Ogre eats icy acorns while riding on his unicorn.

(TEACHER: Write this phrase on the chalkboard and circle the words that begin with o, e, i, a, u. Then read it aloud, emphasizing the long vowel sounds. Place the straight mark— above the vowels.)

The End

Help students to notice that although the vowels are out of the traditional ABC order, the messages still contain the letters a, e, i, o, u. Point out that the alligator has only short vowel sounds and the ogre has only long vowel sounds. Will this make a difference? (Create an aura of mystery as you appeal to the wonderful imaginations at this developmental stage.) The long and short vowels will be discussed again in December.

Let's Learn the "Alligator Itch"

Oh, we itch, itch, itch (*itch elbows*)
And we twitch, twitch, twitch
(*wiggle body*)
On, and on, and on. (*keep itching
and twitching*)

Yes, we itch, itch, itch (*itch elbows*)
And we twitch, twitch, twitch
(*wiggle body*)
When Uncle Alligator says his sounds:

    A – Alligator (*itch ankle*)
    E – Elbow (*itch elbow*)
    I – Itch (*itch foot's instep*)
    O – On (*itch with opposite hand*)
    U – Uncle (*itch under nose*)

Ah, Eh, Ih, Aaah, Uh! RAH! RAH! RAH!

Here Comes the Ogre

Here comes the ogre, oh! oh! oh!
Riding a unicorn on the snow. (*two*
    fists together, moving hands up
    and down as if riding a horse)
The unicorn stops by a great big
    tree (*encircle arms overhead*
    and sway)
And eats icy acorns, 1, 2, 3. (*reach*
    up to pluck acorns and put
    fingers to lips as if eating; repeat
    three times)

Run to find the alligator. (*run in*
    place)
Skip to find the alligator. (*skip in*
    place)
Jump across the ditch. (*high jump in place*)
Feed him icy acorns (*bring hand to mouth*)
Sent by ogre's unicorns
To stop that itch! (*rub elbow gently and*
    look amazed because itching stops)
Stop that itch!
    A – Acorns
    E – Eat
    I – Icy
    O – Ogre
    U – Unicorn
A, E, I, O, U! RAH!

SPOTLIGHT ON MATH

Plymouth Rock Toss

For this activity, you need two small beanbags (the "rocks"), one box with three holes ("Plymouth Rock"), and labels (1, 5, 10) under the holes.

Two or three students can play at a time. One student tosses the beanbag at "Plymouth Rock" (the box) three consecutive times and all players help to add up the score. The player with the highest score is the winner. Repeat several times.

- The "Plymouth Rock Rabbit" can help with rote counting to 100 by fives. Have students put their hands up to their heads to represent rabbit ears. Flap one hand and say, "Five," flap the other hand and say, "Ten," flap the first hand again and say, "Fifteen," and so on. This can be done to music. Have students "rock" and when the music stops, they say, "Five," and flap one ear (hand); rock again, stop the music, and students say, "Ten." Repeat until you reach 100.

- Be sure to find Plymouth, Massachusetts on a map or globe. There is a huge rock (boulder) monument to honor the Pilgrims who sailed on the Mayflower and reportedly landed there in 1620. Perhaps a student has been to Plymouth and can tell about the giant boulder (that's a new vocabulary word, too). The school librarian can help in finding a picture of the monument.

Turkey Gobble Game

This game works with the concept of NEAR and FAR. Select an object in the room that is going to be partially hidden from view. Send one person out into the hall (or into the coatroom or bathroom) while another person partially hides the object. Everyone should be very quiet while the person who is "It" is called back into the room and asked to search for the object. As the person gets "nearer," the class begins to say, "Gobble, gobble." The farther away the person gets, the fainter the "Gobble, gobble" becomes. When the person is right next to the object, the "Gobble, gobble" should get loud. (Determine with the students the appropriate volume for their turkey talk as they play to reinforce the concept of near and far.)

Storybook Characters at Work

Gather a bunch of easel brushes (about 10 or 12) in a container. Use familiar storybook characters to tell who is going to be painting at the easel today. For example, The Three Billy Goats are painting this morning so they will need three brushes. (You can remove the brushes one by one as the children help count aloud 1, 2, 3.) Return the brushes and note that Cinderella and the Prince, Snow White, and Little Red Riding Hood are coming to the easel today to paint. How many brushes will we need to get for them? You can take out one brush, and the students will need to "add on" three more in order to have four. (This can be written on the chalkboard as 1 + 3 = 4 for additional reinforcement.)

Continue with the storybook characters by having students use these characters to make up stories about who's painting at the easel today. What would Cinderella paint at the easel? (A pumpkin, a coach, the palace, her wicked stepsisters, and so on.) Who is going to be Cinderella today? (Have students sign up to be storybook characters to paint what they think the characters would paint.) Who will be The Big Bad Wolf and what will he paint? Who will be Mother Goose and what will she paint?

Paintbrushes for a Family of Seven, Please

The Seven Dwarfs are coming to paint, so you can set aside two brushes. How many brushes do we need to "add on" for the dwarfs? (2 + __ = 7.) Suppose that we have the seven brushes set aside and four dwarfs come along? Let's put four by the easel. How many more make seven? (4 + __ = 7.)

- Use the concept of the family of the Seven Dwarfs, who come along in different sets, to reinforce the math family of seven which can be represented in different sets: 1 + 6, 2 + 5, 3 + 4, 4 + 3, 5 + 2, 6 + 1.

- Point out the set pattern. As the first amount grows larger, the second amount gets smaller. Is this true for other number families? Let's try six, five, eight, and so.

Soup's On

Do the students want alligator soup or ogre soup today? We won't really eat alligator soup or ogre soup, but we can make the favorite soup of Uncle Alligator (short vowels) and the ogre (long vowels). What is their favorite soup? You guessed it—the alligator likes Chicken Vegetable Alphabet Soup with all those letters in it, and the ogre likes plain Vegetable Alphabet Soup with all those letters in it!

The students will need to put their problem-solving math skills to work to figure out the following:

How many styrofoam cups will we need?

How many plastic spoons will we need?

How many cans of soup will we need to open?

How many cans of water will we add?

Will we have alligator soup one day and ogre soup another day?

Will we cook it in a slow cooker on HIGH or will we use a pot on the stove?

How many spoons will we need to stir the soup?

How will we get the soup from the container into the cups?

How long will it take to cook?

How long will it take to eat?

The students have a lot to figure out, but math will enable them to organize, to work things out, and to solve problems. (NOTE: The math concepts include one-to-one correspondence, volume, temperature, time, going from larger to smaller containers, and liquid measure.) Five or six students can be served from one can of soup. Remember that you are working with the *experience* rather than with a full-blown lunch (although some crackers might be nice, too!).

Let's Talk About Great Big Numbers

Ever wonder what alligators and ogres like for dessert? It would have to be something that uses their special sound and, since they both like to eat, the amounts would have to be very large. (For example: the alligator might eat 100 Apples, 60 Eggs, 75 Icky snails, a ton of Olives, and a peck of Underwater turtles.)

- Have students use grocery ads from newspapers to determine sizes such as bushel, 5-pound bag, 16-ounce can, and so on. This will get them interested in large numbers. Perhaps they can begin to bring in large empty containers to show some of these amounts.

- Have students put together a menu "fit for the ogre" and "fit for the alligator." Use large amounts (quantity) and, of course, words that contain their special long and short vowel sounds. Print the menus on alligator and ogre shapes. An ogre ice cream treat may be just the thing to top off this activity!

It's Time to Make Graphs

A graph is a great big picture of information. We can find something out "at a glance" when we use a graph. It's a way of collecting, organizing, recording, and "reading" data.

Since it is good for the young child to begin with known information and work toward more abstract concepts (or the unknown), graph information that is relevant to the student. For starters, you can make a graph of "Our Favorite Color" or "Our Class Birthday Graph." (See the reproducible activity sheets.)

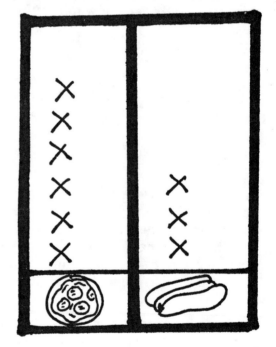

Once students get the hang of it, they like to graph other information and to make their own individual graphs. They can start with simple graphs that require a "forced choice" such as, "Which do you like better—pizza or hot dogs?" Later, they can go to three items. Finally, they can use two or three categories and one for "Other." For example, "My favorite storybook character is Snow White, Johnny Appleseed, The Big Bad Wolf, or Other." Students are sharpening their process skills by working with graphs.

HANDS-ON SCIENCE

The Edges of Leaves

Some edges of leaves are jagged like saws, some are rounded, some are pointed, some are frilly. Examine the edges closely and classify the leaves by the contour of their edges. Leaves can also be classified by size and color. Can students find other ways to classify leaves? It's time to set up your Autumn Table and to bring in leaves.

Ask students to look for leaves on their way to school. Have a large container available because some students bring in bags full. Again, these can be categorized by shape, size, color, texture (rough, smooth, silky), and degree of dryness/moisture. If the batch of leaves gets too large, have a committee select those that are to remain and those that can be returned to nature via the playground.

Be sure to have a magnifying glass available and, if possible, a microscope, so that students can examine the stems and vein patterns.

Who Eats Leaves?

People usually don't eat leaves from trees but we do eat other plant leaves, such as cabbage leaves (cole slaw) and lettuce leaves (green salad). Animals and insects nibble at leaves. Sometimes trees have to be sprayed with insecticides in order to save the tree from being destroyed by nibbling insects. A good picture book to read is *The Very Hungry Caterpillar* by Eric Carle. It has real holes in the pages to show how the caterpillar ate through leaves as well as other items.

A Fashion Show in the Sky

Trees wear seasonal leaf hats and, in autumn, they put on their brightest, showiest, splashiest, most colorful hats of leaves. During the autumn season, people travel to New England just to see this fashion parade of leaf hats that come in many shades of reds, oranges, and golden yellows.

Your students can have their own Autumn Tree Fashion Parade. Make colorful leaf hats using a circular shape of oaktag as a base. Get bright shades of tissue paper (orange, red, yellow, purple, maroon, blue, green) and have students gently tear them into small pieces. These can be glued to the circular base by using a brush dipped into watered-down white glue. Allow these to dry. Use ribbon or thick, bright orange yarn to tie them under the chin. Then strut in an Autumn Tree Fashion Parade. Wow! Be sure to plan your route in advance (through other classrooms and the office) so that everyone can see the show—and then march outdoors to show the trees. They're watching, too!

Leaf Identification Books

Choose a leaf shape and make a book about that tree. Identify the tree by name on the cover. Show the tree in different seasons. If possible, include a real leaf that has been pressed between sheets of wax paper.

CHILDREN'S BOOK WEEK

The Wonderful Storybook Quilt

Cover the bulletin board with a large sheet (or sheets) of colorful construction paper in red, orange, or dark blue. Find wallpaper, wrapping paper, or cloth material that has a small overall design (calico print) and cut strips for a border and for a grid. Then measure and cut a variety of colors from construction paper to fit within the squares. Have students select a color and make their favorite storybook character on it by using felt pens. Glue the squares onto the grid. Have students put their initials in the lower right-hand corner. Now the class has a storybook quilt—and students can gather around this spot to tell their story. You might want to save the wonderful quilt for Spring Open House.

Bring in a special hat or a variety of hats and refer to these as "The Storyteller Hats." Students can wear the different hats as they tell different stories. The "hats" seem to magically help students remember the stories and to send an elaborate word or two to make them even more interesting.

Plan a Book Festival

Make an arrangement with a teacher of an upper grade to send students to your classroom this week for a Book Festival. Older students can read stories to small groups, they can record stories on cassette tapes, and they can help the young children make books. (The younger students can dictate their stories to an older student, who can write the words underneath the picture that has been drawn.) Try to arrange for this event to be videotaped, and play it in the morning in the entryway as students arrive for school. It's another way of broadcasting and celebrating Children's Book Week.

There's Magic in Threes

Have three students work together to memorize and tell a story. The story can be divided into the beginning, middle, and the ending. Students can use real props or puppets or dress up as the storybook characters. When the storytellers perfect their performance, they can go "on the road" (other grades can sign up for a time to have the storytellers visit their classroom). Again, try to videotape the event, or at least capture it on a cassette tape recorder.

Invite a Storyteller to Class

Check with your local library to see if there are storytellers in the area who would be willing to visit the classroom to tell a story. Invite parents or area college students to come in to read during this week, too.

A THANKSGIVING POPCORN POWWOW

Thanks to the American Indians, the Pilgrims were introduced to corn. Somehow it was discovered that when corn "seeds" were exposed to intense heat, the inside of the seed POPPED right out. This popped corn (or popcorn) tasted delicious and is also nutritious. Corn was a staple of the diet in those days, and people ate popcorn as a breakfast cereal. Today, dentists tell us that popcorn (minus the butter) helps to polish our teeth. It also contains few calories when eaten plain.

Popcorn Powwow Time

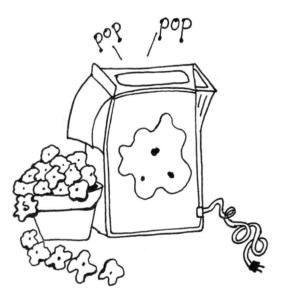

For a different kind of Thanksgiving Festival, arrange to have a popcorn party. The students can engage in a sensory learning experience as they discover and describe the sight, smell, sound, taste, and feel of popcorn.

First, have these materials available: popcorn seeds, electric popcorn popper, styrofoam cups or bowls, a scoop, a large pan or bowl, newspapers to spread on the work area, napkins, butter and salt (both optional), and experience chart paper with headings already printed at the top, such as "The Day We Had a Popcorn Powwow," "The Sight, Sound, Smell, Taste, and Feel of Popcorn," "How to Make Popcorn," and "Food Fit for Pilgrims, American Indians, and Me."

Now, pour some seeds into the popper (be sure to follow the particular directions that come with the popper), and just wait. As the seeds begin to pop, ask the students to think of a word or words that describe that sound, that wonderful smell, that explosion or blizzard going on inside of the popper (the plastic lid enables students to see this). A measure of popcorn can be served in styrofoam cups for students to enjoy. Then elicit descriptive words that tell how it looks, feels, and tastes.

Next, it's time to divide into committees. A teacher-aide, parent volunteers, or upper-grade student volunteers can be of invaluable help here. On the experience chart entitled "How to Make Popcorn," the student committee can write the experience by telling what they did first, second, third, next, and so on. Pictures to accompany the text are very helpful. "The Sight, Sound, Smell, Taste, and Feel of Popcorn" committee will have to elicit this information individually from classmates and bring back a word to print on the chart. The "Food Fit for Pilgrims, American Indians, and Me" committee might want to visually represent the past and present event.

Keep the popcorn popping during the powwow (supervised by an adult) and try to involve everyone in this experience. This is important because many students may only be familiar with microwave popcorn and don't see the popcorn kernels (seeds) in action.

Plan ahead so that there is plenty of time to enjoy the popcorn, complete (or almost complete) the experience chart pages, and clean up after the powwow.

Activities for the Powwow

Here are more suggestions to add variety to the powwow:

- Ask parents to loan their popcorn poppers so that small groups can have one to use and observe (each with adult supervision). This cuts down on traffic.

- When the powwow is over and everyone is settled down, bring out a large bag each of cheese popcorn and caramel corn. Have students taste them and decide which of the three (plain, cheese, caramel) they like best. It's a great opportunity for graphing!

- Red and purple popcorn? If you decide to use melted butter, you can add food coloring to it and have a variety of shades of colored popcorn.

- Let's count the seeds and then count the popcorn. Did they all pop?

- Make enough popcorn so that you have some to eat for breakfast (with milk) the next day, just like Pilgrim boys and girls.

- How many ways did we use math when we made the popcorn? Try to list them (number of cups or bowls used; number of batches of corn popped; number of seeds that popped when we experimented with counting them before and after; measuring how many to put into the popper; determining how long it took for the corn to pop from beginning to the last pop;

determining how much space the unpopped seeds took up in comparison with how much space the popped corn took up; recalling the step-by-step procedure for making the popcorn).

- Make popcorn-shaped cards with the capital letters P and C printed on them. Students can cover the letter C with the corn kernels, and then insert the corn kernels into the popper, and cover the letter P with the popped corn. Students can take home the cards and some seeds in a plastic bag so that they can remember to share their pow-wow experience with family members.

- Find library books about popcorn and share them with students. You might try *The Popcorn Book* by Tomie dePaola and *Popcorn* by Frank Asch. Then, at a later time, have students create their own books about popcorn.

WHERE'S YOUR BIG CARDBOARD LOOM?

Remember the loom that was suggested in the September section? You may now want to take advantage of the natural items from the environment and weave them into the loom.

Set up the great big loom and slit the ends and string it. Students can stand while they work on it. The items woven into the loom can be seasonal, such as dried grasses, long cat tails, weeds, dried corn stalks, dried leaves, wheat, and so on. These can be woven along with yarns that are the color of the countryside now—browns, beiges, autumn gold, dull green. It's a most effective work of art for the classroom.

THE FRIENDSHIP TREE

For the real classroom tree, have students make construction paper "faces" of American Indians and Pilgrims and tie them to the branches. Place the tree in the middle of a table, and have an abundance of picture books that reflect the changing season, the Thanksgiving holiday, and the subjects you are studying. This table can also be the November home for a display of a wide variety of gourds, squash, pumpkins, Indian corn, cornstalks, and other seasonal items that give the classroom a homey, yet aesthetically pleasing touch.

WHAT'S GOING ON AT THE COLOR TABLE?

This month, you may want to investigate and explore one or two of the secondary colors—perhaps autumn gold or violet or mauve or beige. Go to a paint store and ask for paint strips so that students can see the wide variety of tones in a single color referred to as "beige," for example. These are interesting names as well, such as Buffy Beige, Mud Mush, Putty Tan, Almond Autumn, and so on. Have students bring in samples of items they find at home and explore the classroom for items as well. Ask parents for help with this activity. Even a broom fits into the Autumn Gold category—you'll be amazed at the array of items that will fill up the color table when you select a secondary shade.

A DRIED WEED BOUQUET

Encourage students to bring in dried seeds that they find outdoors. (This may require a country ride for you or interested parents in order to get samples, but it's worth it.) Place the weeds in a large wicker wastebasket. Set out construction paper that has been cut into wide strips. There should be several shades of brown, tan, and gold. Students can select the background sheet (12″ × 18″) from among a variety of autumn colors as well. Have students construct their own weed bouquet with the wide strips of autumn tones—you'll be amazed at the beautiful results. Frame them and display them for all to admire and enjoy.

Reproducible Activity Pages for November

Meet Uncle Alligator (short vowel sounds)
Meet the Ogre and His Icy Acorns (long vowel sounds)
The Alligator Itch (short vowel sounds)
The Ogre's Icy Acorn Chant (long vowel sounds)
Say-a-Story (creative thinking—letter T)
Play-a-Story (creative dramatics—letter R)
The Number Rabbit (counting by fives to 100)

Hats, Pumpkins, and Corn (matching
objects, numerals, number words)
Signs-of-Autumn Math (addition facts)
Basic Shapes: Halves (concept
reinforcement)
Class Birthday Graph (graphing)
Rectangle Rex (math shape)
The Turkey in the Straw Gives Thanks
(Thanksgiving holiday)
November Names (working with letters
t, p, m, f)
The Johnny Appleseed Memory Game
(increasing memory span)
**Autumn Leaves Come in Different
Shapes, Sizes, and Colors**
(math/science—classification)
Timmy Turkey Gobbles Up Good Books (reading)
Storybook Characters in Action (children's literature)

MEET UNCLE ALLIGATOR

Uncle Alligator thinks that he owns the vowels, and he gets itchy elbows when someone wants to take them away from him. Today, you can trace the vowel letters and color Uncle Alligator's vowel suit. Can you think of a word that begins with each short vowel sound?

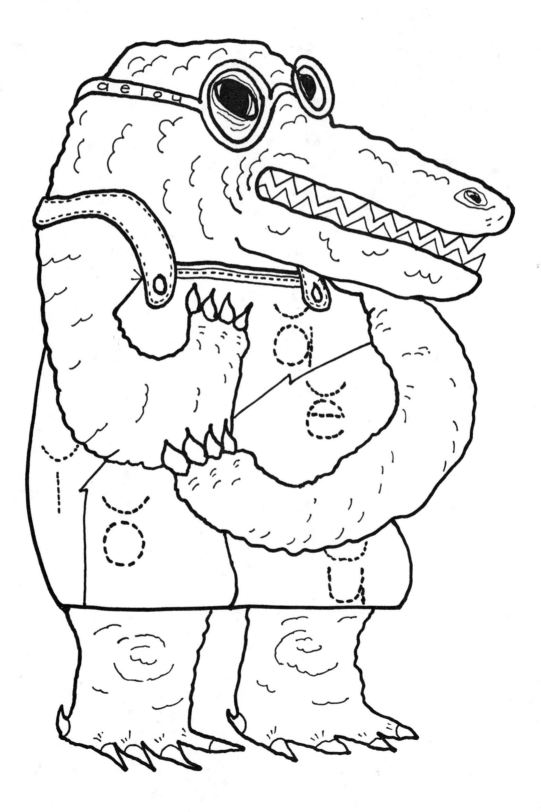

MEET THE OGRE AND HIS ICY ACORNS

The ogre is greedy and wants to own all of the vowel letters. He will fight for them. Trace the vowel letters and color his handsome portrait. Can you think of words that begin with the long vowel sounds?

THE ALLIGATOR ITCH

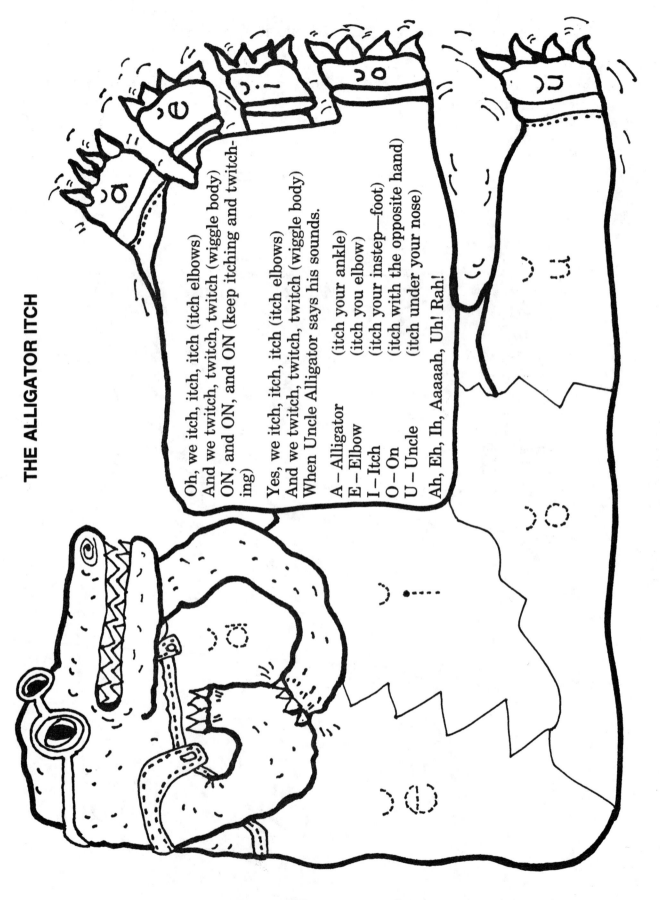

Oh, we itch, itch, itch (itch elbows)
And we twitch, twitch, twitch (wiggle body)
ON, and ON, and ON (keep itching and twitch-
ing)

Yes, we itch, itch, itch (itch elbows)
And we twitch, twitch, twitch (wiggle body)
When Uncle Alligator says his sounds.

A – Alligator   (itch your ankle)
E – Elbow   (itch you elbow)
I – Itch   (itch your instep—foot)
O – On   (itch with the opposite hand)
U – Uncle   (itch under your nose)

Ah, Eh, Ih, Aaaaah, Uh! Rah!

THE OGRE'S ICY ACORN CHANT

Here come the Ogre, oh, oh, oh.
Riding a unicorn on the snow, (ride in place)
The unicorn stops by a great big tree
And eats icy acorns, 1,2,3.
Run to find the alligator. (run in place)
Skip to find the alligator. (skip in place)
Jump across the ditch. (jump in place)
Feed him icy acorns
Sent by Ogre's unicorns
to STOP THAT ITCH!
STOP THAT ITCH!

Ā Ē Ī Ō Ū

A – acorns
E – eat
I – ice
O – ogre
U – unicorn

RAH!

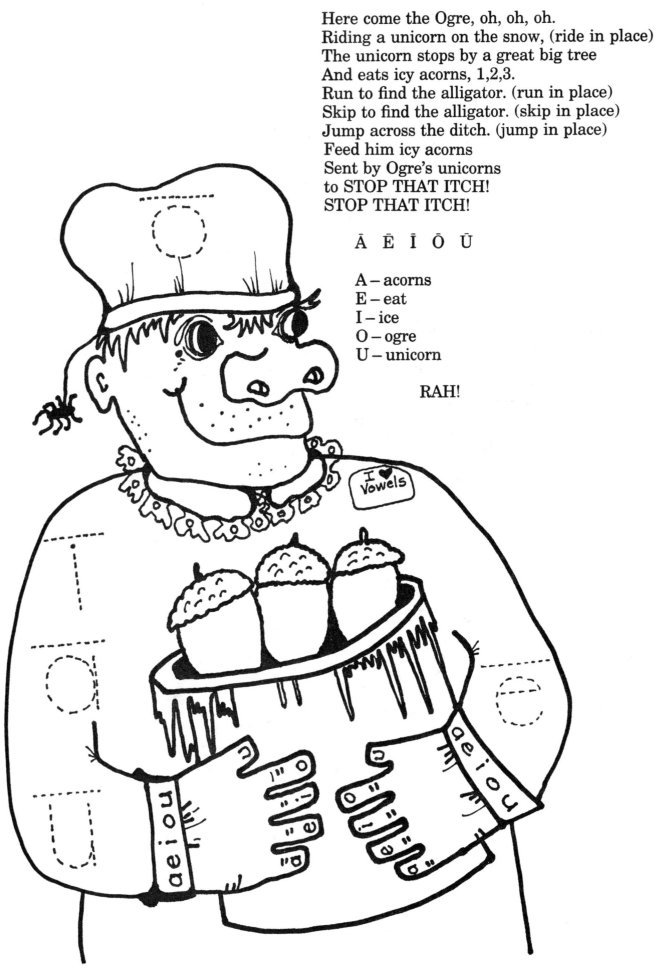

SAY-A-STORY

The telephone is ringing. Who will answer it—the tulip or the turtle? What will the message be? What if it is the wrong number? Can the telephone talk? There is going to be a lot of talking in this story. Use your imagination.

Today we are working with the letter T.

telephone

tulip

turtle

Tell yourself the story as you color the pictures. Then say the story out loud to good listeners.

PLAY-A-STORY

The three animals are very still. When the wind blows, two of the animals start rocking back and forth, back and forth, but they don't go anywhere. The rooster does not understand this. He wants to play, skip, and hop. How is he going to play with the rocking horse and the rabbit? You can help solve the problem. Use your imagination, and have fun!

Today we are working with the letter R.

rocking horse

rooster

rabbit

Color the animals, and think about how you are going to move around when you tell your story.

THE NUMBER RABBIT

This rabbit's ears twitch because she is listening for numbers. Today she heard you counting by fives. Trace and write the numerals to 100.

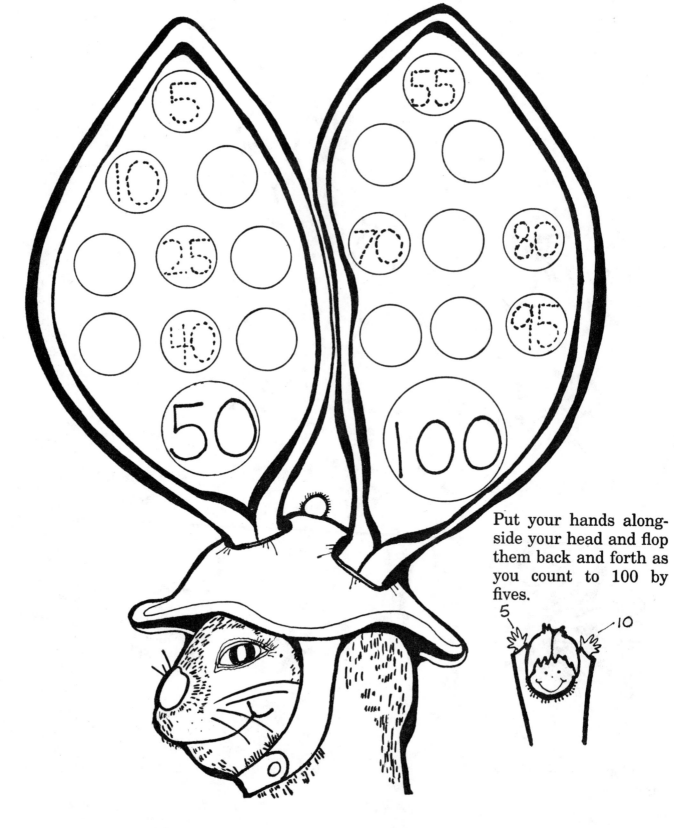

Put your hands along-side your head and flop them back and forth as you count to 100 by fives.

HATS, PUMPKINS, AND CORN

Count the number of dots on the Pilgrim hat. Draw a line to the matching pumpkin numeral, and then to the number name on the corn. The first one has been done for you. Use your harvest colors to make the foods look healthy.

SIGNS-OF-AUTUMN MATH

Complete the addition facts. Count the number of autumn items in each square. Connect them to the addition fact with the same answer. The first two have been done for you. When finished, color the autumn items with your favorite colors.

Name _____

Date _____

BASIC SHAPES: HALVES

Do you recognize the basic shapes—triangle, rectangle, square, and circle? Today we are going to divide them in half. Use your pencil and ruler, and make sure that both sides are EQUAL, or the same size. Then, color the halves.

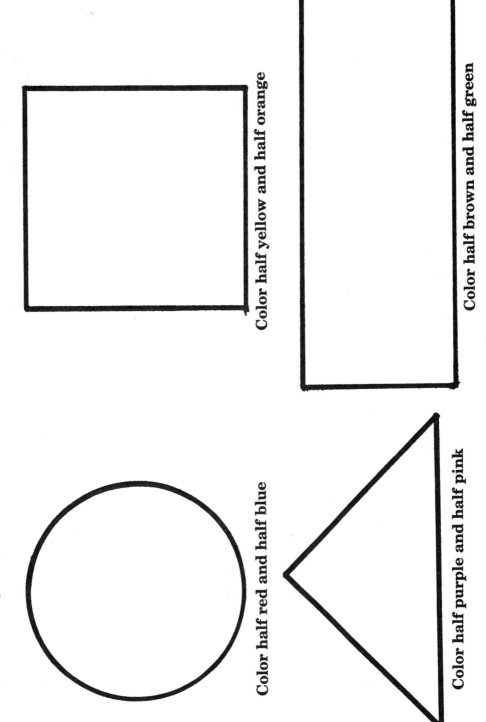

Color half yellow and half orange

Color half brown and half green

Color half red and half blue

Color half purple and half pink

CLASS BIRTHDAY GRAPH

Make a class graph. How many students were born in January? Color that many squares. Do the same for all the months. Use a different color for each mouth. Which month has the most birthdays? Which has the least? What other things can you learn from your graph?

how many? / month	Jan.	Feb.	Mar.	Apr.	May	June	July	Aug.	Sept.	Oct.	Nov.	Dec.
7												
6												
5												
4												
3												
2												
1												

RECTANGLE REX

Rectangle Rex loves rectangles. To-day he is shopping for rectangle shapes. Can you help him? Draw an item in each rectangle for which he's looking. He likes bright colors, too!

Draw an item (rectangle shape) that you can hold in your hand.

Draw an item (rectangle shape) that you can use in your house.

Draw an item (rectangle shape) that can move on streets and highways.

THE TURKEY IN THE STRAW GIVES THANKS

This Thanksgiving turkey hid some Thanksgiving messages in the straw. Now he can't find them. Can you help?

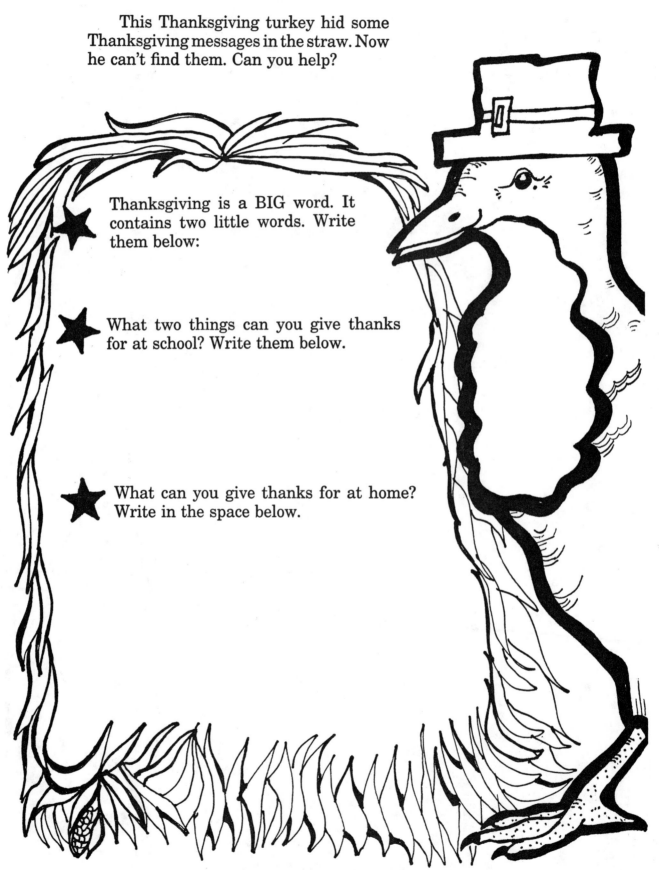

Thanksgiving is a BIG word. It contains two little words. Write them below:

What two things can you give thanks for at school? Write them below.

What can you give thanks for at home? Write in the space below.

Name _____

NOVEMBER NAMES

Date _____

November has so many names.
Mayflower, Indians, Pilgrims, games,
Corn and squash and turkey, too.
We give thanks for ALL of you!

DIRECTIONS: In the spaces below, trace the letter. Then use your crayons to draw something that begins with that letter. Sound out the letters! Be sure to color the friendly Indian, too.

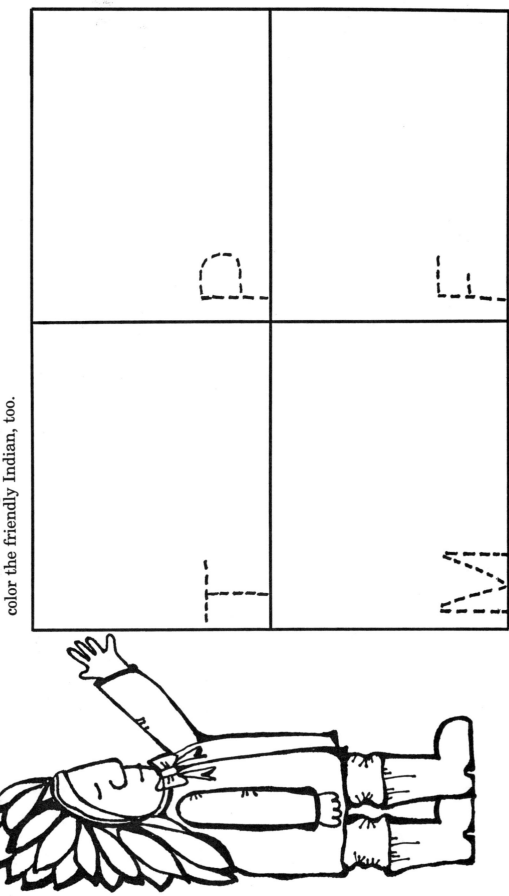

THE JOHNNY APPLESEED MEMORY GAME

In each box below, there is a picture about apples. Color each picture, and cut the boxes apart on the lines. TO PLAY: Shuffle the cards. Lay them face down and turn over two cards. If the cards match, you may keep them. If the cards do not match, turn them face down. Try to remember where each picture is hidden as your partner takes a turn. The winner is the player who has the most matching cards.

To add a little excitement, Johnny Appleseed has included an apple worm. That's a "wild" card and matches up with any other card that shows a whole apple on it.

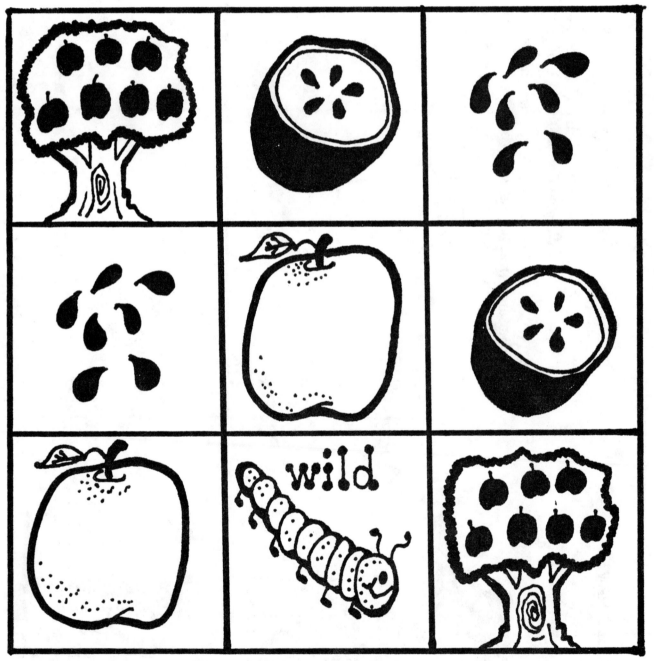

Name _____ Date _____

AUTUMN LEAVES COME IN DIFFERENT SHAPES, SIZES, AND COLORS

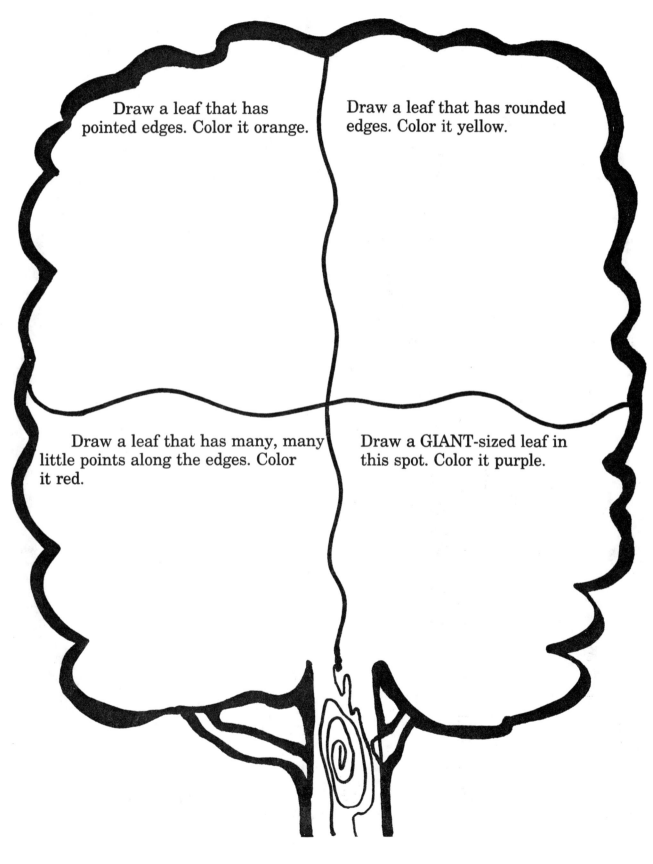

Draw a leaf that has pointed edges. Color it orange.

Draw a leaf that has rounded edges. Color it yellow.

Draw a leaf that has many, many little points along the edges. Color it red.

Draw a GIANT-sized leaf in this spot. Color it purple.

Children's Book Week is in November. Cut out Timmy's body and head, and put them together at the X with a paper fastener. Then, each day when you read a good book, color a feather and paste it onto Timmy. When Timmy is all dressed up, can you remember the story that each feather represents? Try it. Remember to color Timmy with bright colors.

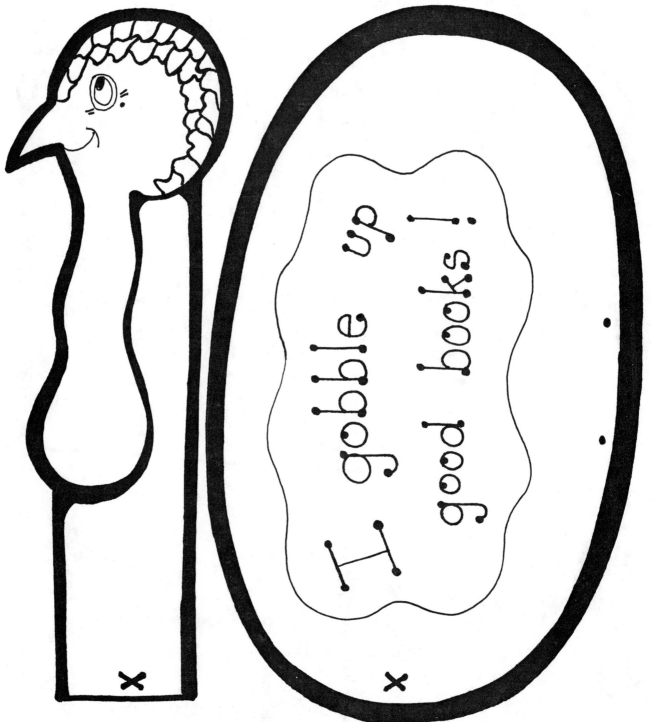

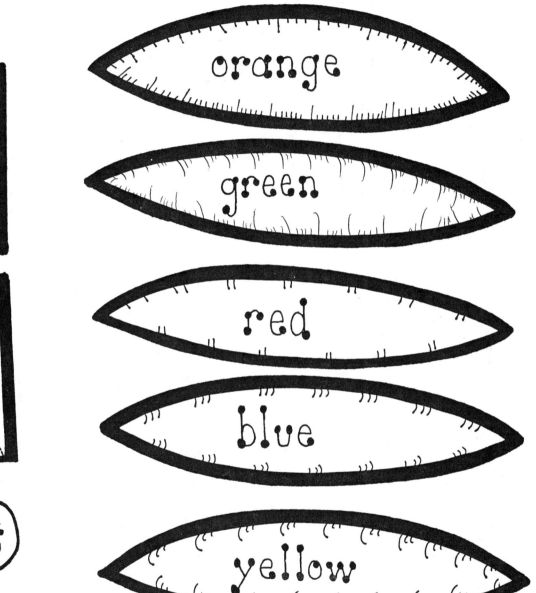

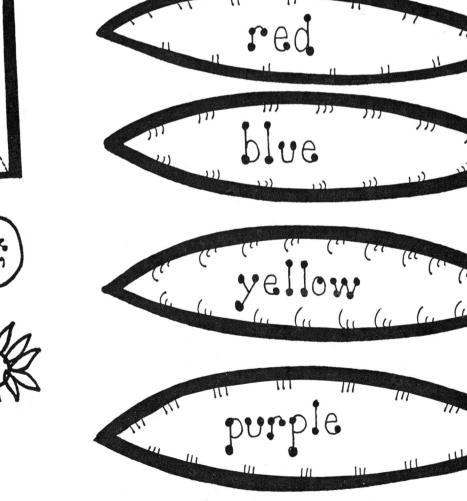

Name _____

Date _____

STORYBOOK CHARACTERS IN ACTION

I would like you to meet three different book characters I have met during this month. With my crayons, I will (1) draw a picture of each one, (2) show you something that each character did (action), and (3) show you what happened as a result of what the character did. Then you can choose your favorite character from these three, and listen while I retell the story to you.

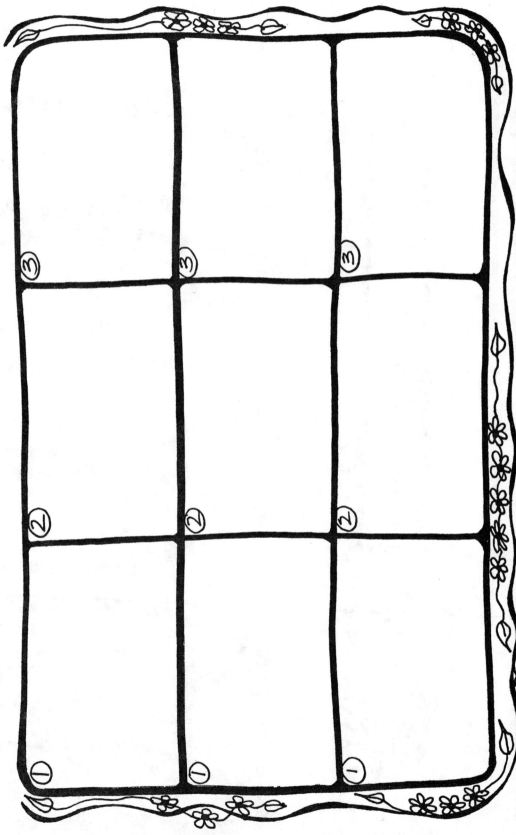

December

ALL BUNDLED UP FOR A MONTH TO REMEMBER

December helps to make school the "best thing" that happens in the lives of some youngsters. If it snows, expect a rush to the windows to watch this event. And the traditions to be transmitted at Hanukkah and Christmas make this special month an exciting and happy time. Patience is needed as the first graders prepare for the holidays—but, with gentle reminders, they will continue to do the academic work that is expected of them.

RECOMMENDED CHILDREN'S BOOKS FOR DECEMBER

- *Merry Christmas, Strega Nona* by Tomie dePaolo (Orlando, FL: Harcourt Brace Jovanovich, 1986). There is so much to do for Christmas. Will it ever get done? Strega Nona has her doubts and has to cancel her magic in order to get ready for the holiday. She finally decides to cancel her Christmas celebration. Can Big Anthony save the day? Won't there be any magic for Christmas, or does Christmas seem to have a magic all its own?

- *Cranberry Christmas* by Wende and Harry Devlin (New York: Four Winds Press, 1976). Mr. Whiskers, who sweeps only in the spring, enlists the aid of Maggie and her Grandmother to transform his cottage because Christmas is coming to Cranberryport, and so is his sister Sarah! Children will meet grumpy Mr. Cyrus Grape, a newcomer to the area, who wants no children iceskating on his rink. Hmmm, this book lets us know that it pays to clean house in more ways than one. As a bonus, Maggie's favorite cranberry cake recipe is printed on the back cover and is fun to make with children for a holiday treat.

- *The Mommy Exchange* by Amy Hest, illustrated by Anne DiSalvo-Ryan (New York: Four Winds Press, 1988). In Jason's House, they get spaghetti twice a week, but in Jessica's house, they get it once a week and it's swirly. Jason is an only child, but Jessica's family has twin babies. With the approval of the two mommies, the children decide to switch homes for awhile. They're both in for a big surprise in this "the grass is always greener on the other side of the fence" humorous tale.

- *I Love Hanukkah* by Marilyn Hirsh (New York: Holiday House, 1984). This book takes the reader along with a young boy and his family as he learns the customs and traditions of the Hanukkah holiday. This is an excellent teaching/learning story.

- *Another Mouse to Feed* by Robert Kraus, pictures by Jose Aruego and Ariane Dewey (New York: Simon and Schuster, 1980). Mr. and Mrs. Mouse have a huge family, can just about remember everyone's name, and have to work several jobs to feed the family. But they manage; until an orphan mouse is left on their doorstep. That's the end! Or is it the beginning? Now the mouse children decide to pitch in and help, and everyone's life is enriched.

- *Apple Tree Christmas* by Trinka Hakes Noble (New York: Dial Books, 1984). Winter's coming, and the family needs to pick apples and prepare them for winter. The old apple tree is a source of joy to the daughters—a thick vine provides a swing for Josie, and one limb makes a perfect drawing board for Katrina. But a winter storm strikes early and, alas, it strikes the apple tree! How can this sadness be turned into joy? It happens in this touching story that is enriched by beautiful illustrations.

- *Jewish Holiday Cookbook* by Susan Gold Purdy (New York: Franklin Watts, 1979). This is an excellent resource book for the teacher. There are recipes for cookies, fruit dishes, potato latkes, challah (braided bread), and Mother's Chicken Soup!

- *The Puppy Who Wanted a Boy* by Jane Thayer, illustrated by Lisa McCue (New York: William Morrow and Co., 1958, 1985). This delightful story, told from the point of view of a little puppy named Petey, tells how he sets out to find a boy for Christmas. He encounters many dogs who absolutely will not give away their boy. It turns out to be a joyful Christmas for all, however, when Petey suddenly finds an abundance of little boys!

- *Merry Christmas Ernest and Celestine* by Gabrielle Vincent (New York: Greenwillow Books, 1983). The appealing duo of bear and mouse are back, and this time it's the holiday season and there's no money for a Christmas party. Celestine convinces Ernest (and the reader) that it can be done without a lot of money. This important message comes through to young children, who like to listen to the reassuring tale again and again.

- *Morris's Disappearing Bag* by Rosemary Wells (New York: E. P. Dutton, 1975). Christmas presents received by brothers and sisters can seem more appealing than your own, and Morris the Rabbit finds himself in that predicament until he locates a present that had been overlooked. Suddenly that present is a big hit, and Morris makes the most of his new gift.

SPOTLIGHT ON READING

The Alligator and the Ogre Sort It Out

That's the headline news for this month! Talk about headlines in the newspaper and show samples of headlines. These lines of print are at the HEAD (or top) of the page. Examine your local newspaper for headlines—note that they give you a little bit of information and try to "pull you in" to read the story.

Here's the story that goes with this heading: "Remember those enemies, the Ogre and Uncle Alligator, who both wanted all of the vowels, a, e, i, o u, and sometimes y ? Well, they have sorted it out and are now very good friends. How could this happen? Here's how. The Ogre brought his icy acorns to the ailing Uncle Alligator for a treat and they cured his itchy elbows. This made Uncle Alligator feel so good that he wanted to become friends with the Ogre rather than be his enemy. He invited the Ogre to supper. The Alligator served apples, elbow macaroni, Indian bread, octopus, and underwater bugs. (TEACHER: Note that each menu item begins with a short vowel sound.)

"Uncle Alligator told the Ogre that he wanted to share their letter food, which is why he chose the menu carefully. 'This is not MY letter food!' exclaimed the Ogre. 'I don't eat this stuff! I eat acorns, eagles, icicles, opossum, and unicorn hair.' (TEACHER: Note that each menu item begins with a long vowel sound.)

'But I thought you wanted to fight with me about the vowel letters,' gasped Uncle Alligator. He was very puzzled, but he kept talking. 'I like Indian bread and apples, and you like icy acorns—but they both begin with the letters i and a.'

"The Ogre was very surprised! So was the Alligator! And then they both began to laugh. They laughed and laughed until they rolled on the floor. They had discovered the secret of the vowels. The vowel letters have two sounds. The Alligator liked short sounds and the Ogre liked the long sounds—just like some children like chocolate ice cream and some like strawberry.

"The Alligator and the Ogre are now the best of friends and they read together every day. They both love vowels—and they share them rather than fight about them. THE END . . . or is it the beginning?"

Go on a Vowel Search

Give each child a page from the newspaper. Have them go on a vowel hunt and circle all of the words that begin with a, e, i, o, and u.

Next, give each child a different page from the newspaper. Have four students take out a red crayon and circle only the letter "a" every time they see it—whether it is at the beginning, in the middle, or at the end of a word. Other students can use blue to search for the letter "e," green to search for the letter "i," pink to search for the letter "o," and brown to search for the letter "u." Have them count the letters that they circled and put that numeral at the top of the page. Then compare the numerals—they will vary considerably since each student has a different page. The main purpose of this activity is to practice location skills, and to see how busy those vowels are.

Then print a sentence on the chalkboard and go on a vowel search. Circle all of the vowels in each word. From this, determine whether the vowel is short and belongs to Uncle Alligator or if it is long and belongs to the Ogre. (Remember the phrases in headline form: "Uncle Alligator—Itch on Elbows" and "Ogre's Unicorn Eats Icy Acorns.") See the reproducible activity pages, too.

Base (or Root) Words

In order to teach the concept of a base (or root) word, use the chalkboard. First, print a recognizable word in with a mixture of letters. For example, "xyprday." Have students sound out the letters or raise their hands if they recognize by sight the little word "day" in the word. Use their reading vocabulary words or spelling words for this exercise; it strengthens attention to detail and skill in letter and word recognition.

This is a good skill "game" to play with the group. Give it a catchy title such as "Base Wordo," "Finder's Keepers" (print the word on a card and let the child keep it), or "Detective Duty" (circle the word and put a handle on it to represent a magnifying glass). This approach appeals to the young child's imagination and they will not tire as easily.

Shirp and Chirp Words

For digraphs, it will pay dividends if, again, you can appeal to the children's imaginations as you teach them. Two bird hand puppets (made from paper bags) will work wonders. The puppets are named Shirp and Chirp and their message is: "Oh, those tricky letters are at it again! How they like to try to fool us." Then the puppet, Shirp, proceeds to teach the students that when they see the letters "s" and "h" side by side in a word, it is okay to try to decode it (sound it out) by saying "sssssss" and "hhhhhhh." But, when it doesn't work, try remembering Shirp's name and sound (which is a very quiet Shhhhh) and see if it works. Shirp enjoys quiet sounds, so "s" and "h" got together and made a special sound just for him.

Read a list of words to the students and, if it contains Shirp's sound, have them put their fingers to their lips:

Shirp   Chirp

shade	single	Saturday
silly	shoes	shingles
shadow	carrots	show

Have the students repeat the sounds of "s" (top teeth resting on bottom teeth) and the sound of "sh" (top teeth over bottom teeth). Say the following so that the students can feel their jaws move back and forth:

s   sh   s   sh   s   sh   s   sh

Now, Chirp is the sound that birds make. Since Chirp the puppet had no voice and couldn't sing, the letters "c" and "h" got together and decided to create a special sound just for Chirp. They gave it to Chirp for a birthday present. When we see "c" and "h" side by side in a word, it is okay to try to decode (sound it out) it by saying "kkkkk" and "huhhhh" OR even "sssss" and "huhhhhh." But we know that it is Chirp's sound when it doesn't make any sense.

Read a list of words to the students and, if it contains Chirp's sound, have them flap their "wings" (arms):

chipmunk	chilly	shadow
careful	chunk	chew
silly	parrot	chocolate

Print the word "church" on the chalkboard and let children know that the special "made up" sounds called digraphs are not always at the beginning of the word; they can even be in the middle or at the end.

Use the newspaper to search and circle words that have the "sh" and the "ch" letters printed side by side. Then try to figure out if they belong to Shirp and Chirp, or if they are saying their own sound.

We're having a lot of fun trying to figure out these word puzzles—that's the message you need to convey to the students. You are similar to a cheerleader—rallying the group and enthusiastically moving them forward. Remember that your attitude is critical to the reading process and to the progress of the child. One of your many roles as a first grade teacher is to motivate the students to want to learn.

Take Five—and Read

December is an extremely busy month for everyone because there is much preparation for holidays, and often children don't get as much rest as usual because of pressures at home. So, if you have not already done so, this is a good month to begin to build in some silent, uninterrupted reading time for the entire group. Get a new group of picture books from the library each week. Try to include some holiday books (Hanukkah and Christmas) in your book choices.

Wordless picture books are excellent for this time of year because children can just look at the pictures or make up their own story as they turn the pages.

Begin with a five-minute time segment. Have students select a book and go anywhere in the room with it as long as they are quiet. They cannot get up to change their book nor can they interrupt the group. After the five minutes, have students return the books and then return to their seats. A little treat *after* the quiet reading time is a good reinforcement technique for desired reading behavior.

SPOTLIGHT ON MATH

Pennies, Nickels, Dimes, Quarters

- Have a variety of real coins for the students to explore. Give each student a penny, for example, and have them take a good look at it. Let's discover the following: Who's picture is on the penny? (Abraham Lincoln) Who was he? (the 16th President) What are the four numbers on his right? (the date the coin was minted; these will vary, so it is possible to tally and then graph this data) What is the word on his left? (Liberty) What does it say along the top of the coin? (In God We Trust) Turn over the coin. What building is shown on the back? (the monument to Abraham Lincoln) Does anyone know where that is located? (Washington, D.C.) The Latin inscription *E Pluribus Unum* appears on the back of the coin. What does it mean? (one nation made up of many).

- Explore the nickels, dimes, and quarters in the same way. Young children can become fascinated with these coins that they are using every day, yet are not examining. It may help them with the value relationships, too, if they know the names of the people on the coins (nickel—Thomas Jefferson; dime—Franklin Roosevelt; quarter—George Washington). What one thing do all of these people have in common? (all former U.S. Presidents).

There are other coins in our money system. John F. Kennedy is on one half dollar; who is on another? (Benjamin Franklin; "Miss Liberty" walking). And there is a silver dollar (used at one time before we went to paper currency), and a relatively new coin dollar that never caught on with the public (the Susan B. Anthony coin). One major reason for its rejection was that it was about the same size as the quarter and caused much confusion; another reason was that it was not truly round and vending machines rejected it.

Some coins have a single letter indicating where they are minted (such as D for Denver and P for Philadelphia).

- Do coin rubbings. (See the reproducible activity pages.)

- Later, bring in foreign coins to examine. Compare them to U.S. coins in size and weight, and speculate about what might be on these coins in terms of information.

Coin-Eaters

A vending machine likes to "eat" coins. Have students list the various coin-eaters, such as: pay telephones; vending machines for soda, candy, and other food; bubble gum machines; laundromats; parking meters; and so on. We even have machines that will make change for us. Take a survey of how many students have had the opportunity to use coin-eating machines.

Set Up a Measuring Interest Center

You can set up a center for dry measure, and have everything housed in a large, under-the-bed-size box to help contain the contents. You will need colorful plastic measuring spoons (¼, ½, ¾, 1 teaspoon, 1 tablespoon), plastic measuring cups, a large spoon, various-sized measuring containers (1 pint, 1 quart), and mixing bowls. For the dry measure, you can use sand, cornmeal, lentils, navy beans, beans, or any combinations thereof. Students can be encouraged to measure on their own, and also to do specific activities. Activity cards can be placed in the box, too.

Filling Holiday Orders

During this month there is an abundance of colorful advertisements of items that hold special appeal for children. Many catalogs are received via mail and are also helpful. Take advantage of this to work with money and/or number facts.

Materials: Cut out a wide variety of items, some single and some in groups. Cross out the price. Place them in a bag and label it "Holiday Toy Bag." Next, make up a set of flashcards for the numerals one through ten. Place these in a bag and label it "Number Bag."

Procedure: Have a student reach into the Number Bag and pull out a flashcard. Call out the number. Write it on the chalkboard. This is the customer order for the amount. Next, have a student reach into the Holiday Toy Bag and pull out an advertisement. Count the number of items in the ad. Call out the number for the item. Write it on the chalkboard. Now comes the problem-solving. How many does the customer want? How many more will you need to fill the order?

For example, if the numeral eight is extracted from the Number Bag, and an ad showing three marbles is extracted from the Holiday Toy Bag, how many more do we need to make eight? Write on the chalkboard: 3 + ____ = 8.

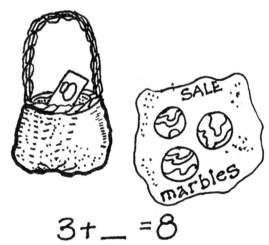

$$3 + \underline{\quad} = 8$$

Keep filling orders over and over again throughout the month as students work with addition and subtraction facts to 10. For additional challenges, you may want to work with numbers to 15 or 20.

All and Almost All

The concept of "almost all" is very close to, but not the same as, "all." You can demonstrate this concept by filling a jar with water and then emptying half of it. Is this "almost all"? No. The jar is still half full. Even one-fourth is not the same as "almost all." But we're getting close when there is just a ring of water left in the bottom of the jar.

The "all" and "almost all" concept can be practiced with items in the room. Some possibilities include directives such as:

Place (all or almost all) of the books in a stack.

Place (all or almost all) of the pencils in a row.

Place (all or almost all) of the papers on the counter.

Close the door (all or almost all) of the way.

Close the drawer (all or almost all) of the way.

Other possibilities for learning this difference include an inventory such as:

Have we (all or almost all) been served our juice and crackers?

Have we collected (all or almost all) of the papers?

Are we (all or almost all) ready to listen to a story?

Did we (all or almost all) finish cleaning out our desks?

Who painted at the easel this week? (All or almost all) of us?

Who will buy lunch today? Is that (all or almost all) of us?

We have two more days in the month. Is the month all over or almost all over?

Shape of the Month

A can is a cylinder shape with two flat edges. Have students begin to bring in a variety of empty cans that once contained soup, vegetables, fruits, oatmeal, and so on.

- A cylinder shape with one flat edge removed makes an excellent container. Cover several of these shapes with self-sticking colorful paper and redecorate your classroom. They can be used to contain broken crayons, used pencils, scissors, rulers, glue, and so on. Students will think of many more uses for them.

- A giant cylinder shape can be painted and placed on its side. With a cozy rug and a stack of books, this becomes a pleasant reading capsule.

- Be on the lookout for cylinders (some with automatic moving parts) that help us wind things, such as film for the camera, inner workings of cassette tapes, movie projectors, pencil sharpeners, paper towels, toilet tissue, yarn, and so on. Go on a cylinder hunt. Find cylinder shapes in magazines and newspapers and be ready for a big surprise, because we do tend to take cylinders for granted!

- Have students collect cardboard cylinders of various sizes and make a new invention.

HANDS-ON SCIENCE

Magnets come in different shapes (bar and horseshoe) and sizes. A magnet is any piece of iron or steel or original magnetite (lodestone) that has the property of attracting iron or steel. Check with the middle school or high school science department in your school district to see if they will loan a set of magnets to your class (if you have no magnets available). Ask parents if they are willing to help supply the class with several magnets, too.

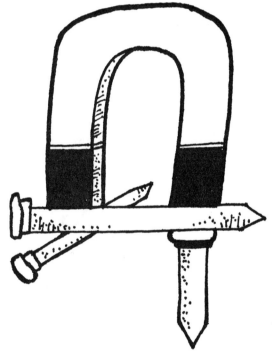

At this age, children can learn that magnets have a north-seeking pole and a south-seeking pole. Also, they can learn that magents that are opposite (north and south) will attract, and magnets that are alike (north and north, or south and south) will not attract (or will "repel," a new vocabulary word). They need to know that by dropping a magnet, it is weakened. Therefore, care must be taken not to drop the magnet itself.

It is a good idea to set up a Magnet Investigation Area in your room ON THE FLOOR (not far for things to drop that fall from the magnet) and also on a rug (minimum noise disturbance for the rest of the class).

Most students may already be aware of magnets because of the popularity of magnets in households that serve the purpose of securing messages, artwork, etc., to the outside of the refrigerator. However, students do need an opportunity to explore with magnets in order to find out what items the magnet will attract and what items the magnet will not attract. What are the similarities? They can begin an "Attract" and "Does Not Attract" list. Have a plastic tub filled with items that students can use for their explorations, such as a ruler, pencil, staples, brass fasteners, string, nails, scissors, cotton, cardboard, sponges, plastic pieces, aluminum pie plate, minature toys, and so on. Next, let the students leave the Magnet Investigation Area and explore in the classroom.

HOLIDAY TIME

Let's Go International with Our Games

At this festive time of year, there are celebrations all over the world. Borrow a large globe for the classroom so that students can get an idea of where these countries are that we are talking about. Let's learn some of their games:

- *Country:* Canada. *Game:* Ajaqaq. The Canadian Eskimos play this game during the winter months. *Materials Needed:* A straight stick, approximately 6 inches in length; a 24-inch length of string; a circular jar rim. Tie one end of the string to the stick. Tie the other end to the jar rim. *Procedure:* Use two hands. Hold the stick with one hand and toss the ring into the air with the other hand. Try to catch the ring on the stick. One point is scored for each catch. The first person to get a score of ten wins the game. Then repeat with two or more players.

- *Country:* Japan. *Game:* Portrait Painting. *Materials Needed:* Felt-tipped markers or crayons; scissors; thin cardboard; two pieces of 18-inch lengths of yarn or string. *Procedure:* Each player cuts a piece of cardboard, larger than his or her face. Cut holes in each side so that the cardboard "canvas" can be tied around the back of the head. Select a leader.

Select two artists. Others sit and watch. The artists tie on their "canvas." The leader then gives directions, such as:

"Paint your right eyebrow."

"Draw your left eye."

"Put on your eyelashes."

When finished, the leader parades the artists around so that all can enjoy the portraits. Then they are removed for the artists to enjoy. Repeat with the other children.

- *Country:* Brazil. *Game:* Chicken Fight. *Materials Needed:* A handkerchief or scarf for each player, and a long piece of string to mark the 6-foot circle playing area. *Procedure:* Two players enter the ring with a handkerchief tucked under their belts. They need to hop on their right foot, with their right arm held across their upper chest touching their left shoulder. Each player tries to grab the other's scarf with the left hand. CAUTION: If a player's left foot touches the floor or if the right arm unbends, then the scarf must be given up. The player with the most scarves wins.

Happy Hanukkah

Hanukkah is a Jewish holiday that is observed during mid-winter. It is known as the Festival of Lights because candles are lit in homes and in synagogues (places of worship) in observance of a feast. The celebration covers a period of eight days. Some of the symbols are:

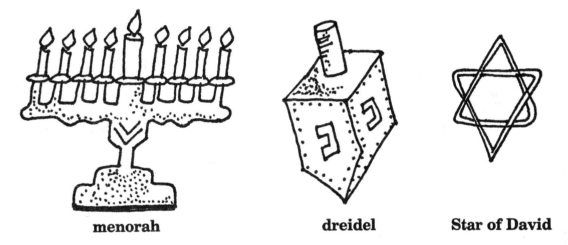

menorah   **dreidel**   **Star of David**

Draw from the Dreidel Box

Cover a large cardboard box with paper. Use a felt-tip pen to make one dreidel symbol on each of the four sides:

gimel   hay   nun   shin

Wrap tiny gifts. Tie a string around them and put the string outside of the box. Place an equal number of strings on all four sides. Spin the dreidel, or point to the dreidel symbols drawn on the chalkboard. Pull the string from that side of the box. Wait until all have a turn. Then open the gifts. (These could be raisins or nuts, or a new pencil, crayon, eraser, etc.)

Merry Christmas

December 25 is the celebration of Christmas Day. In the U.S., it is a time for being with family and friends, for sharing, and for giving gifts. The figure of jolly Santa Claus in a red suit who climbs down the chimney with a sack filled with toys is a familiar sight.

- How can we share? Some schools may decide to have a Mitten Tree in the main lobby or entrance. Parents donate mittens and the tree is decorated with them each day. Just before vacation, the mittens are removed and donated to an organization that works with needy families. Perhaps students in school might receive them as well.

- Make greeting cards and mail them to a local hospital, perhaps to the children's ward.

- Make a cassette recording of Christmas carols and send it to a nursing home in the community.

Classroom Holiday Spirit

Make a festive tablecloth. Use gleaming white shelf paper and transform it into a designer tablecloth by using red and green felt pens. Each student can draw one item on the paper cloth.

Drinking Red, Eating Green!

The menu calls for "Sparkling canned or frozen raspberry punch; a doughnut with a scoop of green sherbet in the hole in the middle." Enjoy!

Holiday Customs Around the World

We can learn about other people and how they celebrate during this season. Find a book about holidays at the library to share with your students.

- SPAIN: "The Urn (Vase) of Fate." Each person writes his or her name on a piece of paper and places it in the big urn. On Christmas night, the people go to the village square. Two names are drawn out at a time. Each pair will become good friends during the next year. (Wouldn't this be worth a try?)
- SWEDEN. Christmastime begins on December 13 and is called St. Lucia Day. The oldest girl in the family dresses in white, puts a wreath of seven lighted candles (beware!) on her head, and serves coffee and buns to the family in their bedrooms.
- MEXICO. A piñata (peen-YAHT-uh) is made of papier-mâché in the shape of an animal. It is filled with candies, fruits, and small gifts. The piñata is hung above the heads of the children. One at a time, the children are blindfolded and swing at the piñata with a bat or stick. When the piñata breaks, everyone shares in the goodies.
- AUSTRALIA AND NEW ZEALAND. It's summertime and families celebrate by having picnics at the beach!
- FRANCE. On Christmas Eve, children put their shoes in front of the fireplace. They hope that Father Christmas (Pere Noel) will fill them with presents.
- RUSSIA. Father Frost, dressed in red, comes bringing gifts for the New Year on January 1. Real fir trees are decorated with ornaments and tinsel for this occasion.

Christmas Symbol Booklet

Red and green are traditional Christmas colors. Some ancient beliefs are that green is the symbol for everlasting life (evergreen trees) and red is the symbol for the blood that Christ shed. Include these items in your class booklets:

- *Holly and Evergreens*—In ancient times, people believed they brought good luck.

- *Ornaments*—The first Christmas trees were decorated with real fruits, lighted candles, and flowers. The candles were not safe and the trees had to be carefully watched. The candles gave way to lights, and German glassblowers began to make lighter ornaments.
- *Poinsettia*—The first poinsettia was brought to the United States from Mexico in 1828 by Dr. Joel Poinsett. He was the first U.S. ambassador to Mexico.
- *Stockings*—Many years ago, people hung their stockings by the fireplace to dry them. Legend has it that St. Nicholas dropped bags of gold into the stockings. Today, we hang stockings in the hopes that they will be filled with fruits, nuts, and tiny gifts.

- *Santa Claus*—The friendly, jolly, red-suited, bearded gift-bringer.

- *Greeting cards*—This custom began in England in the 1800s. Today, it is a time to exchange greetings with friends old and new, near and far.

- *Bells*—The custom of ringing bells began as a way to drive away evil spirits.

- *Mistletoe*—This is a symbol of love. People believed that it could keep them healthy and happy, so the mistletoe was hung over their doorway. Those who entered got a kiss as a symbol of love.

DECEMBER COOKING TREATS

Uncle Alligator's and the Ogre's Secret Recipes

The December holidays are times for cooking and baking. Our vowel friends are so fond of sharing now, instead of fighting, that they want to help us make a special holiday treat. Here they are, just as they wrote them:

Uncle Alligator's Orange Elbows

1. Boil elbow macaroni until firm. Drain.
2. Pour melted cheese over the macaroni.
3. Sprinkle with a pinch (ouch!) of paprika.
4. Serve warm, to tender hearts.

The Ogre's Icy Acorn Supreme Delight

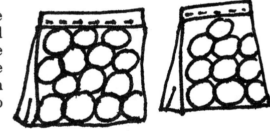

Make tiny scoops of chocolate ice cream (one scoop per person) and place them into plastic bags. Store in the freezer. Then remove. Place in a cone or on a dish. Sprinkle with chopped nuts. UMMM! Designed to melt your heart.

Ren Bear's Choc-o-Nut Candy

Ren Bear, the Baker Bear, has the following treat for you to try.

Ingredients: 1 10-oz. package of semi-sweet chocolate chips
1 14-oz. can condensed milk
2 tablespoons margarine
1½ cups chopped pecans
1 9- or 11-oz. bag miniature marshmallows

Procedure:

1. Put chocolate chips, condensed milk, and margarine in the top part of a double boiler. Cook on medium heat until everything has melted. Don't stop stirring.

2. Remove from heat. Stir in nuts and marshmallows.

3. On a cookie sheet lined with wax paper, drop spoonfuls of candy. Refrigerate for several hours before serving.

Gingerbread Dough

Ingredients: 9 cups unsifted flour
1 tablespoon grated lemon rind
1½ tablespoons cinnamon
1 tablespoon ginger
¼ teaspoon salt
1½ cups light brown sugar
(pack firmly)
1¼ cups margarine
2 cups corn syrup

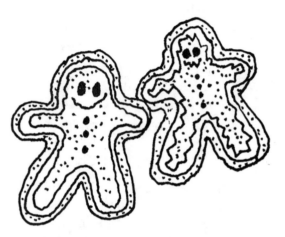

Procedure:

1. Combine flour, lemon rind, cinnamon, ginger, and salt in a large bowl.

2. In saucepan, stir together corn syrup, margarine, and brown sugar. Mix well.

3. Pour liquid mixture into flour mixture and blend.

4. Form dough into a ball. Knead until smooth.

5. Roll out dough on foil-lined cookie sheets to ¼-inch thickness. (Use flour on the rolling pin for easier rolling.)

6. Cut out cookie shapes.

7. Bake cookies in 350°F. oven for 12 to 16 minutes, or until cookies are lightly browned and firm.

8. Cool cookie sheets before removing cookies from foil. Eat before the cookies run away!

"Ginger up" your holiday with gingerbread, a gingerbread house, ginger snaps, ginger ale, and serve gingerly—with great care.

Reproducible Activity Pages for December

**Alligator and Ogre Words (long and
    short vowel sounds)**
**Say-a-Story (creative thinking—
    letters E, B, T)**
**Play-a-Story (creative dramatics—
    letter M)**
My Holiday Story (creative writing)
December Reading (bookmarks)
**We Can Go Shopping (working with
    money)**
**Ren Bear's 100 Muffins (counting
    and measuring)**
**Cookies by the Dozen (the concept
    of 12 as a "dozen")**
**The Measurement Elf (measuring
    in inches)**
**Math Shapes: Cylinder (concept
    reinforcement)**
Magnets (working with magnets)
**Make an Electromagnet (working with
    an electromagnet)**
**Sharpen Your Holiday Memories Game
    (increasing memory span)**
Santa Bear (skills reinforcement)
**Mrs. Santa Bear (group sharing; oral
    expression)**
The Writing Cat (writing readiness)

ALLIGATOR AND OGRE WORDS

Now that these two are good friends, they work together to make words. The Alligator takes care of the short vowel sounds, and the Ogre is happy with the long vowel sounds. Today, they want you to write five words in each chart below. This is the rule: The word must have the vowel as its first or second letter. Can you do it? They think you can!

Name ———————————————— Date ————————————————

SAY-A-STORY

Oops! This bear is practicing to be the Easter Bunny Bear, and he got mixed up! He's shown up for the wrong holiday. It's time to trim the tree and wrap the presents. How will you solve this one?

Even our letters are mixed up. Today, we are working with e, b, t.

As you color the items, think carefully about how you will tell your story to good listeners. Also, how will you turn this into a happy ending?

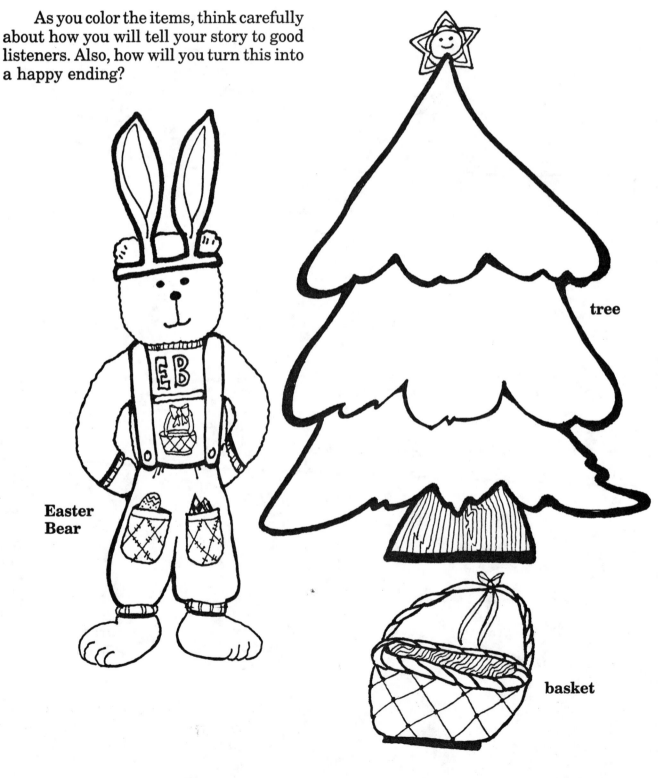

Easter
Bear

tree

basket

PLAY-A-STORY

When someone puts on a mask, we can't see that person's face. Here's the mystery: Someone keeps taking the money! They think they won't get caught because they are wearing a mask. But, is that a make-believe mouse or is it a police officer hiding in a mouse costume? You decide. This is your story. Good luck!

Today, we are working with the letter "m."

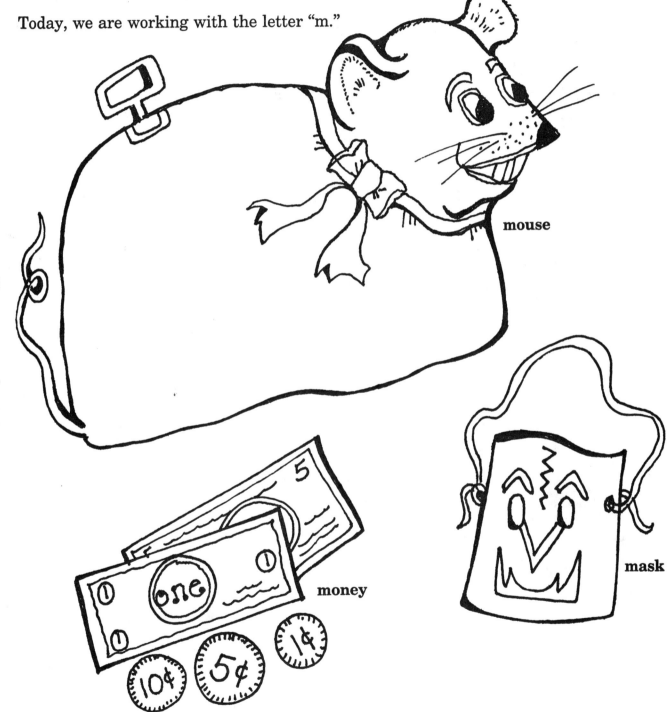

mouse

money

mask

Slowly color your story items, and think about how you will catch the robber. How will you act and move as you thrill your audience? When you use a storytelling mask, you can play more than one part.

My Holiday Story

by _____

Guard My Place

name _____

READ

name _____

Name _____   Date _____

WE CAN GO SHOPPING

Count the money in each bag. Draw a line from the money bag to the item that you can buy for that amount. These items are brand new, so use your crayons to make them look bright. The first one is done for you.

REN BEAR'S 100 MUFFINS

Ren Bear is very busy making one-hundred (100) muffins. Print the numerals on the muffin cups below to see how many he has made. How many more does he need to make to get to 100? _____ Also, Ren Bear can't remember which is bigger—a teaspoon (tsp.) or a tablespoon (tbsp.). Do you know? Do you have a sample of each spoon? Color the bigger one red and the smaller one green in Ren Bear's thought balloons below. Thank you! Color Ren Bear and his muffins, too.

COOKIES BY THE DOZEN

Goodie Bear needs to put one dozen freshly decorated cookies into the box. Oops! Goodie has forgotten HOW MANY items are equal to one dozen. Can you help? Use your bright crayons to decorate one dozen cookies. Three are in the box to get you started, so you will need to add on. In Goodie's thought balloons, use your red crayon to color the correct answer.

THE MEASUREMENT ELF

Santa Claus likes to know what size you are, so he sent this elf to help you measure. You will need a measuring tape and a friend to help. Record the information on this chart. Stay to the nearest inch. The elf likes graphs, too. He suggests that you make a big class graph of the information recorded for each person. Then you can make comparisons in size.

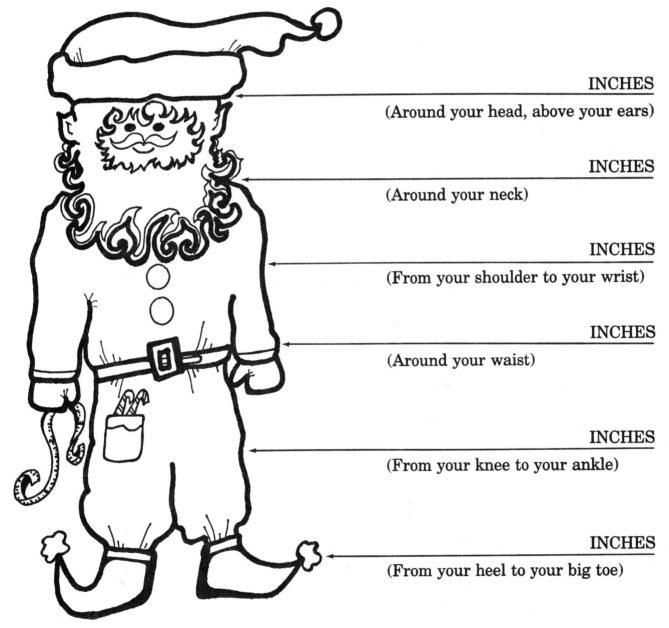

_____ INCHES
(Around your head, above your ears)

_____ INCHES
(Around your neck)

_____ INCHES
(From your shoulder to your wrist)

_____ INCHES
(Around your waist)

_____ INCHES
(From your knee to your ankle)

_____ INCHES
(From your heel to your big toe)

Name _____ Date _____

MATH SHAPES: CYLINDER

A cylinder shape is useful. It can roll or help things to roll. Both ends are flat for easy storage and for storing things inside of the cylinder shape.

Here are three ways that a cylinder is useful for helping something to roll:

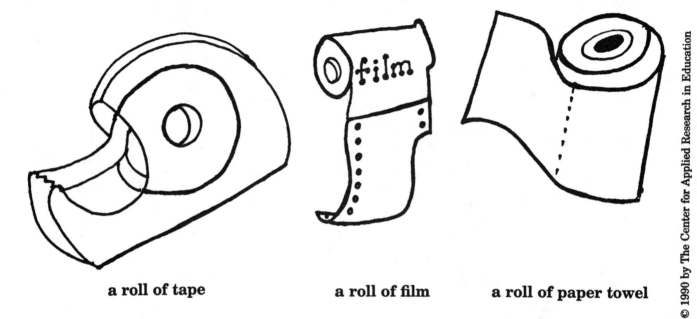

a roll of tape   **a roll of film**   **a roll of paper towel**

In the spaces below, show three ways that a cylinder is helpful in the kitchen when it is in the shape of a can:

1.	2.	3.

Name _____   Date _____

MAGNETS

Magnets attract some things and do not attract others. Draw four items that the magnet WILL ATTRACT and four items that the magnet WILL NOT ATTRACT. Compare your drawings with those of your classmates.

will attract

will not attract

Make a paper–clip.
magnet chain. How
long is it?

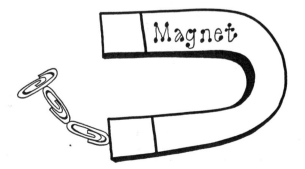

Name _____

Date _____

Make An Electromagnet

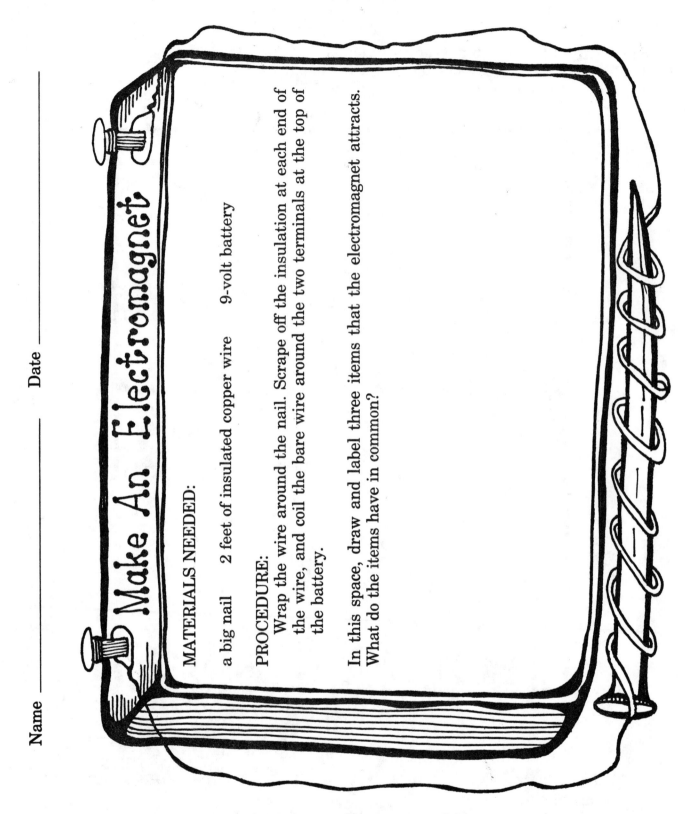

MATERIALS NEEDED:

a big nail   2 feet of insulated copper wire   9-volt battery

PROCEDURE:

Wrap the wire around the nail. Scrape off the insulation at each end of the wire, and coil the bare wire around the two terminals at the top of the battery.

In this space, draw and label three items that the electromagnet attracts. What do the items have in common?

SHARPEN YOUR HOLIDAY MEMORIES GAME

Color the pictures and cut the boxes on the lines. Each picture goes with the holiday season. To play the game, lay the cards face down and turn over two at a time. If the cards match, you may keep them. If they do not match, turn them back over. Try to remember where each picture is hiding as other players take their turns. The winner is the player with the most matching cards.

SANTA BEAR

This bear needs lots of practice in order to become a good Santa. We need practice in school, too. Here's what you can do. Color Santa Bear, cut him out, and paste him onto a paper lunch bag. Then, put your practice papers inside the bag. You can practice your name, your numbers, or even write a letter. At the end of the week, take home all of your papers.

MRS. SANTA BEAR

Color the bear, cut her out, trace her shape around a sheet of heavier paper, and glue or staple the edges together. Be sure to leave the bottom edge open. Insert your hand between the two pieces of paper, and tell Mrs. Santa Bear all about YOURSELF. She's a good listener. She likes to listen to stories about bears, too.

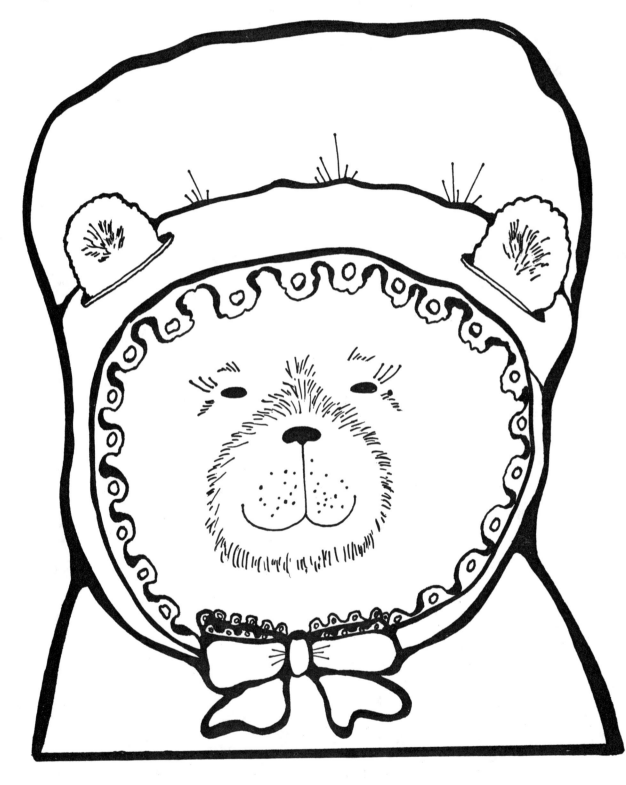

THE WRITING CAT

Candy, the writing cat, is still working very hard on printing. She needs to practice, practice, and practice these strokes. Can you help Candy? On the back of this paper, show Candy how well you can print your letters from A to Z.

January

A BLANKET OF SNOWY-DAY IDEAS

Hello, January! We're back to school after a long holiday and it's very quiet. Take advantage of this quiet atmosphere to re-establish routines or to make changes. Praise children daily for their work, their art, their stories—and they will pour on the effort just to please you. A first-grade teacher is a powerful "significant other" in the life of the youngsters, who are watching and learning from you. Your patience and understanding will pay dividends later.

RECOMMENDED CHILDREN'S BOOKS FOR JANUARY

- *All in a Day* by Mitsumasa Anno, et al. (New York: Philomel Books, 1986). This wonderful story shows what is happening to children around the world. In the U.S., it's Christmas Eve; in England, children are sleeping; in the U.S.S.R., people are celebrating; and in Japan, it's early in the morning. Four other countries are represented, too. As the reader turns the pages, we follow each of the eight families throughout a day. Peace is the theme of the book, and there is an impressive list of noted illustrators. This is a marvelous teaching book for use throughout this month.

- *Anno's Counting Book* by Mitsumasa Anno (New York: Thomas Y. Crowell, 1975). This book begins with the concept of zero and ends with 12. It is an excellent book for an introduction to the months of the year, as well as the seasons. A tally is kept at the side of the page as each month goes by and as the same scene changes. This is an excellent teaching book, and there is always something new to add or subtract—depending upon whether you go forward or backward.

- *Midnight Snowman* by Caroline Feller Bauer, illustrated by Catherine Stock (New York: Atheneum, 1987). This is a good book for children who live in an area where it never snows, but only rains. Suddenly when a snowfall surprises the whole town, it brings everyone outdoors for a memorable snowy-day experience.

- *January Brings the Snow, a Book of Months* by Sara Coleridge, paintings by Jenni Oliver (New York: Dial Books, 1986). This book is in rhyme. The watercolors are subdued and seem to glow on the page. January is a good time of year to review the months with such a lovely book.

- *Ed Emberly's ABC* by Ed Emberly (Boston: Little, Brown, 1978). It's a good time to review and reinforce the alphabet, and this book focuses upon the construction of the letters in a way that delights the reader. Children also enjoy finding all of the items on the page that begin with a particular letter. The book may also give children inspiration for making alphabet pictures and books of their own.

- *Arthur's Prize Reader* by Lillian Hoban (New York: Harper and Row, 1978, 1988). The first-grade reading contest is on and Violet is determined to read the most books. Arthur reminds her that she can't read. In this escapade, one message is that "if you can read easy words, then you can read hard words, too." First graders enjoy this adventure.

- *A House Is a House for Me* by Mary Ann Hoberman, illustrated by Betty Fraser (New York: The Viking Press, 1978). This delightful story doesn't stop when the last page is finished. It kindles the imagination of children who discover that an item, any item, is usually a house for something. A glove is a house for a hand, a shoe is a house for a foot, a wrist is a house for a watch, and so on.

- *Don't Forget the Bacon* by Pat Hutchins (New York: Greenwillow Books, 1976). Children immediately identify with the message of this book. A boy is sent to the store with verbal instructions for four items. Along the way, the list becomes so jumbled in his head that "six farm eggs" becomes "six fat legs" and then "six clothes pegs." After enjoying this book, children can use it to help the boy by "drawing" his grocery list or writing it down. Maybe they will be helped, too.

- *The Pooh Story Book* by A. A. Milne, illustrated by E. H. Shephard. New York: E. P. Dutton and Co., 1965. This book contains three separate Winnie the Pooh stories. Children meet old friends Eyeore, Piglet, and the loveable Pooh! January is a good time for renewing old acquaintances and for making new ones. For story time, students can bring in their own teddy bears, who always make story time quieter because they listen so well.

- *Owl Moon* by Jane Yolan, illustrated by John Schoenherr (New York: Philomel Books, 1987. Late one night, as shown in the beautiful illustrations of the book, a little girl and her father go owling in the silent snowy country. It's a quiet, watchful trip on a cold night that makes you feel warm inside. This book earned a Caldecott Award Medal.

SPOTLIGHT ON READING

The January Review

Children returning from the holiday recess are generally subdued, so this is a good time to re-establish learning links. There needs to be time set aside for review of letter-sound relationships, sight vocabulary, and phonetic strategies to help pronounce words. Many children will have lost ground over the recess, but this is soon regained once reading routines and teaching strategies become a part of their daily reading pattern.

- Play "Nana's Bandana." Use a bright piece of cloth with the four ends tied in a knot. You (or a student) hold up the bandana and start the alphabet review by saying, "Nana's Bandana can hold a _____" (word that begins with the letter *a*). The bandana is passed to another student who must say, "Nana's Bandana can hold a _____ and a _____" (the *a* word and a word that begins with the letter *b*). Continue passing the bandana around the class. Here are some examples:

  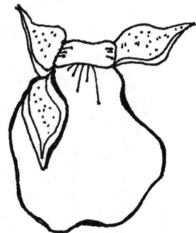

  "an apple and a baby"
  "an apple, a baby, and a cat"
  "an apple, a baby, a cat, and a dog"
  "an apple, a baby, a cat, a dog, and an eagle"
  "an apple, a baby, a cat, a dog, an eagle, and a frog"

  Continue all the way through *z*. As the children continue to pass Nana's Bandana, they pretend that it gets heavier and heavier, so that they have to lug it around!

- Play "Feed the Caterpillar." You will need a total of 26 two-pound coffee cans (one for each letter of the alphabet), but you can begin with just five and add a few more cans each day. Cover the cans with colorful prepasted paper, make a giant caterpillar head from construction paper to place in front of the "A" can, glue one alphabet letter on each can, and place the caterpillar along the edge of the floor or counter. Students can bring in all of their holiday greeting cards to cut up, and can cut colorful pictures from magazines to insert into the cans in order to feed the caterpillar. (This caterpillar eats *everything,* not only food items. So an airplane in the "A" section is fine.) If it's difficult to find a lot of coffee cans, you might want to use lunch bags.

- Mix the caterpillar cans and have students put them back in ABC order.
- Students can take one can from the caterpillar to their seat and work with the contents to reinforce the letter-sound relationships.
- Students can play this group game. "I'm thinking of something that begins with this letter (show can) and it _____ (hint)." Students get three guesses before another hint is given. The one who guesses correctly gets to select a can, an item, and give the hints. Often, several children will select this as an indoor recess game.

Meet the Ugh Bug!

It's a brand new month, a brand new year, and here's a brand new creature to meet—the Ugh Bug! The Ugh Bug is the "exception to the rule." Explain to students that sometimes we try to use rules to help us figure out new words, but the rules don't work all the time; there are exceptions. When this happens, everyone says "Ugh!" That's how the Ugh Bug got its name!

Some of the rules, with exceptions, are:

"Use *i* before *e,* except after *c,* or when sounding like *a,* as in neighbor and weigh."

"When two vowels go walking, the first one does the talking."

"CVCV pattern—first vowel is long" or "The letter *e* at the end of the word makes the first vowel say its name."

These rules work most of the time, but there are exceptions. See the reproducible activity pages.

How does the Ugh Bug feel about always being an exception to the rule? Not very well. In fact, horrible! Students will begin to sympathize with this character because the bug feels so badly and cries because nobody likes it. Students will tend to be more patient about finding reading rules that don't work. You can begin to make a list of words for Ugh Bug.

Make Ugh Bug puppets from colorful socks. Students can wear the puppet on one hand while reading independently in order to show Ugh Bug that it's okay when you find a word that doesn't follow the rules. Teach the word to Ugh Bug, too.

Review the Alligator and Ogre Vowel Sounds

Print the name of the new month, sing out the vowels and the long and short sounds, and find out how many belong to each one. Some students may be interested in looking through a brand new calendar for the new year in order to find out how many long and short vowels are at work.

Learn to Sight These UFOs

Some words are used with high frequency (or upper frequency—UFOs) and need to be learned by sight. Place these words on satellite or planet shapes and hang them from the ceiling fixtures (if allowed by your school). Students can take a yardstick or pointer, and point to the ones they can name. Keep practicing until the children know all of them. Make flashcards of these words on UFO shapes:

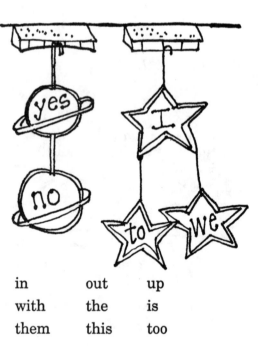

I	you	yes	no	in	out	up
down	and	to	we	with	the	is
can	look	school	today	them	this	too

Double Final Consonants, but One Sound

Some words have two final consonants but only one sound. For example, the word "ball" is pronounced "b aw l" rather than "b aw l l." Be on the lookout for letters with double final consonants, and keep a list of them on the chalkboard. Students can add to them. Here are some starters:

all	hiss
ball	kiss
call	miss
tall	

"S" and "Z" Sounds at the End

- List words on the chalkboard that end with the letter *s*. Pronounce them, and see if they have a final sound of *s* or *z*. Use experience chart paper to make "Final S" and "Final Z" words. Some starters are:

this	has
his	is
yes	cats
plows	makes

- Say the plural of animal names. If they end with an *s* sound, students can hold up a curved hand (an *s* has curves); if they end with a *z* sound, students hold up a straight hand (a *z* has straight lines). Here are some starters:

bears (z)	rabbits (s)
elephants (s)	dogs (z)
horses (z)	giraffes (s)
cats (s)	lions (z)
frogs (z)	

- Make "An S and Z Animal Book." Put a capital S or Z on the page for plural endings. Have students show the book to others and see if they can figure out why this is an S and Z book.

SPOTLIGHT ON MATH

Happy New Year

Since it is a new year, it is represented by a new number. On the chalkboard, write the numerals that represent the old year. Then write the numerals that represent the new year. How many digits have changed? Work it out.

Review your vocabulary of "time" words. Place them on a shape of a time capsule. You can use such words as the specific days of the week, months of the year, clock, hand, hour, minute, o'clock, half-past, today, yesterday, tomorrow, day, night, noon, evening, and so on. Have students play a game centering around the time capsule words, such as "I'm thinking of a time word that goes tick-tock and lets us know when it is time to eat lunch." (clock)

Calendar Review and New Teaching

There are beautiful calendars on the market today, and many businesses give out calendars free of charge. Bring to class a big new calendar for the year and go through it. Count the number of months and review their names. Count and review the names of the days of the week, count and review the total number of days in each month. Find students' birthdays to see the day of the week on which they occur. Look for special holidays and national birthdays to celebrate during the upcoming year. This gives students a sense of future time, and things to look forward to along the way.

- Designate the months within your classroom as *focus* months, such as Computer Month, Addition and Subtraction Month, Shape Month, Children's Math Books Month, and so on. There can be designations by week within the monthly focus.

- Take the beautiful calendars from last year and laminate them. These become worksheets that students can use to study the 12 months of the year. Use watercolor pens that can be easily erased or wiped off. Ask parents to donate their old calendars and use the different varieties to compare the holidays and special events that have been marked.

- Have a special January calendar on the bulletin board so that students can work with the calendar daily. Be sure to have them make their own calendar for the month of January to take home. On this calendar, you can mark special days that help busy parents remember when things are due and when special events will be occurring.

R-R-Ring! The Alarm Clock Is Ringing

Bring an old alarm clock into the room and notice how it helps to perk up interest in telling time. Set the alarm clock so that it will ring in five minutes, and continue working. When the alarm rings, show students how to turn it off. The alarm clock can be set to ring for snack time. It can be set to ring approximately five minutes *before* getting ready to go to special classes so that students have ample time to prepare for the shift in their routine. Teach students how to set the clock so that it will ring in five minutes, ten minutes, or fifteen minutes. You may find that students ask to bring in *their* clock next week so that their clock is the one helping our classroom run so smoothly. (TEACHER: Another plus is that the *clock* is telling the students that it is clean-up time, or that recess is over—not you. So when students are engaged in particularly enjoyable activity, the clock gets the frowns and grumbles!)

January Sales

Take advantage of the many advertisements in the local papers that show a wide variety of items on sale. Use stickers to place over the dollar amount and write in the amount that you want students to be working with, such as pennies, nickels, dimes, quarters, and so on. Cut out the items and paste them onto cards, and then "go shopping." Turn over a sale card, and have students show the necessary amount needed to buy the item, using real coins or cut-outs.

Pennies, Nickels, Dimes, and Quarters

Use real pennies, nickels, dimes, and quarters for counting. Note that if we can learn to count by fives, we will have no difficulty with our money system.

- Make a set of coin cards so students can place coins on top of them in order to identify the coin size and value.

- How many different ways can we "save up" for a total of 25 cents or one quarter? Have students arrange coins in various combinations. You may want to use large laminated coin cut-outs.

- Make a "Bank Book" for each student or a BIG BANK BOOK to hang up in class. You can keep track of the cut-out pennies or nickels "earned" for good work papers, good behavior in the hallway, good sports on the playground, and so on. When students have "earned" a designated amount, perhaps a treat is in store. The treat can be a brand-new classroom library book, or new pencils for all, or a new set of colored marking pens for the classroom—or even a classroom popcorn or pizza party!

A Dazzling Snow Cone Store

You need: 1 or 2 quarts of vanilla (or lemon) sherbet, 1 package of ice cream cones, 1 scooper or large metal spoon, and a storehouse of cut-out coins. Make a big sign: "JANUARY SNOW CONES—10 cents a dip." Students will have to show the correct amount of money before they can "buy" a dazzling snow cone.

- For variety, serve Precious Pink Snow Cones (strawberry sherbet) or North Wind Blue Snow Cones (blueberry sherbet), or Signs-of-Spring Snow Cones (lime sherbet) and charge varying amounts for each, such as 5 cents, 15 cents, and so on. Again, students need to show the correct amount before they can "buy" their snow cone.

- On a day when a variety of cones is offered, put different price tags on them. Graph the student "purchases."

Math Shapes in Winter

What shapes do we find in winter? Let's go on a Shape Look as we peer out of the window, or go on a Shape Hunt on the playground. What shape is a snowman? What shape is the shovel? What shape is a tree trunk? What shape is an evergreen tree? Break these large shapes down into smaller shapes, and we find that a snowman is a series of circles. A shovel is a rectangle or square, with a rectangular or circular-shaped handle. A tree trunk is a giant cylinder. An evergreen tree is a series of triangles going in different directions.

- Have an abundance of basic shapes cut out of felt material. Students can construct large objects from small shapes using the felt board.

- Go on a different kind of hunt for shapes on the playground. Look carefully at the playground equipment for squares, circles, triangles, cones, cubes, and so on. What shapes do we find on the swing set? What shapes do we find on the jungle gym? What shapes can we locate on the slide, in the sandbox, on other equipment?

- Children are amazed when they look for tiny shapes that make up big shapes. Keep looking! One author who has a variety of good books for children is Tana Hoban with *Shapes and Things; Cirlces, Triangles and Squares;* and the excellent wordless book *Look Again!*

- For variety, cut students' writing paper into a triangle or a circle for the day. This seems to bring out the very best writing efforts!

HANDS-ON SCIENCE

Sink and Float

Set up an area in the classroom so that students can work with a tub of water and items that they discover will either sink or float in water. The area should be away from other work areas, and strict rules are required here so that the area fulfills its purpose. In some classrooms, only one person at a time is allowed in this area; whereas, in other settings students may work together in pairs. Students need to be aware that it is an area for working and learning, and they, themselves, may be very helpful in setting up the rules for the area.

You will need:

a half-filled tub of water

a sponge for clean-up of spills

newspaper for the table or floor

paper towels

pencil and paper for recording sink/float information

a box of assorted items

a sign-up sheet

Some of the assorted items can include: ruler, twig, pencil, string, eraser, stone, rock, plastic spoon, wooden spoon, silver spoon, paper clip, ball of clay, flat piece of clay, rubber ball, and so on.

The key learning concept at this developmental level may well be that objects can be grouped according to whether they will sink or float. More detailed information may be absorbed later.

MORE DETAILED INFORMATION: The key word here is *density* (a new word). One material floats in another because of the difference in densities. Density is a measure of how closely molecules (another new word) are pushed together. Molecules pushed together form a mass. Dense material has more mass. Gravity pulls more on denser materials, making them heavier—and thus they sink.

Don't Look for Me, I'm Sleeping

Most of the winter sleepers take their long naps underground (process called hibernation). They usually roll up into a ball to conserve body heat. The hibernating animals go into a state where they barely breathe; their heart beats very slowly; and they don't eat or get rid of their waste. This is nature's way of insuring that particular animals will survive. Otherwise, they would not find enough food nor would they be warm enough if they had to spend the long winter outdoors. Many animals hibernate, including the ground squirrel, raccoon, chipmunk, bear, snail, slug, and earthworm. Be sure to get an information book from the library about this fascinating topic.

Hibernating Bears

The *black bear* is the most common bear—with black fur and a brown face. As the days get shorter and the sun shines less, the bear eats more and more in order to gain weight. It hunts for nuts, berries, insects, honey, and some grasses, and goes on an eating spree. The bear stores up food in its body in order to become its very own "stocked refrigerator" for the long winter sleep. The black bear does not go into as deep a sleep state as some other hibernators. The temperature of the bear drops, and it can be awakened by loud noise or by bright light. Females usually give birth to twin cubs during this time. The cubs are the size of baby kittens at birth and weigh about 2 pounds each. (If students cup their hands together, they can pretend to be holding a bear cub. Mold a bear from 2 pounds of clay to feel the weight.) When bears emerge in the spring, the first thing they do is find water and drink, drink, drink until they get their fill.

The female *polar bear* hibernates, but the male remains outdoors. During this time, the female gives birth and takes care of her young. The polar bears (the largest of the bears) have bristles on their paws much like great big brushes;

these enable them to move over the slippery ice and snow. In this way, they can sneak up on a sleeping seal and catch it for dinner. Students can pretend to be the quiet polar bear sneaking up on a seal. Tie hand brushes to students' "front paws" (hands) and "back paws" (feet) and have them walk like a polar bear on all fours!

Simulating the Hibernation of Bears

Act out the following to the tune of "Twinkle, Twinkle Little Star":

pretend to eat berries, honey, etc.

> Time to eat now, big black bear,
> Stuff yourself without a care.

puff cheeks

> You have gained much weight, I see.

waddle in a little circle

> You look like a house to me!

dig with big claw hands

> Time to dig yourself a home,
> Winter's not the time to roam.

crawl into cave, roll into a ball

> Crawl right in and roll up tight,

deep breathing

> You will sleep through winter's night.

*turn out lights; have students nap
for 1 minute or longer*

> SHHHH!

turn on the lights

> Here's the sun, it's getting light,

yawn and stretch

> Nights are shorter, days are bright.

crawl outside cave, blink eyes repeatedly

> Yes, you may go out today,

swallow 3 times, sniff the air while wiggling nose

> Get three drinks and sniff the day!

Make a Chipmunk's Burrow

The chipmunk takes the "layered" approach to hibernation. It does not store body fat like the bear, so it must store acorns, nuts, grains, and dried grasses. It digs a burrow for its winter home and stores its food on the ground, lays grasses and leaves upon the food, and then climbs upon that and curls up for its nap. Then it periodically awakens long enough to reach down to get food. When the food is gone, it's time for spring.

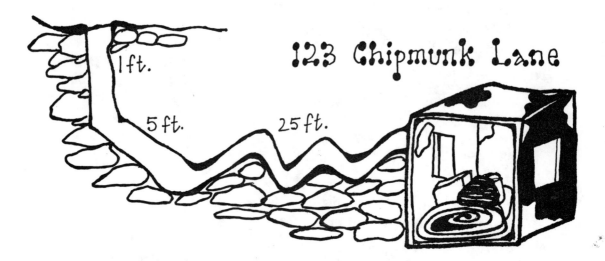

Make a "burrow" along the wall. The chipmunk digs straight down for about 1 foot (students can measure with a ruler), then it slopes its ramp for about 5 feet (students can measure with a ruler, yardstick, or both), and then it winds its way for about another 25 feet before it sets up its winter home. In the classroom, the winter home can be a large box that students can crawl into. Outfit it with a snug rug, pillows, and lots of good books to read. Then, students can crawl into this special place and hibernate with a good book. Give the burrow a special name, such as Chipmunk's Burrow or The Hibernation Cave or 123 Chipmunk Lane. Occasionally, the "chipmunk" might share some nuts with the class for a very special treat—but only a few because it needs enough to get through the winter.

Do Stuffed Bears Hibernate?

No, indeed. January 18, the birthdate of A. A. Milne, creator of Winnie the Pooh, is a beary, beary special day for stuffed bears. They are all invited to come to the classroom, dressed in their finery, and each one must find a library book to share with the class. The bears can also tell a story, or a riddle, or even perform tricks with the help of the owners. To the delight of everyone, honey is served on graham crackers at about 11 o'clock.

- Have a collection of library books with bear themes for Bear Browsing Time.
- Serve blueberries and milk after reading *Blueberries for Sal* by Robert McClosky.
- Sit in a circle, hug your stuffed bear tight, and listen to the record "Brown Bear, Brown Bear, What Do I See" by Bill Martin, Jr. Then have each student tell what he or she sees.

- Students can make a paper doll bear for their stuffed bear by using wallpaper samples, construction paper, scissors, and glue.
- Bring out the checkered tablecloth and have everyone eat a picnic lunch in the classroom today (provided by room parents, or have students bring in "brown bag bear lunches").
- Have a variety of bear story records available for quiet listening time.
- Make prize ribbons for the biggest bear, the funniest bear, the friendliest bear, the most huggable bear, and so on.
- Make headbands of bear ears and have students claim a "bear name" for the day: Honey Bear, Cuddles, Big Paw, and so on.
- Use sponges with brown and honey-colored paints, and great big sheets of kraft paper so that everyone can make a big teddy bear. Allow this to dry. Later, or the next day, the students can carefully cut the bear shape with their scissors. These bears can be assembled on a bulletin board, on the door, or in the hall, and can have cartoon bubbles alongside their heads to let us know what they are saying and thinking about what we're studying in school. This information may be written or dictated by the student.
- Write a class experience story (on bear-shaped paper) from the point of view of the bear about the day's (or week's) activities.
- Each student can write a letter to a real hibernating bear and include a picture to show the bear what it is missing.
- Interview a bear with a toy microphone. (The owner can interpret for the teddy bear as it whispers in the owner's ear.)

Keeping Warm in Winter

Unlike bears or birds, people don't have fur and feathers to keep them warm in winter and cool in summer. We need all the help we can get in the form of food, clothing, and shelter all year long.

- Eskimos make clothing of animal skins, such as deer and fox. The skins prevent the cold air from reaching their bodies. They also wear boots made of animal hide and stuff them with grass and moss for insulation. How many students have a parka (winter jacket) that has draw-strings around the middle that can be tightened to keep air out or loosened to allow air in? How many have strings on clothing, such as hoods and boots? Bring in a pair of chunky ski boots, if possible, and have students practice tying shoelaces.

- A person's body temperature is usually between 96° and 98° Fahrenheit. When the temperature is at the freezing point (32° Fahrenheit), people need the proper clothing (gloves, boots, hat, scarf, jacket or lined coat, ear muffs, and so on) to keep warm. Use your flannelboard and make a cut-out of a person and cut-outs of clothing. Each day, students can dress the weather person according to the temperature and weather conditions.

- *Insulation* is a new vocabulary word for winter weather. We use special insulation material to line the walls of our homes and buildings to keep the warm air in and the cold air out. As a result of our astronauts traveling in outer space and needing to keep warm, scientists have developed special insulated material for use with gloves, socks, and undergarments. This *thermal* material, developed by NASA, is a special aluminized fabric that is lightweight, durable, washable, and able to stretch with body action. Is anyone able to bring in a sample of thermal material? (Sporting goods stores would be one source.)

Let It Snow, Let It Snow

When snow falls in winter, it serves as insulation for the ground and the plants. That is why we speak of a "blanket of snow." For an experiment, take two thermometers outside. Make sure that they have the same reading. Bury one under the snow, close to the ground. Place the other on top of the snow. After 30 minutes, go back outside and get the two thermometers. Which one has the lower reading (indicating colder) and which one has the higher reading (indicating warmer)? Did the "blanket" work?

Martin Luther King, Jr.

On January 20, Martin Luther King, Jr. Day is celebrated as a national holiday. Martin Luther King, Jr. was a black minister who believed in working peacefully to change the laws. He came from a family that required all the children to be home for suppertime—no matter what they were doing. Suppertime was a special time of day for sharing what each family member was doing and thinking. How do we spend suppertime at home? Could we take a lesson from his family and spend this time together for sharing?

- Martin Luther King, Jr.'s nickname was "ML." These are the initials of his first and second names. Let's say our initials and learn them.

- On the very first celebration of this national holiday in 1986, hundreds of balloons were released by children. Perhaps balloons could be released from your school.

- Bells were also rung on the very first celebration day. Be sure to ring bells in your classroom in celebration of peace.

- Do something kind for someone today. Let someone else get ahead of you in line, pick up a pencil from the floor and return it, be sure to say "thank you" and "excuse me."

- Put everyone's name on a tiny piece of paper. Fold the papers in half and put them into a basket. Each person can reach into the basket and draw a paper. Silently read the name of the person who is to be your "special" person for the day. Do something nice for that person. Say something nice to that person. At the end of the day, gather together in a circle and talk about all the nice things that were done for each other today. Can anyone guess who their "secret pal" is? Maybe we could have a "secret pal" time at least once a week.

- Find some children's books that have received the Coretta Scott King Award for themes that promote peace and brotherhood in children's literature, and read them aloud. Some suggestions are: *Everett Anderson's Goody-Bye* by Lucille Clifton (New York: Holt, Rinehart & Winston, 1983); *Mufaro's Beautiful Daughters* by John Steptoe (New York: Lothrop, Lee & Shepherd, 1987); and *Justin and the Best Biscuits in the World* by Mildred Pitts Walker (New York: Lothrop, Lee & Shepherd, 1986).

- Above all, let's convey the message to treat people fairly regardless of the color of their skin, their height, their weight, their looks, and the way they dress.

HAPPY NEW YEAR

This is a brand new year and it is a custom to make New Year's Resolutions. This means that we put forth more effort and try to change our behavior in an area that needs some help.

Butch the Bird

Butch the Bird needs help. (See the reproducible activity pages.) Butch was not allowed to migrate because he would not settle down and study. So the Wise Old Owl decided that Butch had to improve his math, reading, and writing skills. Now that Butch is on his own for the winter, he is asking for help. Students may also need to settle down and work on one of these areas, so by helping Butch, they are also helping themselves. The Wise Old Owl will return in the spring and be on the lookout for good effort and some practice and progress.

A Quiet Corner

Set up a quiet area in the room where students may go and time themselves for five minutes to see just how much of their work they can accomplish correctly during that time. Or, bring in a two-minute sand-timer and put it on a student's desk to see how much can be accomplished before "time runs out." Often this time-on-task method assists the student who is easily distracted. Also, the competition is with the student's own previous progress.

Perhaps a bird puppet or a stuffed toy bird (kept in a cage with paper, pencils, and books) will help capture the imagination of the first graders who will work harder to help Butch catch up with the other birds!

Reproducible Activity Pages for December

Snowbear's Special Words (compound words)

Oops! Claire Bear Is Spilling the Beans (ABC review)

Meet the Ugh Bug (exception to vowel rules)

Ugh! The Rules Don't Work (exception to vowel rules)

January Bookmarks (reading)

Special! Half-Price Sale (subtraction with money)

Price Mark-Up! The Big Sale Is Over (addition with money)

Check Your Coins (penny information and nickel news)

The Juggling Bear (addition facts for 12)

Compare Yourself to an Alligator (height and weight)

The Good Breakfast Match (increasing memory span)

Sink and Float (science facts)

Snowflakes (working with six)

Martin Luther King, Jr. (parade planning)

Let's Review Room Rules Before the Monster's Visit (room rules)

My New Year's Contract with Butch the Bird (extra effort)

SNOWBEAR'S SPECIAL WORDS

When you put two words together to make a big word, that word is called a COMPOUND word. Use the word "snow" to help Snowbear make these special words. You can use the back of this sheet, too. Snowbear will give you a hint: start with "snowman."

1.

2.

3.

4.

5.

6.

Name _____   Date _____

CHECK YOUR COINS

PENNY INFORMATION

1. The name of the man on the penny is

_____.

2. He was our _____.

3. This penny was made in the year _____.

4. I noticed that _____

_____

_____.

penny

Do a coin rubbing of a
real penny in the circle.
Then, do a coin rubbing of
a real nickel in the
circle below.

nickel

NICKEL NEWS

1. The name of the man on the nickel is

_____.

2. He was our _____.

3. This nickel was made in the year _____.

4. I noticed that _____

_____

_____.

THE JUGGLING BEAR

Jordie the Juggling Bear is working on his number facts. Today, he is working on the 12 family. You can help Jordie by filling in the number facts. He is helping you to get started, and you can help him finish.

Name _____ Date _____

COMPARE YOURSELF TO AN ALLIGATOR

Weigh yourself. Measure your height. Count your teeth. Then compare yourself to an alligator. Do you weigh more or less? Are you heavier or lighter? Who has more teeth? Find a book on real alligators and make other comparisons such as skin, favorite food, and so on.

Alligator - Age 5

Weight – 350 pounds
Height – 5 feet long (60 inches)
Teeth – 20 per jaw

Name

Age _____

This is a picture of me.

Weight _____ pounds

Height _____ feet

_____ inches

Teeth _____

Other

THE GOOD BREAKFAST MATCH

Color each picture below. Then cut the boxes apart on the lines. TO PLAY THE GAME:
Lay the cards face down on a grid. Turn over two cards. If the cards match, you may
keep them. If the cards do not match, turn them back over. Then the next player takes a
turn. Try to remember where each picture is located. The player with the most matching
cards wins the game.

SINK AND FLOAT

You will need a tub of water and materials from the classroom for this experiment. Complete the diagram that shows the results of your experiment. Do these items have anything in common? What? On the back of this sheet, make a list of all the sink and float items.

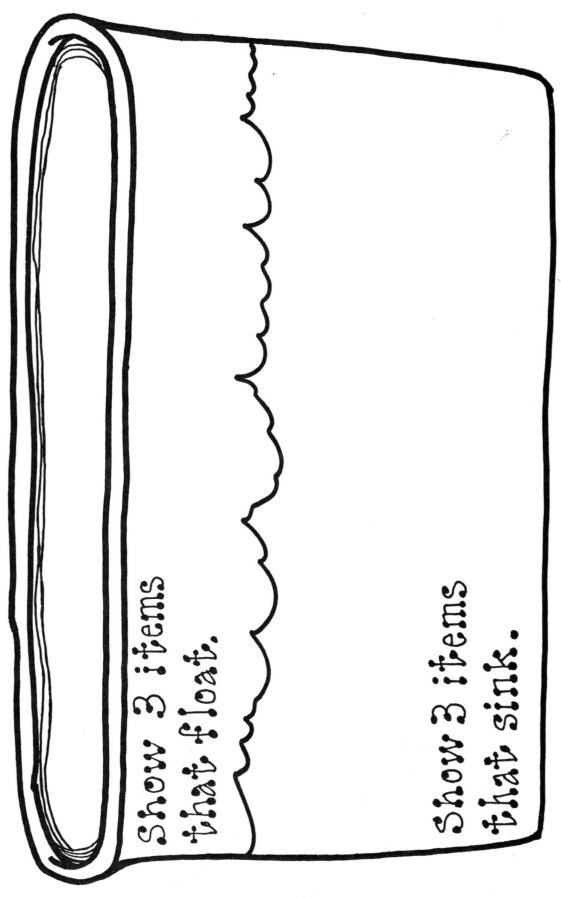

Show 3 items that float.

Show 3 items that sink.

Name _____ Date _____

SNOWFLAKES

Snowflakes have six sides. There are no two alike. Each little part is a crystal of ice. Look at some snowflakes through a magnifying glass to get some ideas for designs. Then make six different snowflakes with six different colors.

MARTIN LUTHER KING, JR.

On January 20, 1986, the first Martin Luther King, Jr. Day was celebrated. Martin Luther King, Jr. was a black minister who believed in equal treatment for ALL people, regardless of the color of their skin. In the boxes below, use your crayons to show how to join in the celebration. How many will you actually do?

ring a bell

fly a balloon

love
peace
justice

make a flag

have a parade

LET'S REVIEW ROOM RULES BEFORE THE MONSTER'S VISIT

This purple and orange monster is friendly and wants to visit our school. It wants to be good, but does not know what our rules are. Let's write six rules on its pet rock.

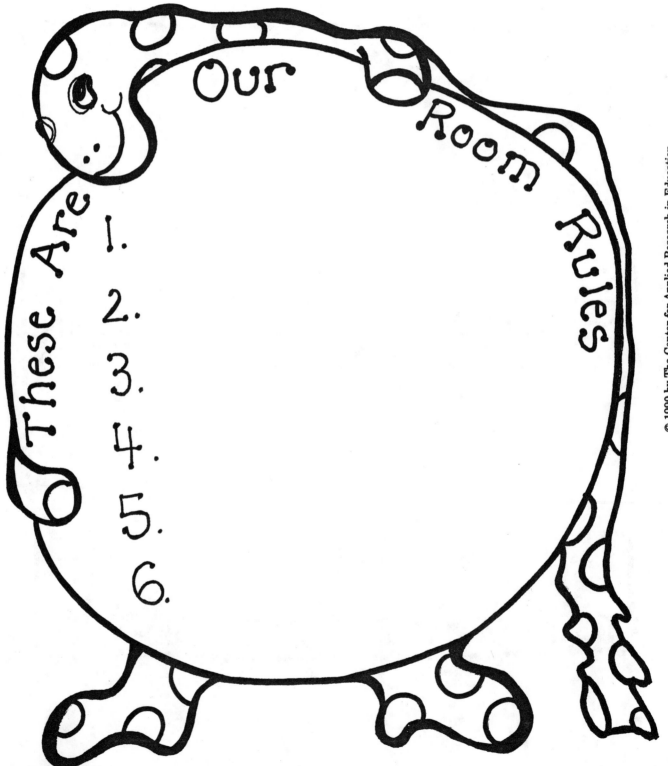

MY NEW YEAR'S CONTRACT WITH BUTCH THE BIRD

Butch the Bird needs help! He was not allowed to migrate because he would not do his work. But if he sees YOU working, then he will work, too.

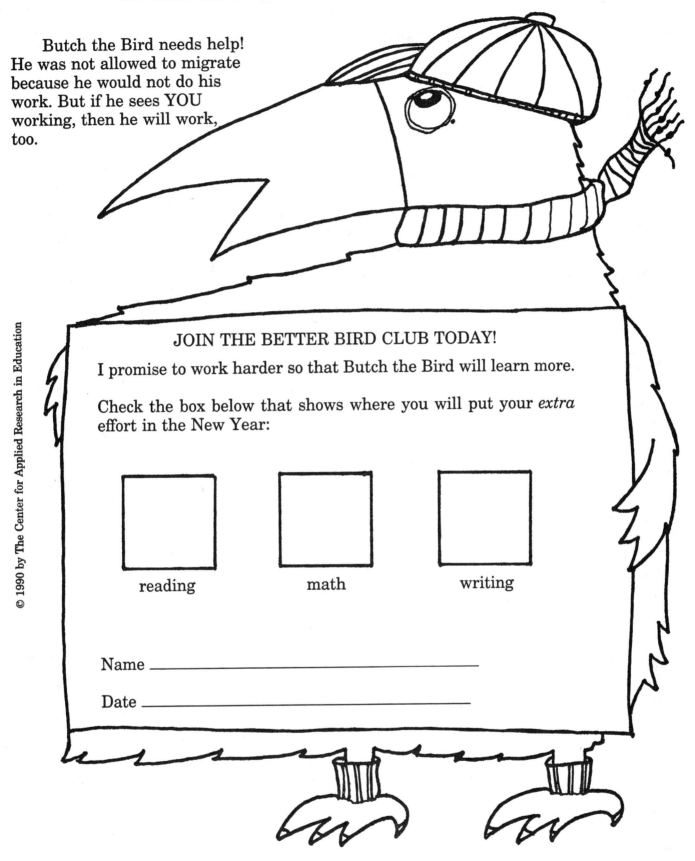

JOIN THE BETTER BIRD CLUB TODAY!

I promise to work harder so that Butch the Bird will learn more.

Check the box below that shows where you will put your *extra* effort in the New Year:

reading   math   writing

Name _____

Date _____

WE'RE FALLING IN LOVE WITH LEARNING

February is special because we are emphasizing caring—dental health care, general health care, and expressing care for others by making and delivering hand-made valentines that nurture both the giver and the receiver. By now, small-motor coordination has noticeably improved and students are better able to print, and to button, buckle, and zip with less effort. Artwork at the easel reflects this new developmental passage—so bring out the new paints and brushes!

RECOMMENDED CHILDREN'S BOOKS FOR FEBRUARY

- *Why Mosquitoes Buzz in People's Ears* retold by Verna Aardema, illustrated by Leo and Diane Dillon (New York: Dial Press, 1975). In this African tale, the mosquito sets off a chain of events that gets more jumbled up and more amusing as each colorful new animal is introduced. Finally, Mother Owl reacts by refusing to hoot and wake up the sun. All of this has left the mosquito wondering if anyone likes it. What's your answer? This beautifully illustrated book is a Caldecott Medal winner.

- *The Great Valentine's Day Balloon Race* by Adrienne Adams (New York: Charles Scribner's Sons, 1980). Orson Abbott, the Easter Egg artist, decides to enter the Valentine Hot Air Balloon Contest. His mother and father pitch in and help to launch the project. How will he decorate it? What will he name it? Can he really do it? You bet!

- *The Jolly Postman and Other People's Letters* by Janet and Allan Ahlberg (New York: William Heinemann, 1986). Following the postman around all day can be an exciting adventure, especially when he visits old favorites such as the witch, the three bears, Goldilocks, and others. The mail is in real envelopes inside the book pages and can be removed. Some are typed, some are printed, some are on letterhead stationery, and some are air mail. Even the postage stamps and post office cancellations are fun to scrutinize. This delightful book can launch the entire class into a month of letter-writing activities.

- *Little Rabbit's Loose Tooth* by Lucy Bate, pictures by Diane DeGroat (New York: Crown Publishers, 1975). This is a favorite story with first graders who are all in the process of losing baby teeth to make way for permanent teeth. What does the tooth fairy do with teeth? Is there a tooth fairy? This gentle tale lets the reader decide.

- *Everett Anderson's Friend* by Lucille Clifton, illustrated by Ann Grifalconi (New York: Holt, Rinehart & Winston, 1976). This is one in a series of the Everett Anderson books. In this story, we explore with Everett, a latchkey child, the mixed feelings that children have when new neighbors are moving in next door. In this case, Everett knows he will not like the new people in 13A, but perhaps he's in for a surprise.

- *Whistle for Willie* by Ezra Jack Keats (New York: The Viking Press, 1964). Peter tries to whistle until his cheeks get tired, but he just can't master the art of whistling. Suddenly, one day it happens. And when it does, his dog Willie is happy, and his mother and father are proud— and like anything else that's new, Peter just can't get enough of it. This book has many delightful illustrations. Look for the many other good books by this author, too.

- *The Best Valentine in the World* by Marjorie Weinman Sharmat, illustrated by Lilian Obligado (New York: Holiday House, 1982). Ferdinand Fox decides to make a special valentine for Florette—not red like everyone else's, but a purple valentine. He works on it for months, and imagines that Florette is working with the same intensity on one for him. When he delivers it to Florette, she claims that she has forgotten Valentine's Day, so he leaves in a huff with his valentine. How do these two resolve this problem on a day when people should be hugging, not fighting?

- *Zerelda's Ogre* by Tomi Ungerer (New York: Harper & Row, 1967). An ogre is usually big on brawn, but short on brains. This hungry ogre spies Zerelda going to market and decides to devour her. In his impatience, he falls from a rocky ledge and knocks himself unconscious. Zerelda takes pity and uses up most of her supplies to fix him a delectable dinner. Is it possible to tame a hungry ogre? The pictures enrich the story, and children especially like the illustrated menu of the midnight snack at the ogre's castle.

- *Albert's Toothache* by Barbara Williams, illustrated by Kay Chorao (New York: The Trumpet Club, 1974, 1989). How can Albert the turtle have a toothache when no one else in the family has ever had a toothache? Turtles just don't have toothaches! He must be making it up. Finally, Grandmother Turtle, a good listener, comes over and gets to the bottom of it. Children who are in the process of losing teeth and cutting second ones seem to relate very well to this story.

- *A Chair for My Mother* by Vera B. Williams (New York: Greenwillow Books, 1982). Grandma was all right and the cat got out, too, but everything else in the house was ruined in a fire. This is one little girl's story about starting over again with the help of family and neighbors. A money jar is set aside so that when it is filled with coins, they will buy a big comfortable chair. This is a story of waiting, being patient, and hoping. The ending is worth the wait!

SPOTLIGHT ON READING

"Love" Is an Exception to the Rule

That's right! In sorting out the rules for the Ugh Bug, the Ogre's Unicorn came across the word "love." If love followed the CVCV rule that the first vowel is long or, stated another way, that the e at the end of the word makes the vowel say its name, then it would be pronounced as "l-OH-v." But it isn't. It is pronounced as "l-uh-v."

And if love followed the rule that the vowel o is either long or short, it would be pronounced "l-oh-v" (long) or "l-ah-v" (short). But it doesn't follow that rule either. So, love belongs to the Ugh Bug!

Help children to rejoice and celebrate (especially during this month of love and valentines) in the Ugh Bug's new-found glory. Make a valentine mailbox or container for the Ugh Bug and make and send it a valentine with the word "love" on it—because it is the Ugh Bug's word.

Happy "Voweltine's" Day!

The Alligator, the Ogre, the Unicorn, and the Ugh Bug are all having a great big party this month. It's not on February 14, which is Valentine's Day. It's on February 13, which is being declared as VOWELTINE'S DAY. Even YOU are invited to participate. On this day, these are the rules:

- You must wear something red.
- You must tie a piece of colored yarn around your finger.
- You must draw a picture of your favorite snack and print the words underneath.
- You must read at least one story or look through one picture book.
- You must say all of the long and short vowel sounds.
- You must take a drink from the water fountain and swallow three times for good luck.
- You must draw a picture of Ugh Bug and print the letters "l o v e" underneath it.
- You can do the Alligator and Ogre chants again. (See December's "Spotlight on Reading.")

Happy VOWELtine's Day!

- You can try to make up a love chant for Ugh Bug, who is seriously considering changing its name to Love Bug. Do you think it should? Take a survey and record your results. Spread the good word on Voweltine's Day!

Let's Look at Picture Clues

Go through a storybook showing only the pictures. Do not read the text at first. Have the children predict the text. Do they want to see the very last picture, or do they want to be surprised by the ending? Next, read the story aloud so that the visual and the verbal message are conveyed simultaneously. Then discuss the story and find out:

- Did the pictures give us some idea of what the story is about?
- What new information did we learn by reading (names of people, places, conversation, feelings, and other things not conveyed by the pictures)?

Be sure to point out the importance of the words for conveying information. Also, point out that the main idea (message, moral, values) of the story comes through with the words. Have students look through a wide variety of picture books, and select some that they would like to have read aloud. REMEMBER: Most picture books are written with a third-grade vocabulary level, so students need to have these books read aloud to them.

Have students make wordless picture books to convey a story.

Let's Go Exploring for Punctuation Marks

Punctuation marks, usually at the end of sentences, are "signals" to the reader. On the chalkboard, review or teach the following:

- The period (.) is the stop sign. You wait before continuing.
- The exclamation point (!) expresses emotion. Your voice gets louder.
- The question mark (?) conveys to the reader or listener that a question is being asked. Your voice goes higher at the end.
- The comma (,) is found within the sentence. It means you should pause before continuing.
- Quotation marks (" ") point out conversation (talk) to the reader.

Distribute a page from the newspaper to each student and have them circle all of the punctuation marks that they can find. They are usually, but not always, found at the end of a sentence. This exercise serves to alert students to the many signals that are given to the reader. It makes them much more aware of the marks as they continue to master the reading process.

Sentences at Work

Use the chalkboard to show that sentence meaning can be changed by word order and punctuation marks. Begin with:

"Jim can go out to play." (sentence)

"Jim can go out to play?" (question—asking for clarification without changing word order)

"Can Jim go out to play?" (question and change of word order)

"Jim can go out to play!" (exclamation mark—expression of emotion)

"Can Jim go out to play?" asked Bobby. (question—direct conversation)

Make flashcards using the punctuation marks. Have students learn what these signals mean. Make sentence strips, but leave out the punctuation marks. Have students select the appropriate marks for the sentences. Now, perhaps, they are ready to write some of their own, too.

Beginning and Ending Consonants

By this time, most of the class will be able to work with beginning sounds of many or all of the letters. They need to be able to spot ending sounds in order to help them make sense of words. For example, if a student knows the sound of a letter at the beginning of a word, help him or her focus upon the ending letter as well.

- Begin by making new flashcards, such as:

  t____k   b____g   r____f
  l____s   p____t   d____h

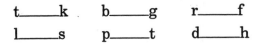

- If a set of ABC cards is displayed in the room, have a student point to first one and then another. A partner then has to make the sound.

- Use a deck of ABC flashcards and have students take TWO. Put them side by side and make the sounds. Next, put them in reverse order and make the sounds. For example: T P   P T. Help students to make up short words using these beginning and ending sounds. Score one point for each word.

SPOTLIGHT ON MATH

Calendar Subtraction

There are 12 months in the year, and we have just completed one, so we flip over the calendar. How many months are left? Write the subtraction statement on the chalkboard: $12 - 1 = 11$. Be sure that students are familiar with the "language of subtraction" which includes words such as minus, subtract, take away, remainder, left.

More Subtraction Practice

- You can help to set the scene by telling students that the classroom has been transformed into a zoo. Instruct eight students to go (gallop, waddle, slither) to a designated area in the classroom. You can count the "animals" and put a big "8" on the chalkboard. The zookeeper (you) is going to gently put a long piece of string (or clothesline) around five animals and lead them away. How

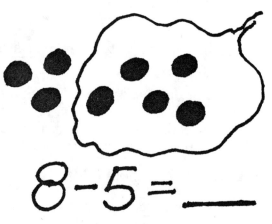

many are left? (Answer: 3) So, on the chalkboard, help the students to understand this number sentence: 8 − 5 = 3. Replay the activity again, so that everyone understands the idea of "taking away." Repeat this, using other animals and other number statement combinations.

- Put a number of objects on a table. Ask students to take away a certain number. Put the number sentence on the chalkboard.
- Put a number of objects on a table. Ask students to take a piece of colorful, bulky yarn and encircle a designated number of the items. These are the ones that we are taking away. Then, on the chalkboard, have students help write the number sentence. In subtraction, we ALWAYS write the total number of objects first, then the amount that was removed, and then the amount that is remaining. Teach students this formula:

First number recorded—TOTAL
Second number recorded—TAKE AWAY
Third number recorded—REMAINDER

Snowball Subtraction

In individual plastic sandwich bags, place ten cotton balls. Each student can get a bag of cotton "snowballs," empty them on the desk or workplace, and follow along with you as instructions are given to "count ten, take away four, and count the remainder." This is recorded on the chalkboard so that students are working at a concrete level with manipulative items, and at an abstract level with the numeral representations.

- If practice is needed with the nine family, for example, simply leave one cotton snowball in the bag and work with nine. This can be done for eight, seven, and so on.

Computer Keyboard

Make a cardboard replica of a computer keyboard. Ask students to focus upon the numerals. Which one is farthest to the left (1) and to the right (0)? What numeral comes before ___ and after? Also work with the plus and minus key locations, as well as other keys on the keyboard.

One Minute Is a Long Time—Or Is It Short?

The focus is upon duration of time. Have students sit perfectly still for one minute. It seems like a long time. Then, have students play a game (Simon

Says, for example) and interrupt after one minute has passed. It seems like a short time. Students begin to learn that the passage of time seems to vary—it sometimes seems long and sometimes seems short.

- Have students list all of the things that would seem long for one minute:

> waiting in line for a drink of water
>
> waiting for the assembly program to begin
>
> waiting for recess to begin
>
> waiting to go to lunch when you're hungry

- Have students list all of the things that would seem short for one minute:

> watching a favorite television program
>
> listening to a good story
>
> playing a game

Shape of the Month: The Cone

What things can we locate that are cone-shaped, and what function do they serve? For example:

funnels (transferring from large to small containers)

ice cream cones (a container for ice cream)

witch's hat, clown's hat

cardboard cones for holding yarn or macrame

nose cone (the front of an airplane)

windsock

megaphone

Cone

Have students make math megaphones. They can communicate addition and subtraction facts through them. One student can call out a number and another student can give an addition or subtraction fact that corresponds with the number.

HANDS-ON SCIENCE

One of the Five Senses: Taste

Children learn science concepts more effectively when the senses are involved. This month, we are going to focus upon the sense of taste. Since February is Dental Health Month and we are focusing upon the mouth and teeth, it seems like a natural progression to investigate our sense of taste.

According to researchers, taste buds located in clusters on the tongue are responsible for our being able to distinguish tastes that are bitter, sweet, sour, and salty.

Have a large mirror with a big handle available so that students can stick their tongue way out and see the taste buds located on their tongue. The buds toward the back appear larger and may be easier to see. Have students twist and turn their tongue as they observe it, so that the crevices reveal the taste buds. (See the reproducible activity pages.) Note that students do not need to handle their tongue with their hands for this activity.

Tasting Party

Have items available so that students may taste them in order to get the flavor. Perhaps this activity can be spread out over a period of time so that the mixture of items does not upset anyone's stomach. Have bite-size pieces of salty items, such as pretzels, potato chips, and corn chips. Have samples of salted and unsalted nuts, and see if students can tell the difference between the two.

Repeat this type of procedure for sour items (rhubarb, lemon drops, pickles); bitter items (iced tea, bitter chocolate); and sweet items (lemonade, candy, pastry).

I've Got a Sweet Tooth

When we say that someone has a sweet tooth, we mean that the person likes to eat sweets. Make a favorite list of "sweet tooth" food. What do too many sweets do to our teeth? This is the month when much information is available in newspapers and magazines on the subject of tooth care.

Are Fruits and Vegetables Sweet, Salty, Sour, or Bitter?

Have a salad-bar approach to this activity with bite-size pieces of apples, oranges, grapes, pears, celery, carrots, cucumber, radishes, and any other items that seem appropriate. In what categories do students place these items? Is there general agreement or do some people appear to perceive some things one way while other people perceive them another way?

My Favorite Food

Students can divide a paper plate into four sections and label each one as salty, sweet, sour, or bitter. Have them find a colorful picture in a magazine to paste in each category on their plate, or show three samples of each, or just paste one picture of their ultra-favorite in each category.

DENTAL HEALTH MONTH

The Tooth Fairy Club

- During the month of February, let's pay special attention to the care of our teeth. Discuss proper brushing (up and down), flossing, and rinsing. If you have not already done so, have a Tooth Fairy Club. Make a giant-size, gleaming-white tooth from shelf paper, and print on it the names of those who have lost their baby teeth. An individual tooth-shape necklace made from white construction paper and strung with yarn can be made for each child, and proudly worn by those who have lost a tooth.

- Our first set of teeth (milk teeth) start to fall out at about age five or six. We have 20 teeth in our first set and will have 32 teeth in our second set. Work this out in terms of tens and ones: 20 is equal to 2 tens and 0 ones; 32 is equal to 3 tens and 2 ones. Subtract 20 from 32 and that's how many more second teeth we will have. How many? 12 (or one dozen).

- Engage in creative thinking by asking children to imagine what the Tooth Fairy does with all of those teeth that she is collecting. Remember, a fairy has the use of magic, so anything can happen! Maybe the teeth show up as jewels in a king's or queen's crown, or as buttons on sweaters. Perhaps they are stuffed into cracks in palace walls to help keep them from tumbling down. Maybe birds use them to trade for sunflower seeds. Let the children's imaginations soar!

Crunch, Bang, Tear, Rip, Grind!

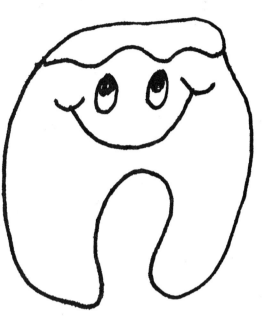

Is that a dinosaur stomping through the forest? No, it's our teeth at work. Our teeth are busy chewing and breaking down our food before we swallow it. Also, our teeth have names. We have 8 incisors that cut; 4 canines that rip; 8 molars in the first set that grind; and 12 molars in the second set that help grind.

Have a large mirror available so that students can locate these teeth and note their shape and size. Have them use their tongue to locate these teeth rather than use their fingers. (See the reproducible activity pages.)

The New Toothbrush Society

This is it. This is the month to run errands, help with the dishes, clean your room, take out the garbage, and so on. Why? Because this is the month we're working for a brand-new toothbrush. What color is yours going to be? (TEACHER: Send notes to parents to remind them that brushes harbor germs, and should be tossed out after a child has been ill. The toothbrushes should be replaced regularly. Engage parents in this New Toothbrush Society activity so that each child will receive a brand new brush.)

CHILDREN'S LITERATURE AND BLACK HISTORY MONTH

The Coretta Scott King Award

This award was established in 1969 and first awarded in 1978. Coretta Scott King is the widow of Martin Luther King, Jr. The award is given annually to Black authors and illustrators whose work promotes world unity and peace. Also, their creative work should serve as an inspiration to young children.

During February, be on the lookout for some of these wonderful books. Some authors are: Virginia Hamilton (*People Could Fly*), Lucille Clifton (*Everett Anderson's Good-Bye*), and Mildred Taylor (*Friendship*). Some illustrators are: John Steptoe (*Mother Crocodile; Mufaro's Beautiful Daughter*), and Jerry Pinkney (*Patchwork Quilt*). There are others also, so be sure to check with your local librarian and enjoy these stories with the children.

A Cooperative Book

Make books that show people working together to solve a common problem. This can be done as a total class project. Select a problem that is real in your community or in your school or in your classroom.

VALENTINE'S DAY

- Have each student make a valentine mailbag, using a brown lunch bag. It can be decorated with red and white designs. The student's name should be prominently displayed on the bag. That way, students can mail their own valentines.

- Decide where your class mailbags are to be located in the classroom. One place to tape them is along the rim of the chalk tray. This way, they are away from student work areas, and students can mail their valentines during indoor recess, or with a partner during morning work-time. (They're practicing reading and location skills.)

- A class list of names, sent home with students, is of tremendous help to parents. They can assist the child with the print on the outside of the envelopes.

- Students can make their own valentines, too. Have an area in the room with red and white paper, paper doilies, glue, glitter, felt pens, and scissors.

- Students can make a cloth valen-tine from red-checkered material, or red plaid, or a calico print. If two shapes are cut, they can sew and stuff them. Use a needle to string red yarn through the top center. These can be hung at home as a cheery valentine greet-ing.

- For those who are working along in the Reading Sections with the Alligator and the Ogre, February 13 can be celebrated as VOWELTINE'S DAY and students can work with long and short vowel sounds on this special occasion. Don't forget to make a valentine mailbag for the Alligator and the Ogre.

- Above all, try to remember to wear bright red for the Valentine's Day celebration on February 14. (Have bright red ribbons handy for those who are wearing yellow and purple!)

HI THERE, GROUNDHOG!

Shadow, Go; Cloudy, Howdy!

The groundhog is another name for a woodchuck. According to legend, the hibernating groundhog comes out of its burrow on February 2. If it sees its shadow, it gets frightened and scurries back into its burrow. This means six more weeks of winter (check this on the calendar). If it's cloudy and the groundhog does not see its shadow, it does not get frightened, and stays outside. This means a mild spring. February is also a breeding time for the groundhogs, so that may have something to do with why they surface from their burrow.

Some Groundhog Facts

The adult groundhog weighs about 10 pounds. Find something that weighs 10 pounds (like a sack of potatoes), put it into a brown burlap sack, and glue on colorful felt features for eyes, nose, and mouth. Have the students hold the "hibernating groundhog" during storytime as a special reward. The groundhog is also 2-feet tall. How does that compare with our height? Let's get the yardstick and measure.

The groundhog burrows and tunnels under a rock or a tree stump. It closes itself in from the inside by pushing dirt back up into the entryway. Often, other animals come along and "rent out" the upper part of the burrow during the winter. Other animals could include a fox, skunk, or rabbit. Use creative dramatics to enact "The Groundhog Rental Company." The groundhog could interview the fox, skunk, or rabbit to make sure that it will make an ideal renter. What qualities would an ideal renter have? (Quiet, no late night noises, no blaring of the television, etc.)

PRESIDENTS' DAY

Who Is Our President Today?

Have students look carefully through a stack of newspapers and magazines for pictures of our current President. Cut them out. Then have someone lie on a piece of kraft paper and draw a thick black outline around the person's body. Carefully cut and glue (overlap) the Presidential pictures onto the paper figure before you cut out the figure along the edge. Now we have a good look at our President in color, black and white, and in many different settings.

Display this in the room for all to study. Alongside of the figure, have the students write an experience chart story about the President, including name, White House residence, spouse, children, pets, home state, and so on.

The Father of Our Country

February 22, 1732, is the birthdate of George Washington. He was the first President of the United States. His native state was Virginia; locate this state on the map. How close are you to this state? Did you know that Washington, D.C. is named in honor of George Washington? How many have visited our nation's capitol? Take a classroom trip together via the lovely picture book *The Inside-Outside Book of Washington, D.C.* by Roxie Munro (New York: E. P. Dutton, 1987).

Many school buildings across the country are named after George Washington. Are there any in your city? Many school buildings have a portrait of George Washington hanging in the entryway. Is there one in your building? After studying pictures of George Washington, have students paint his "portrait" at the easel. A student could pretend to be Mr. Washington, and sit for the portrait, wearing a cotton or white felt wig. The portrait painter could wear a beret for inspiration!

The Book Lover

February 12, 1809 is the birthdate of Abraham Lincoln, the 16th President. His native state was Kentucky, and this can be located on the map. How close are you to this state?

Among the most touching stories about Abraham Lincoln are those that deal with his childhood. Born in a log cabin, he was determined to learn to read, and he read by the light of the fireplace glow. He practiced writing on a real shovel with a piece of coal. Secure a large shovel, and have students take turns writing a lesson (alphabet, or name and date) on the shovel with a piece of chalk. Erase it with an old cloth.

Make an extra-large construction paper "stovepipe hat" and secure it to the bulletin board (and even above), with Abe's large face touching the floor. Students can paint features and beard onto a circle for the face. Have each student read a storybook or a picture book in honor of Abraham Lincoln, and write the title on the hat. Imagine how fortunate we are today to have a wealth of books from which to choose. Make sure that this is pointed out to the students. Students can point to the title they wrote

on the hat and tell the story aloud to the other students. It is said that Abe Lincoln was an excellent storyteller.

Elect a Class-President-of-the-Week

This might be a very good time to elect a class-president-of-the-week. Students can nominate the president, who would have such duties as leading the Pledge of Allegiance, and leading the singing of a patriotic song. The vote could be by ballot (an X after the person's name, or by writing the person's name on an "official" ballot slip of paper), or by quietly telling you as you keep a tally.

At this developmental age, a weekly change of leadership is a good experience for students.

A SPECIAL SWEET TREAT

Make this sweet treat in honor of Valentine's Day (honey, for sweethearts) and for Presidents' Day (cherry tarts, for George Washington). YOU NEED: one cup honey, ½ cup cream, frozen cherry tarts, a toaster oven, a mixing bowl, a wooden spoon, and an oven pan.

PROCEDURE: Heat the honey in a pan in the toaster oven, which is set on warm. Remove from the toaster oven when warm and slowly blend in the cream. Heat the tarts in a medium-warm oven. Remove, and put a dab of the honey-cream mixture on top. Yummy!

HOW IS BUTCH THE BIRD DOING?

Remember Butch the Bird who couldn't migrate? Is he settling down to learn his reading words, his math facts? Is his writing improved? (Perhaps the January reproducible activity pages could be used again.) How is Butch's behavior in class? Does this need to be worked on?

Remember that the Wise Old Owl is returning in the spring and hopes to see progress so that Butch can migrate with the other birds next year.

Let's remind the students to put forth a bit more effort for Butch the Bird. Perhaps a scrawled message from the Wise Old Owl giving some praise and encouragement might be a boost right about now. Or a scrawled message from the Wise Old Owl giving some very specific directives may be of help, also.

Remind students that the Wise Old Owl is keeping an eye on Butch the Bird and is depending on them for help.

The students might write a letter to the Wise Old Owl, in care of Sunny South Lane, Deep South, USA to explain just how they plan to help Butch the Bird during the month. A reply from the Wise Old Owl (who knows all) could be received in about a week. If you know someone in a southern state who could mail the Owl's response in the self-addressed stamped envelope to the class, it would give a ring of authenticity to the letter writing.

Reproducible Activity Pages for February

The Great Ugh Bug Vowel Discovery (a
    valentine love page)
Happy Voweltine's Day (long and short
    vowel words)
Reading Shovels (practicing words)
Say-a-Story (the hard sound of c)
Play-a-Story (rhyming words)
"The Cat's Meow" Favorite Book Award
    (reading)
Piggy Bank Coins (working with tens)
Valentine, I've Got Your Number! (addition)
Tick Tock O'Clock (a memory game)
Cary Clown's Clock (the hour and half-past
    the hour)
Patriotic Cherry Pies (working with half)
Our Sense of Taste (science)
Shadow, Go! Cloudy, Howdy! (Groundhog
    Day)
Dental Health Month (dental health; rhymes)
The Six-Year Molar Club (dental health)
Matching Hearts (a memory game)

THE GREAT UGH BUG VOWEL DISCOVERY

Guess what? The word "love" is an exception to the vowel rule. So, it belongs to the Ugh Bug.

Guess what again? This has made Ugh Bug sooo happy that it is sending you a great big love "voweltine." Color the picture and then cut it out.

HAPPY VOWELTINE'S DAY

Alligator and Ogre are sending vowel words to each other. Can you join in the fun? Get your pencil ready for some words that rhyme.

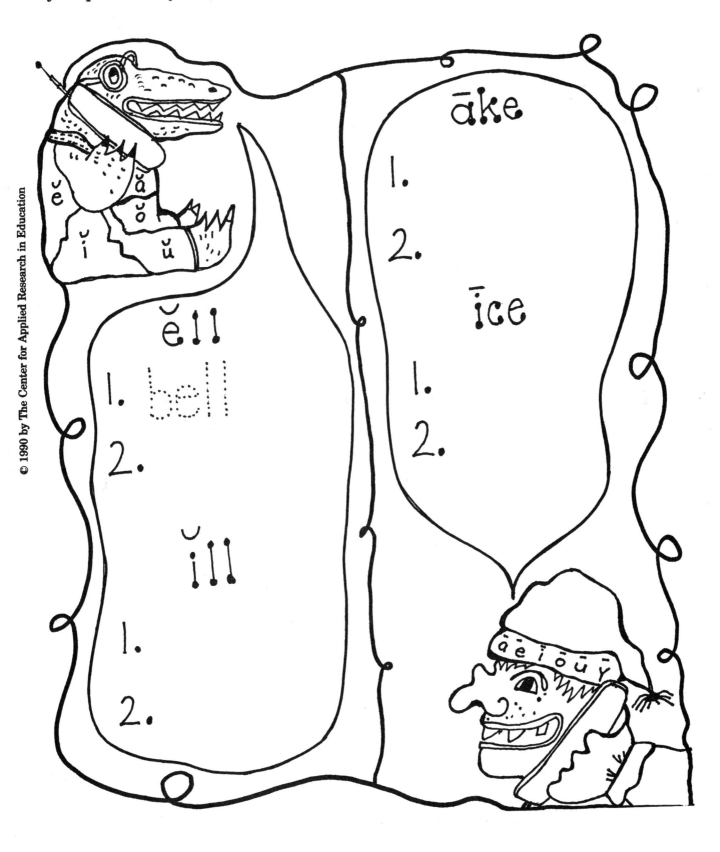

ăke

1.

2.

īce

1.

2.

ĕll

1. bell

2.

ĭll

1.

2.

READING SHOVELS

Abraham Lincoln did not have paper and pencil like you do. He practiced his words on a big shovel, using a piece of slate or chalk. You can use these shovel shapes to help learn words for reading. Use the shovels in this way: SHOVEL ONE—Words I Know; SHOVEL TWO—Words I Need to Study.

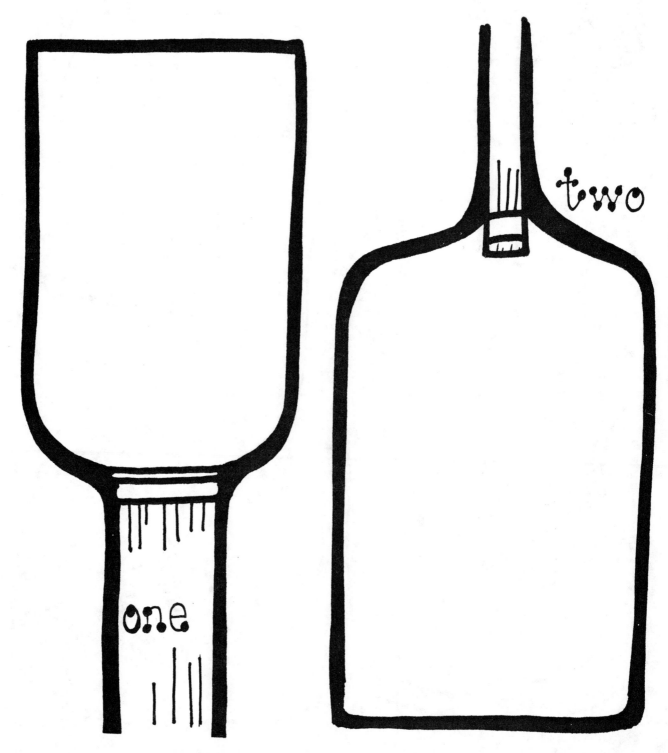

SAY-A-STORY

There is something strange going on here. There is only one carrot left. There were three. Someone keeps eating the carrots. Is it the cat? Is it one of the rabbits on the cup? Only you can solve this mysterious problem.

Today we are working with the hard sound of the letter C. It sounds like K.

cup

carrot

cat

As you color these items, think about how you will carefully write and tell your story.

PLAY-A-STORY

Today we are working with rhyming words. This rich king has lost his magic ring. Did The Thing find it? What is The Thing? This is going to be a magic story. How will it all work out? It's up to you because YOU are the author!

king

ring

The Thing

As you color these items, think of the props that you will need to act out your story. How many times will you have to change your voice to make it high, low, screechy, or soft?

Name _____ Date _____

"THE CAT'S MEOW" FAVORITE BOOK AWARD

The Cat's Meow

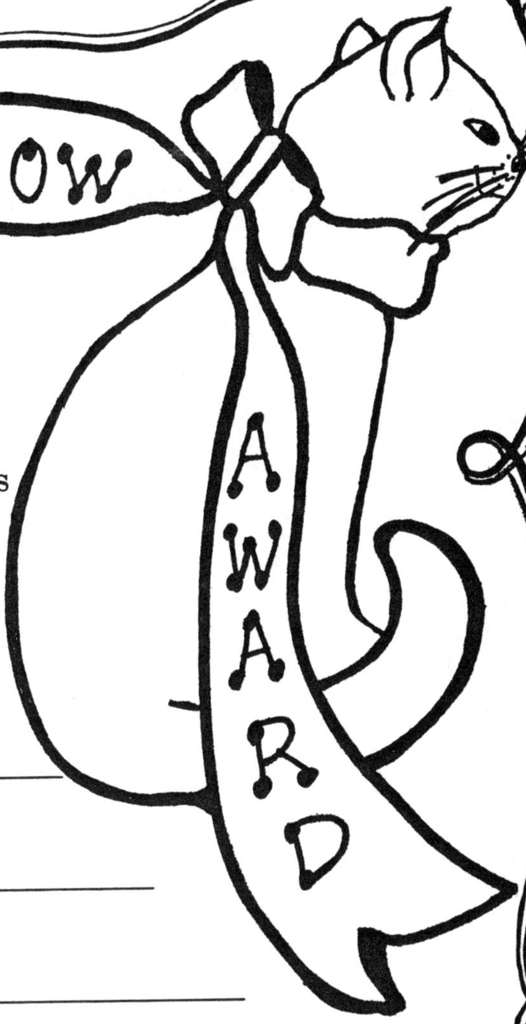

AWARD

When we say that something is "the cat's meow," it means that it is terrific!

What book do YOU think earns this award?

_____

(title)

_____

_____

(author)

_____

(illustrator)

I think this book should receive "The Cat's Meow" Award because _____

_____

_____

_____

On the back, draw a picture of your favorite part of the story. Share it with classmates.

PIGGY BANK COINS

On the left are four different items in a toy store. How much is each one? You can tell by the amount on each price tag. On the right are four piggy banks with dimes inside. Count the coins by tens. Then match the toy with the piggy bank coins that will pay for the toy. The first one is done for you. Color the coins silver, color each bank a different color, and color the toys.

VALENTINE, I'VE GOT
YOUR NUMBER!

You can use the valentines below to help with your addition facts. Place the addition answer in the outside rim. To get you started, two answers have been given for you. Trace them, and then fill in the rest. Color the inside hearts red and color the answers pink.

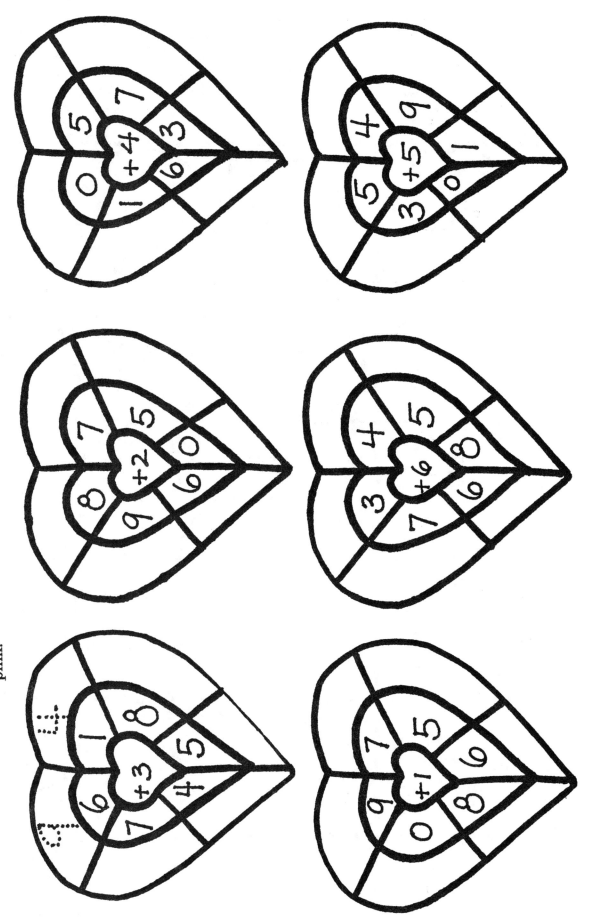

TICK TOCK O'CLOCK

We are working with circular time and digital time. Cut along the lines so that you have 20 cards. FOR ONE PLAYER: Match the digital time to the clock. FOR TWO PLAYERS: Shuffle the cards and place them face down on a grid. Pick up two squares. If they match, keep them. If they do not match, return them. Each player takes one turn. The player with the most matching sets wins. Then shuffle and begin again. Keep track of the TIME it takes to play each game.

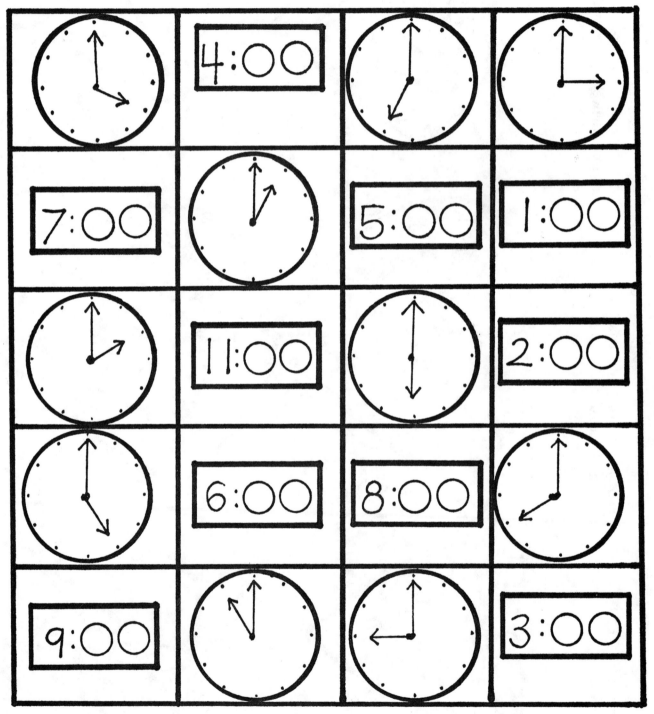

CARY CLOWN'S CLOCK

Cut out the two hands and fasten them with a brad to the center of the clock. Practice telling time on the hour and the half-hour. Fill in the numerals. Be sure to make your clown clock colorful, too!

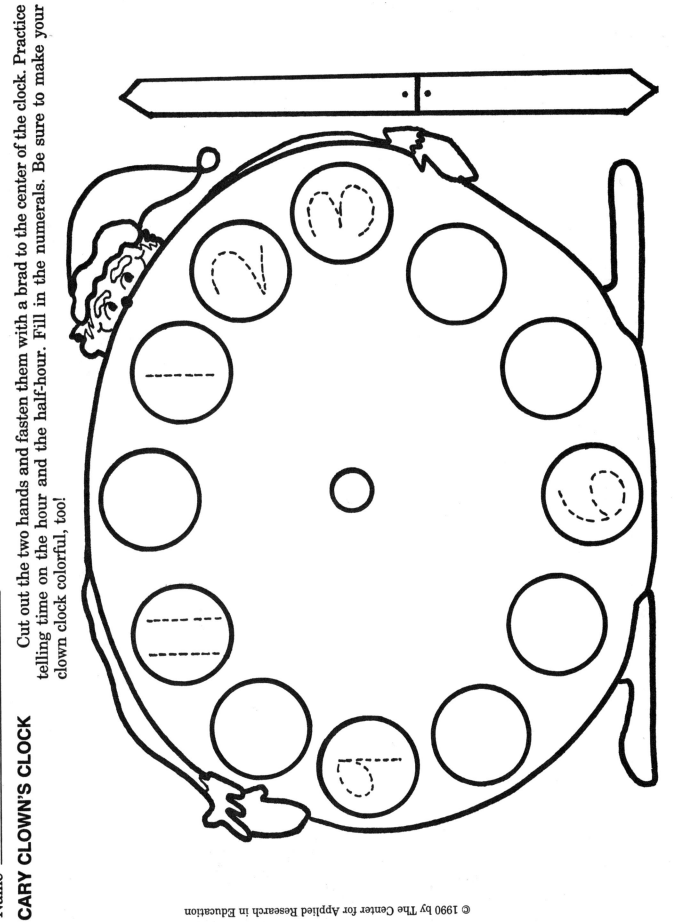

Name _____

Date _____

PATRIOTIC CHERRY PIES

Some of the cherry pies below have been cut in HALF. Find them and color the crust on "1" red and the crust on "2" blue. Also, some of the halves have been cut in half. When you find these pies, make sure to color the crust on "1" pink, "2" white, "3" red and, "4" blue.

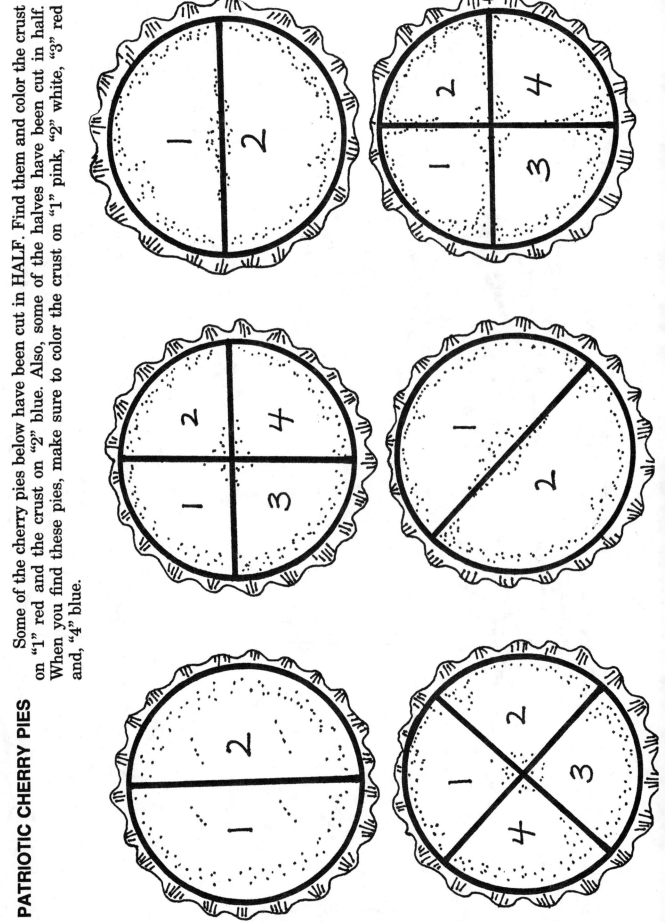

Name _____ Date _____

OUR SENSE OF TASTE

Taste is one of the five senses. We can taste things and tell whether they are sweet, salty, sour, or bitter. On this tongue map, you can see where the taste buds areas are located. Draw a line from the items around the edge of the page to the spot on the tongue where the taste buds would be put to work. On the back of this sheet, can you list other foods that go into these four taste groups?

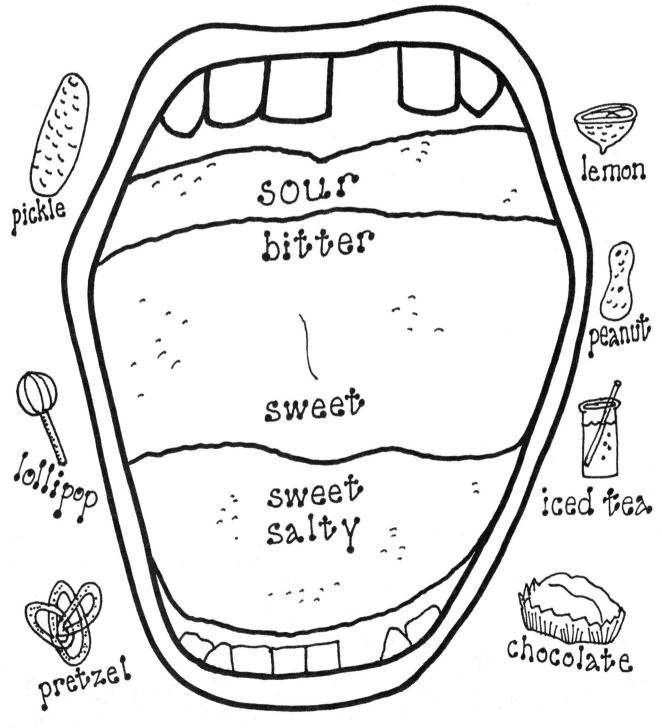

pickle

lemon

peanut

lollipop

iced tea

pretzel

chocolate

sour

bitter

sweet

sweet
salty

Name _____   Date _____

SHADOW, GO! CLOUDY, HOWDY!

Choose the appropriate space above, and show us with your crayons what happened on Groundhog Day where YOU live.

Name _____   Date _____

DENTAL HEALTH MONTH

Allie Alligator wants you to learn her rhymes about tooth care. She wants to know if you have a new firm brush. Do you?

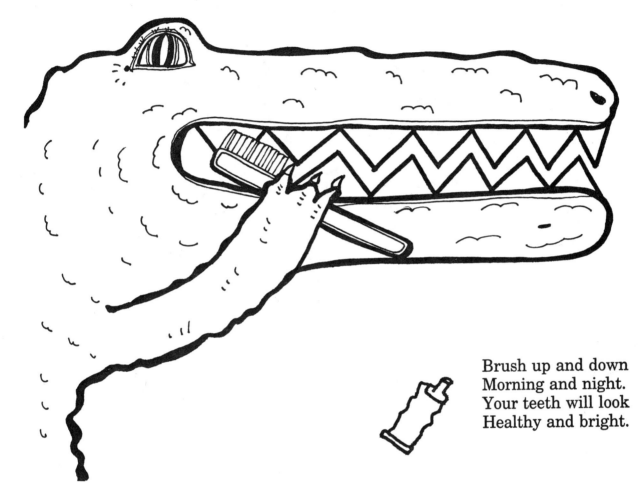

Brush up and down
Morning and night.
Your teeth will look
Healthy and bright.

Floss in and out
Two times a day.
Your healthy gums
Are here to stay.

Wash your mouth out;
It tastes yummy.
Don't swallow it;
Protect your tummy!

The Six-Year Molar Club

New Member

MATCHING HEARTS

There is a valentine heart in each box below. Color them and cut the boxes apart on the lines. Notice that there are two matching cards of each design. You have to look carefully. Lay the cards face down on a grid. Turn over two cards at a time. Do they match? If so, keep them. If not, return them. Your turn is over. The next player repeats this procedure. The winner is the one with the most matching cards. Shuffle, and play again.

March

SWINGING INTO SPRING WITH A TREASURY OF IDEAS

March is bringing seasonal changes and, for the active first grader, this is a good sign because more time can be spent outdoors. Incorporate subject matter into outdoor activities such as walks, hikes, and field trips. Keep curiosity alive indoors, too, with fresh items at the Science Table, the Reading Area, and the Math Center.

RECOMMENDED CHILDREN'S BOOKS FOR MARCH

- *Jim and the Beanstalk* by Raymond Briggs (New York: Coward, McCann and Geoghegan, 1970). Children are familiar with the old tale of Jack and the Beanstalk, and may have been introduced to this book previously, too. It is an updated humorous tale, modeled after the original Jack story. Even if children have heard it, they'll enjoy hearing it again— and it can serve as a springboard for rewriting familiar tales during this magic month.

- *The Hungry Leprechaun* by Mary Calhoun, illustrated by Roger Duvoisin (New York: William Morrow and Co., 1962). Once upon a time, everyone in Ireland was poor, even the leprechauns. A young boy is lucky enough to catch a skinny leprechaun named Tippery, and he takes him home and feeds him. Children will take delight in the mishaps that occur as Tippery tries to regain his magic powers and produces something more edible than gold when everyone is hungry.

- *The Boy Who Didn't Believe in Spring* by Lucille Clifton, illustrated by Brinton Turkle (New York: E. P. Dutton, 1973). Every time the teacher talked about Spring, a boy named King Shabagg scowled because he thought there was no such thing. So, he set about to find Spring, and in the end was pleasantly surprised with his discoveries.

- *Helga's Diary: A Troll Love Story* by Tomie dePaola (New York: Harcourt Brace Jovanovich, 1977). Helga is a lovely troll, but an orphan with no dowry. She sets out to accumulate riches so that she can win the handsome Lars. Can she do the impossible? Trolls are very clever, and Helga is no exception. This is an enchanting tale.

- *Albert the Running Bear Gets the Jitters* by Barbara Isenberg and Susan Wolf, illustrations by Diane deGroat (New York: Clarion Books, 1987). Albert the champion Running Bear is challenged to a race by a new Alaskan Bear named Boris, who uses bully tactics to intimidate Albert. This book serves as an excellent guide for handling the "jitters" that Albert feels. At the end of the book, the author includes a two-page message about stress that teachers will find useful for class discussions.

- *Swimmy* by Leo Lionni (New York: Pantheon, 1968). This timeless tale, with its beautiful watercolor illustrations and exceptional language, is a book that children enjoy hearing again and again. It is especially good to read it to groups who are working together for the first time because cooperation is the theme of this sensitive story, and it serves as a gentle reminder.

- *The Little Red Riding Hood Rebus Book* revised by Ann Morris, pictures by Ljiljana Rylands (New York: Orchard Books, 1987). In this new version of an old tale, words or parts of words are replaced by pictures, numbers, or letters. It's a wonderful beginning-to-read book because children already know the story and the pictures help them to decode the words. The book contains bright illustrations and a helpful rebus dictionary at the end.

- *The Red Thread* by Tord Nygren (New York: Farrar, Straus and Giroux, 1987). This is a wordless picture book. The reader follows the red thread throughout the elaborately detailed, colorful illustrations and finds that, among other things, a bird has the red thread in its beak, a boy is using it to steady himself as he crosses a stream, and a high-wire artist is using it to walk to the moon. The red thread takes us on a magical journey that children like to travel again and again.

- *The Tenth Good Thing About Barney* by Judith Viorst, illustrated by Erik Blegvad (New York: The Trumpet Club, 1971, 1988). The death of a pet or of a friend or a family member can be a devastating experience for a young child. Barney, a cat, has died and is being mourned by the little boy telling the story. This sensitive and tender tale may be helpful to youngsters who are experiencing grief over a loss.

- *The Emperor and the Kite* by Jane Yolen, illustrated by Ed Young (New York: Philomel Books, 1988). This book takes place in ancient China where the youngest daughter of the Emperor is often overlooked because she is so very tiny. She spends her time flying her kite, which is like a "flower in the sky and a prayer in the wind." Her father is captured and sent to prison high up in a tower. This calls for some inventive kite-flying skills by the tiny girl. This is a Caldecott Honor Book.

SPOTLIGHT ON READING

News Flash: Ugh Bug Changed to Love Bug!

This is the month when the leprechauns are busy. They held a secret meeting, had a vote, and declared that Ugh Bug (the one in charge of all the exceptions to the rules) should officially have its name changed to Love Bug (because the word "love" is an exception to the vowel rule). Students can make a special medal and wear it.

Also, the leprechauns voted to award a medal to the Unicorn for discovering that the word "love" is an exception to the rule for both long and short vowel sounds. He was also awarded a pot of gold that mysteriously appeared at the end of the North Rainbow! (See the reproducible activity pages.)

Let's Have an "Apple Dapple" Celebration

The Alligator donated apples (for the short A sound) and the Ogre donated oatmeal (for the long O sound). What do you do with apples and oatmeal? You put them together and call it Apple Dapple. We can make it, too. Here is the easy recipe to make in class. This activity involves reading, measuring, timing, recognizing ingredients, and so on. When it is completed, students can make an Apple Dapple Recipe Book (words and pictures) to take home, and also an experience chart story to reread in the classroom. (See the reproducible activity pages.)

This recipe serves six. YOU WILL NEED: 1 apple, 1 cup oatmeal, raisins, 2 cups water, milk, a slow cooker, a wooden spoon, a measuring cup, a paring knife, serving dishes, spoons, and napkins. PROCEDURE: Put the oatmeal, cut-up apples (with skins), water, and a handful of raisins in a greased slow cooker. Cook for two hours. Students begin to get curious and enjoy the aroma. When done, spoon into serving dishes. You might want to serve Apple Dapple with a little milk. (If there is not enough time for the slow cooker method, use a microwave oven shortcut and cook for two minutes!)

Contraction Subtraction

- Contractions are words that are MINUS some letters, but still make good sense, especially in conversation. Print these two words on the chalkboard: can + not, or cannot. Explain that the apostrophe (quite a helper) will come in and take the place of some letters so that they can get some rest or go out to play. This boardwork may help with the concept:

cannot becomes can't (minus letters n and o)
do not becomes don't (minus letter o)
did not becomes didn't (minus letter o)
would not becomes wouldn't (minus letter o)
should not becomes shouldn't (minus letter o)

Explain to students that in informal conversation, we shorten words but the meaning remains the same.

- Make a contraction flash card set from two different colors, such as green and yellow. Line up the phrase on one side and the contraction on the other side.

- Shuffle the contraction flash cards referred to above. Put them into two piles, face down. Turn over one card from each pile. Do they match? If so, keep them. If not, put them to one side. Next, turn over two more cards. Are they a match? If so, keep them. If not, put them to one side. Now, can any of those that have been put aside be matched? If so, do it now. This drill game can be played singly or with two players. The player with more matched pairs wins.
Play again and again for practice.

The "Pinch" Sound

If something hurts, we say "ow!" or "ouch!" When the letters O and W get together, they often make up their own "pinch" sound which is "OW!" But be careful of this tricky twosome, because sometimes they say the long sound of the letter O. (Love Bug scores again with exceptions to the rule.)

Print some "pinch" words on the chalkboard and ask students to underline the "ow" (pinch sound):

cow   pow   now   how   plow

"OW" sometimes takes on the long sound of the vowel O. Print these words on the chalkboard:

crow   blow   grow   know   flow

The CONTEXT CLUES are important when working with the tricky letters of "ow." Explain to students that when they are trying to sound out a word and it doesn't work with the long sound of the letter O, then go to the "pinch" sound. The sentence will help us with the meaning. We need the context in order to make sense of the words. Here are some to try together on the chalkboard:

I KNOW a new word.	SHOW me your dog.
May I leave NOW?	The CROW can fly.
The FLOWER is pretty.	WOW, this is good!

I Can Replace My Own Name

Use a toy telephone or a puppet to help teach the concept of pronouns. Explain that when talking on the phone, instead of saying, "Hello, this is Mary. Mary wants to talk to Jan," we say, "Hello, this is Mary. I want to talk to Jan."

We use the word "I" instead of saying our own name over and over again. Babies repeat their own name because they're just learning the language and that's fine. But we're grown-up first graders now, so we say "I." You can model more phone conversations, such as:

"Hello, this is Katy. Katy is happy. Katy has a new dress."
"Hello, this is Katy. I am happy. I have a new dress."

Other words can take the place of people's names when we are talking about them. For example:

Tammy is happy! Tammy has a new coat.
Tammy is happy. SHE has a new coat.

Bill and Ted are smiling. Bill and Ted are playing ball.
Bill and Ted are smiling. THEY are playing ball.

Give the cookies to Shelly and Shawn.
Give the cookies to THEM.

Continue to work with pronoun substitutions for names of people, although at this point it is not important for students to know that they are in fact called pronouns.

Echo Reading

You, as teacher, serve as an excellent model for oral reading. Try the following: Read a sentence aloud, then the class reads the SAME sentence aloud. Then you read the next sentence aloud, and the class also reads that sentence aloud—just like an echo.

- You can pair an excellent reader with a reader who needs additional help.

- You can pair two excellent readers to read for pleasure.
- You can pair a reader and a "leprechaun." The reader reads aloud, and the leprechaun whispers the same words.

Green Shape Books

Cut out a large shamrock shape and have students trace it onto green construction paper for the cover of their book. Discuss the color green. Who is wearing green today? Then look outdoors or go on a Spring Green Walk. Is the grass wearing green? Are the trees wearing green? Are the sprouting flowers wearing green stems and leaves? Have students select three or four items that they would like to illustrate on shamrock shapes cut from light green paper. A dark green felt-tip marker can be used to print the title, author, illustrator, and labels (names or sentences).

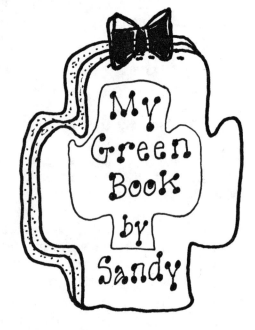

SPOTLIGHT ON MATH

A Change of Weather

March is a good month to chart the weather along with your daily calendar. Cover a bulletin board with white background paper and use black yarn or black construction paper strips to make the grid. Every day, in each square, have a student use a black felt-tip pen to record the numeral for the date and the weather symbol. Use the weather symbol that relates best to the weather at that time. Even if the weather changes during the day, the symbol can remain the same. Students can color in the sun with yellow or orange, and the umbrella with a bright color. This makes a striking contrast on the black-and-white board.

At the end of the month, tally the

number of cloudy, sunny, rainy, snowy, and windy days. Then make a weather graph from this information. Which weather symbol is represented the most? Which is represented the least? Did March "come in like a lion and go out like a lamb?"

Working with Temperature

Gather several thermometers so that students can gain practice reading the temperature numerals. The unit term for measuring temperature is called a "degree." Explain that 32 degrees is the point at which water freezes. If it is raining or snowing and it is 34 degrees, what will happen to the "precipitation" (new vocabulary word) on the roads and sidewalks IF the temperature drops BELOW 32 degrees? That's right, it will freeze or turn to ice. This often makes driving conditions hazardous in certain parts of the country. Is your area one of them?

- Place each thermometer in a jar that is half filled with cold water. Wait until the thermometers have had a chance to stabilize and register the temperature and then record it. Try adding warm and cold water to the jars to make the water temperature warmer and cooler. Students can observe the change in the thermometer reading and record the information. They can make a rebus chart or story with diagrams of the thermometer registering the temperature.

- Place the thermometers in different areas of the room, such as on the sunny window ledge, on the floor in the corner, in the cupboard, and so on, to generate interest in the different temperature readings. Students can also make "predictions" regarding which areas will be cooler or warmer.

Pot o'Gold Nuggets for Leprechauns

- Bring in a 5-pound bag of potatoes (a favorite leprechaun food?) and a scale for weighing. Wrap each potato in green or gold foil, and pretend that each one contains a "gold nugget" that a leprechaun would be happy to find. How much do these precious nuggets weigh singly? Are any almost the same weight or even the exact same weight? Some potatoes are bound to be noticeably larger or smaller than others.

- Use paper lunch bags and add green construction paper arms, head, face, hat, and beard for the jolly leprechaun. Label the bags as follows: "1 lb.," "2 lbs.," "3 lbs.," and so on. Put the pound sign (#) on the leprechaun's hat. Have students sort the potatoes by size and then weigh them. Then mix them together and have students remove a "1-pound nugget" and a "2-pound nugget" and so on, and place them in the appropriate bags. Weigh them. Were the students close? They will improve with practice.

- For St. Patrick's Day on March 17, unwrap the potatoes and cut them in half or in chunks. Then make potato prints. Be sure to use bright green paint and either white or pale green paper for a background.

Let's Practice Handling Coins

- Use a "leprechaun coin purse" (a small one that snaps open and shut) to house the following coins: a quarter, dime, nickel, and penny. Have students remove the coins and identify them in value going from largest to smallest. Keep changing the position of the coins, and continue to work with value from largest to smallest. (Some students have difficulty with the dime and nickel because, although the dime is smaller in size, it has greater value than the nickel.)

- Blindfold students and have them remove a certain coin from the purse without looking. Did they get it right? This exercise has value because students can be taught that people who have impaired vision can learn to handle coins in this way.

- Blindfold students and have them hold out their hands. Put a coin in each hand. Allow them to feel the coins without looking. Can the students tell the value of the coin by the size and/or weight? Keep practicing.

- When do people have to depend upon the feel of coins? This is a good discussion question, and students can help generate some ideas. We use coins for vending machines in semi-dark lighting; we give coins to a cab driver in semi-darkness; we use coins to buy popcorn in a dark theater; and so on.

The Dollar's Wearing o' the Green

Have students examine a real dollar bill using a magnifying glass. What information can they gather from the front and from the back? What signs or symbols are used on the dollar bill? Students can gain practice with the dollar sign ($). From green construction paper, cut up a batch of rectangles and have students make dollar bills using a felt-tip pen.

Students can also work with and count coins that are equivalent to a dollar, such as: 100 pennies, 10 dimes, 20 nickels, 4 quarters, 2 half-dollars.

THE COIN DOLLARS: Try to secure a Susan B. Anthony one-dollar coin from your local bank if you live in an area of the country where they are still in use. Perhaps you may have even saved one? Show students the dollar coin that did not "catch on." Why didn't it? The shape would make it easy to identify by touch, but the size was confusing. Which coin does it most resemble? Would it work in a vending machine? At one time, silver dollars were used. They were big, round, silver, and heavy. If you do not have a silver dollar, ask a parent or a coin collector to visit your classroom so that students can get a good look at this collector's item. In June 1989, a dollar coin was introduced in Canada. A loon is engraved on the coin, which is nicknamed the "loonie."

It's Springtime

Work with the concept of time in circular and digital forms. Have each student make a paper plate clock. Use 12 of the paper plate clocks to make a huge bulletin board clock. Set the hands of the clock in the first position at 1:00, in the second position at 2:00, and so on. Make two very large construction paper hands and tack them together in the middle of the circular clock.

Tack the longest hand so that it is pointing at 12. Call out times ("one o'clock" "five o'clock," and so on) and have a student go to the big clock board and move the smaller of the two hands to the correct numeral. Tack it down. The BIG clock will look just like the smaller clock to which the hour hand is pointing.

Use this clock for practice with half-past the hour, too. Affix the large hand from mid-point to the 6. Have students move just the small hand for half-past.

Note that for half-past two, for example, the little hand is half past the two and moving toward the three. Make sure to continually point out this half-past relationship. In the time that it takes the big hand to travel half-way around the clock (from 12 to 6), the little hand travels half-way between two numerals.

Set the Clock

Make three sets of flashcards—one that shows clocks, one that shows digital time, and one that has such phrases as "time for school" and "time for math." Students can match the times with the activity. They can also use the big class clock on the bulletin board to work along with this.

A Slice of Time

Make wrist-watches from styrofoam balls. Slice the balls into circles. Use a felt-tip pen to print the numerals. Make the hands from felt and glue them on so that they are stationary. For the wrist-band, glue the ball onto a strip of felt material, and use Velcro to fasten it. Each child will have a wrist-watch with a set time. They can learn what that time looks like. Then play the following game where students ask the question and give the answer:

"Who is wearing one o'clock?"

"Is it Jim?" "Not me."

"Is it Andy?" "Not me."

"Is it Lance?" "It's me."

"Who is wearing three o'clock?"

"Is it Liz?" "Not me."

"Is it Lori?" "It's me."

Make an extra set of 12 wrist-watches for different students to wear on special occasions or for a day when that particular time is being taught. Also, make a set of wrist-watches for half-past the hour and have students wear them. By focusing upon one set time that a student looks at all day long, it helps with the visual memory of a particular time. Students are especially happy when the "real" clock on the wall matches the time they are wearing.

Shape of the Month: Pointy and Rounded Edges

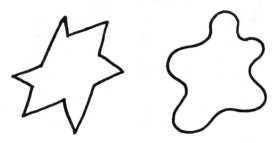

Some classrooms may have commercial math materials that can be sorted by attributes, such as shape. If you do not have these available, then use items from the classroom. In a basket, gather some materials such as a book, ball, crayon, puzzle piece, large plastic paper clip, a sheet of paper, and so on. Students can classify them by whether the edge is rounded or has corners (pointy). If it has a corner, then it means a straight edge. Do some items have both pointed and rounded edges? Yes, a pencil, for one. The eraser end is rounded and the other end has a pointed, sharp edge. Or, the pencil may be round, while the triangular lead has an edge. Help students to classify the shapes by laying down large sheets of colored paper labeled: ROUND, POINTY, OTHER. They can place the item on the appropriate paper.

Use the same items over and over again so that students are successful with this activity. When changing items, however, only change one or two at a time. This creates less confusion and ensures success more frequently.

Make Shape Pictures

This is a good time to empty out the art scrap box and classify the shapes as rounded or pointy. From the pointy shapes, cut triangles, squares, rectangles, diamonds, or shapes that have straight-line edges. From the rounded shapes, cut circles, ovals, and free-form shapes that have curved lines.

Students can use the paper to construct an item (such as a car, house, tree, bird, etc.) that is made from straight lines, and then make the same item from paper with curved lines. These contrasting items can be pasted down on a folded sheet of 12″ × 18″ colored construction paper. (See the reproducible activity pages.)

HANDS-ON SCIENCE

You have probably been working with the five senses throughout the year, and this month you can concentrate on the five senses together. Have a festival of the senses!

Windsock Senses

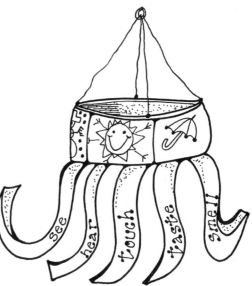

Using a sheet of 9″ × 12″ construction paper, have students create a spring scene that shows something to see, hear, smell, taste, and touch during spring. Then staple the ends of the spring scenes together to make a cylinder. Attach five crepe-paper streamers of different colors to the windsock, and hang them from the ceiling fixtures (if permitted) for a focus upon spring!

Making Sense of the Senses

SIGHT (Eyes): have students look into the eyes of a partner and identify the pupil (black) and the iris (color). If possible, go from dim light to sunlight so that students can see the change that takes place in the size of the pupil—that part of the eye that regulates the amount of light that enters the eye. Encourage students to take care of their eyes—not to rub them or touch them with hands that need to be washed. Working with a partner, one student can act as a seeing-eye friend and the other can be blindfolded or tightly close his or her eyes. Encourage them to move from place to place in the room, to select paper, pencil, and eraser, and return to their desk. Note the amount of time that this takes when our eyes are not able to give us signals. Students are usually relieved to be able to "see" again.

HEARING (Ears): We can shut our eyes, but ears have no lids or doors. Ears are always open. Encourage students to cup their hands around their ears so that sounds will be magnified. CAUTION: There must be no shouting into people's ears at this time.

People who cannot hear use sign language. First graders can pick up signing very readily, so you may want to teach them some signals such as "hello," "good-bye," "thank you," and any other hand signals that could be used in the room. Invite a guest speaker to the classroom to teach students more sign language.

SMELL (Nose): The nose is at work in dark and in light surroundings. Our sense of smell brings us information without using words or pictures. Encourage students to list pleasant and unpleasant smells. Play the "Smell Association Game":

The smell of pizza tells me _____.

The smell of perfume tells me _____.

The smell of toast tells me _____.

The smell of flowers tells me _____.

Students can make up their own smell association sentences, too.

TOUCH (Hands): This sense depends upon direct contact. Encourage students to touch items in the room to determine attributes such as smooth, rough, bumpy, slippery, and so on. Make a chart of these items using pictures from magazines. Also, use clothing material swatches such as corduroy, satin, linen, open-weave burlap, felt, and so on. Have two squares of each and see if students can match them only by using the sense of touch.

TASTE (Taste buds on tongue): This is a chemical sense. Taste buds send messages to the brain to inform us if food is salty, sweet, sour, or bitter. Try a special snack each day to match each of the categories. For example: salty pretzels, sweet cupcakes, sour lemon drops, and bittersweet chocolate.

Students need to be made aware that the tongue also helps people to talk. Do some exercises to find out where the tongue is located in the mouth when these words are said:

teeth

glass

watermelon

bird

lollipop

turtle

Have students make up words and "track" their tongue from the "roof" to the "floor" to the "sides" of the mouth. Also, the teeth are involved for many sounds (th, l, s); and the roof of the mouth (both front and back) assists with speech. For example: The letters d, l, n, and t push the tongue up against the back of the front teeth. (After doing these exercises, students can be seen "trying out" many words on their own, making facial contortions, as they work with the concept of the tongue as a language assistant.)

MARCHING IN WITH OTHER AREAS OF INTEREST

The Arrival of Spring

Are the days getting longer? That is, are there more daylight hours when the children go home from school? If so, that's a signal to the birds to get ready to migrate and to start building their nests. To help the birds, set out a nesting station bag that contains twine, feathers, string, yarn, cotton, etc. (See the reproducible activity pages.) Hang the nesting station in a tree away from the school building. Use a set of binoculars to do some birdwatching duty from the classroom window. Take turns for blocks of five-minute birdwatching duty. While students are on duty, they can use the binoculars to help them locate other signs of spring, too, such as flowers poking up through the ground, bushes beginning to bloom, and trees beginning to bud.

St. Patrick's Day and Spring Green Party Treats

Leprechaun in the Well

>   plain doughnut
>
>   scoop of green sherbet in middle
>
>   green jelly beans for facial features

Lucky 7 Green Things Salad

>   one small lettuce leaf
>
>   one chunk of light green celery
>
>   one small piece of dark green pepper
>
>   one fresh pea
>
>   one green olive
>
>   one pickle slice
>
>   one green bean

The Lucky 7 Green Things Salad is served salad-bar style. Students can take their own dish and, using the serving spoon or scoop, can take one of each item to put on their plate (good for balancing and small motor coordination). If someone absolutely cannot eat something from the salad bar, that student has to do other things so as not to break the spell. Some suggestions: name seven green outdoor items, name seven green items in the room, find seven green things in a magazine, locate seven people wearing something green, and so on.

Start an Indoor Peanut and Popcorn Garden

MATERIALS: Two baking pans, paper towels, raw peanuts, and popcorn seeds. PROCEDURE: Line each pan with two or three layers of paper towels. Soak them with water. Spread raw peanuts in one pan, and popcorn seeds in the other. Cover with clear plastic wrap and keep in a warm place.

Keep a magnifying glass handy. Have students make observations daily and record them on a garden chart shaped like a glove (with a green thumb, of course!).

Wise Old Owl and Butch the Bird Study Buddies

A study buddy is someone with whom to read a story, or to help with math, or to get help from with decoding words, and so on. Partners can be teamed who are on an equal footing, or sometimes partners can be teamed so that one is assisting another in the learning process. Often students can learn from other students what they have been unable to learn from an adult or on their own. Sometimes study buddies select each other, and at times you may want to pair two (or three) students for certain skill-building activities.

To assist with the study process, the Wise Old Owl and Butch the Bird are becoming study buddies. Remember, the Wise Old Owl decided that Butch could not migrate because he didn't pay attention and did not have enough information to travel. Now, the Owl is teaming with Butch to help work on first-grade skills because Butch has made good progress, but needs to continue to practice. (See the reproducible activity pages for study buddy hand puppets.)

March Is a Good Month for Fairy Tales

Because children get caught up with leprechauns and fairies this month, it is a good time to gather together a collection of picture books that deal with fairy tales. *Jim and the Beanstalk* by Raymond Briggs is a tale that follows along the same line as *Jack and the Beanstalk* and makes children hold their sides with laughter. Another tale is *Mr. and Mrs. Pig's Evening Out* by Mary Raynor, which introduces the wolf and the pigs in a different way that causes children to hold their breath right up until the very end. *Mrs. Pig's Bulk Buy* by Mary Raynor is another in the Mrs. Pig series that children take delight in.

Children can try rewriting their favorite tales or telling them with a different twist at the end. They can dictate their stories to an aide or to an older student or use the cassette recorder. Students could even write them on paper and illustrate them, as a picture book.

Above all, read many fairy tales aloud this month. The plots move swiftly, the language is colorful, and the stories are good. They usually have a moral to them. Students can begin to identify some of the "bad guys" (monsters, ugly witches, mean giants), some of the magic (stones, wands, chants), and some of their favorite characters in the tales. Be sure to familiarize the students with *Strega Nona* and *Big Anthony and the Magic Ring,* both by Tomie DePaola.

A Windy Month for Kites

Whether you decide to make indoor kites to hang from the ceiling, or to make a "kite corner" in the classroom, or to hang one from a large bulletin board, or even to fly kites outdoors—March is an excellent month for kites. Kite-flying is becoming more popular, and if you check the Yellow Pages of the telephone directory, you may find a store that advertises kite-making equipment. If so, a visit to that store (by you) may end in some interesting information to bring back to the class. Also, it is possible that someone may come to your classroom to demonstrate the art of kite-making and kite-flying.

Kites come in a variety of shapes and patterns. Brightly colored felt-pens can be used to decorate the kites. Plastic garbage bags cut into strips make excellent lightweight tails or streamers.

Some helpful safety tips:

1. Do not use wire for the flying line. Use string or twine.
2. If your kite gets tangled up in overhead wire, do not try to get it down.
3. If it begins to look stormy, do not fly your kite.
4. Wear gloves to protect your hands.

Add a Little Magic to Creative Dramatics

Ask parents to donate old shoes and boots for the Creative Dramatics Corner. Get a can of green spray paint and color five or six different varieties of shoes or boots for acting out leprechaun stories and fairy tales. Before the paint dries, sprinkle the shoes with green, gold, or silver glitter that you can purchase at a craft store. This will liven up the indoor recess periods for the unpredictable spring weather days.

Spring Green Fingerpaint Gallery

You can work with two or three students at a time with fingerpaint, while other students are busy at their desks with green felt-tip pens or green crayons and paper. Have the fingerpainting area set aside in the corner on the floor or on a table. Students can wear smocks for this activity. Play a soothing, background recording. All students can loosen up with crayons and felt-tip pens before they do their actual gallery painting. Spread newspapers along the front of the room, and allow paintings to dry on them. All work is valued. Frame them, and hang them on the door, in the hall, or on a bulletin board for an art gallery exhibit that catches our eye and reminds us to welcome spring.

A See-Through Window Garden

For this activity, you will need a small plastic see-through bag for each student, potting soil, lima bean seeds, and masking tape. Each student can "plant" a window garden by putting soil in the bag, inserting the bean along the edge so that it can be seen, and adding water. Tape the bags to the windows. Students can put nametags on their window gardens and actually see the growth. Other seeds can be added as well.

Reproducible Activity Pages for March

Some "Ow" Words (working with the "pinch sound" of OW)
Making Unicorn Stew (vowels)
The Contraction Shamrocks (matching words and contractions)
The "An" House (making words that rhyme with "an")
Apple Dapple (language experience recipe)
Weekly Weather (making a chart)
School Clocks (working with time for special activities)

The Octopus Timekeeper (clocks and digital time)

Straight and Curved Lines (working with line segments)

Who Has 25 Cents? (working with coins)

Favorite Food Graph (learning to make a horizontal bar graph)

Spring Windsocks (sight, sound, smell)

Making Beads (language experience recipe)

Pot o'Gold Award (leprechaun award for good workers)

The Leprechaun Look (creative thinking)

Spring Things (identifying spring items)

SOME "OW" WORDS

Sometimes the "ow" sound is called the "pinch" sound. It sounds like it hurts. At other times, "ow" takes on the long "o" sound. Below, the "ow" rocket is taking off. It will visit the powwow (pinch) words. Color those words orange. Then color the rocket and stars.

Name _____

Date _____

MAKING UNICORN STEW

For this special dish, the unicorn needs water and sunshine. You can help by adding the vowel letters. Use your crayons to color the rainbow bubbles, the unicorn, and the kettle. Do you have a prism? If so, try making the rainbow stew. Place a bowl of water in the sunlight. With a prism, catch the reflection of the sun's rays on the water.

THE CONTRACTION SHAMROCKS

Connect the contraction shamrock with the matching shamrock word. Color the sham-rocks that belong together with the same shade of green.

THE "AN" HOUSE

These letters landed on the roof. They can only go inside if they make a word when put in front of "an." Print the family members on the ten lines below. Use your crayons to plant flowers, grass, and trees around the house.

Apple Dapple *

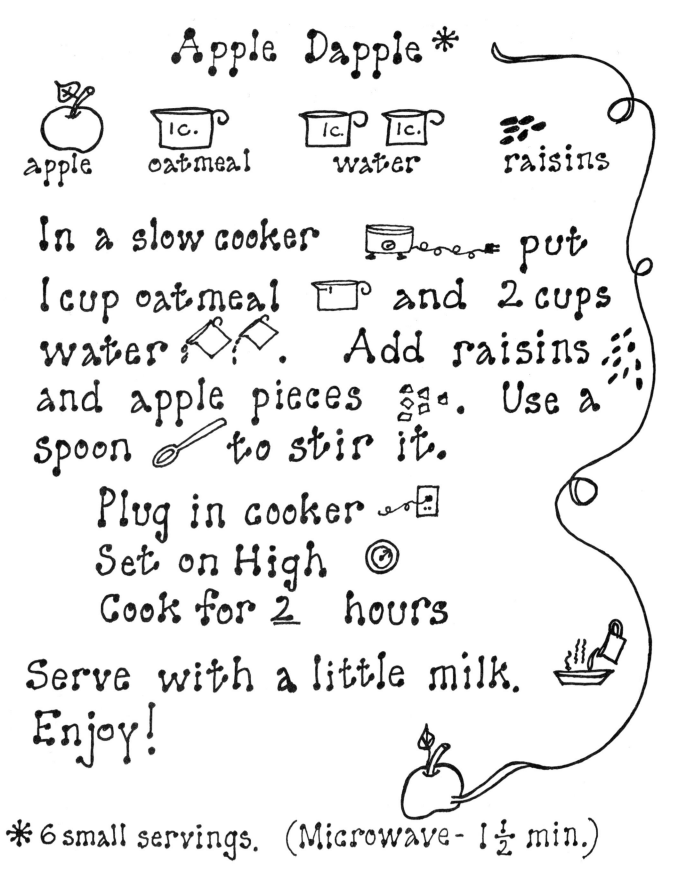

apple   oatmeal   water   raisins

In a slow cooker put
1 cup oatmeal and 2 cups
water. Add raisins
and apple pieces. Use a
spoon to stir it.

Plug in cooker
Set on High
Cook for 2 hours

Serve with a little milk.
Enjoy!

* 6 small servings. (Microwave - 1½ min.)

WEEKLY WEATHER

Put your finger on the Monday square. Go across to the right and stop in the square above the weather symbol that tells what the weather is on Monday. Color that square. Do this daily for each day of the week. What does your weekly weather picture look like?

Name _____

SCHOOL CLOCKS

Use the clocks below to show what time these activities take place in your classroom.
Work slowly and carefully.

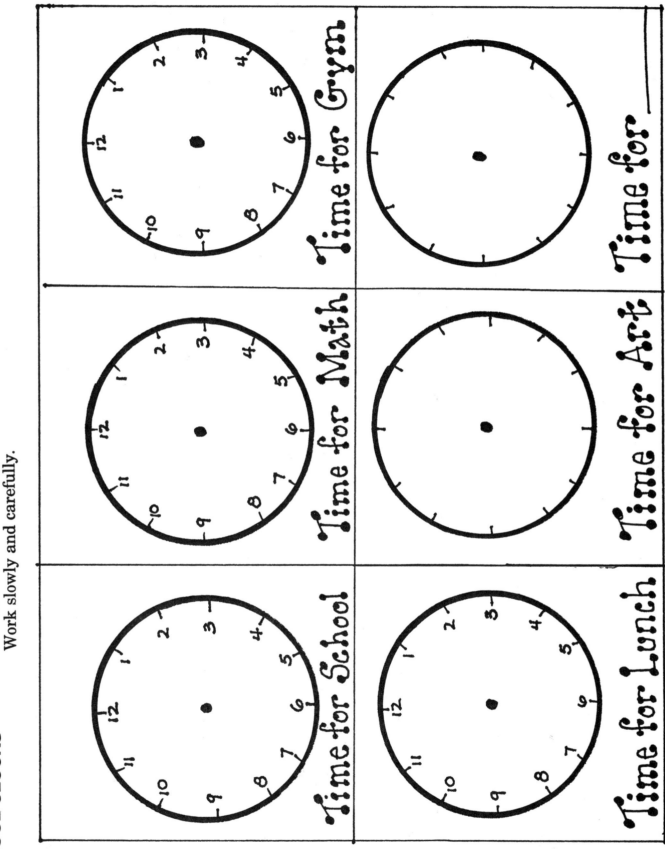

Time for School   Time for Math   Time for Gym

Time for Lunch   Time for Art   Time for _____

Name _____

Date _____

THE OCTOPUS TIMEKEEPER

This cheerful octopus has a watch for each arm. But the octopus needs your help.
Read the digital time and, with your pencil, show that time on the watch. Work carefully.
Then color the octopus.

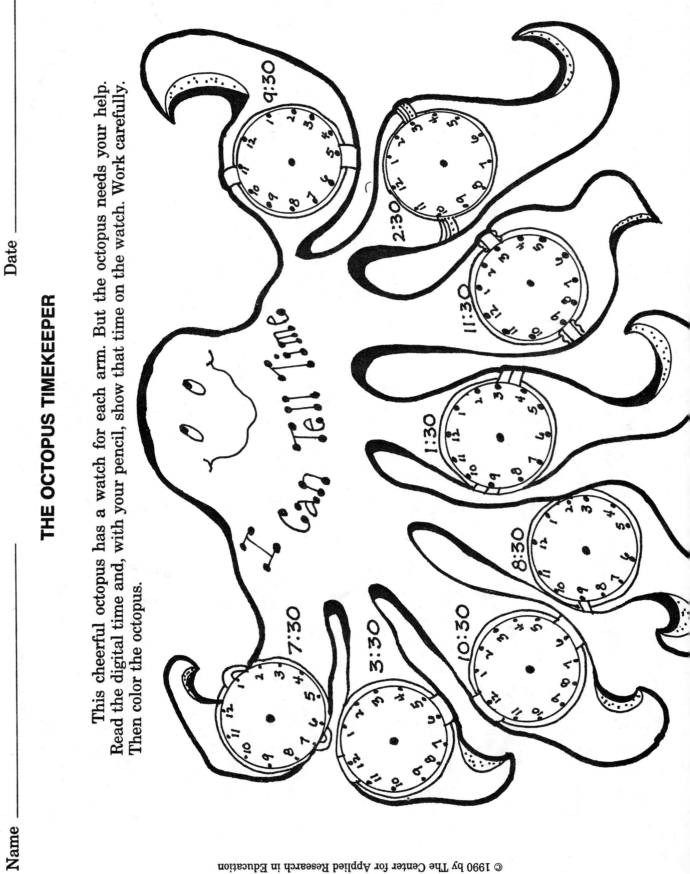

I Can Tell Time

9:30

2:30

11:30

1:30

8:30

7:30

3:30

10:30

STRAIGHT AND CURVED LINES

Find all of the objects with straight edges and color them red. Then find all of the objects with curved edges and color them blue.

Name —————————————— Date ——————————————

WHO HAS 25 CENTS?

Butch the Bird has a quarter (or 25 cents). His friends are showing him their coins. Color the hand or paw of the friends who have money that is EQUAL to that of Butch.

© 1990 by The Center for Applied Research in Education

FAVORITE FOOD GRAPH

I asked _____ friends to look at the food below and to name their favorite. They had to choose just one, and then color in the space that was in the same row as that food. These are the results of my survey. The favorite food is _____, and it was chosen by this many people _____. The graph below is called a horizontal bar graph.

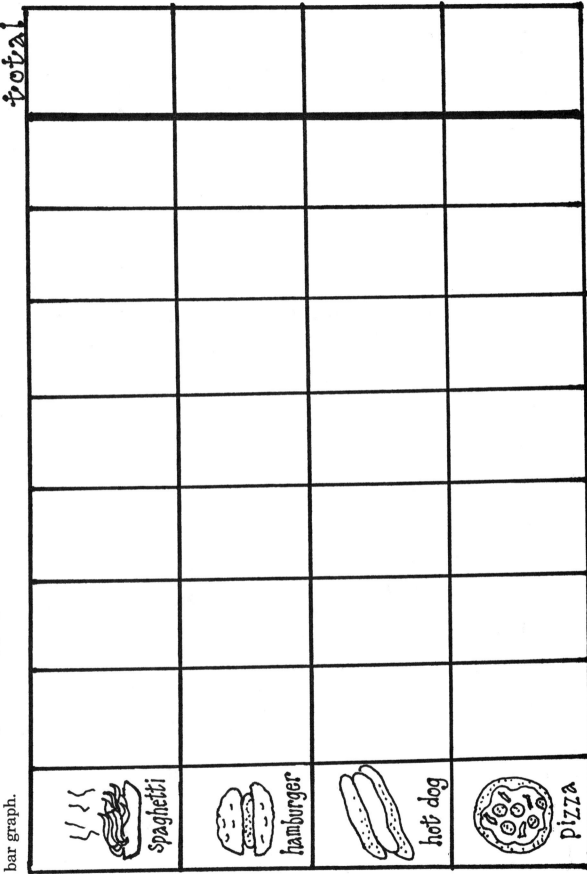

Name _____

Date _____

SPRING WINDSOCKS

On the windsocks below, make two sights, two sounds, and two smells that you associate with spring. Then make your windsocks bright and colorful.

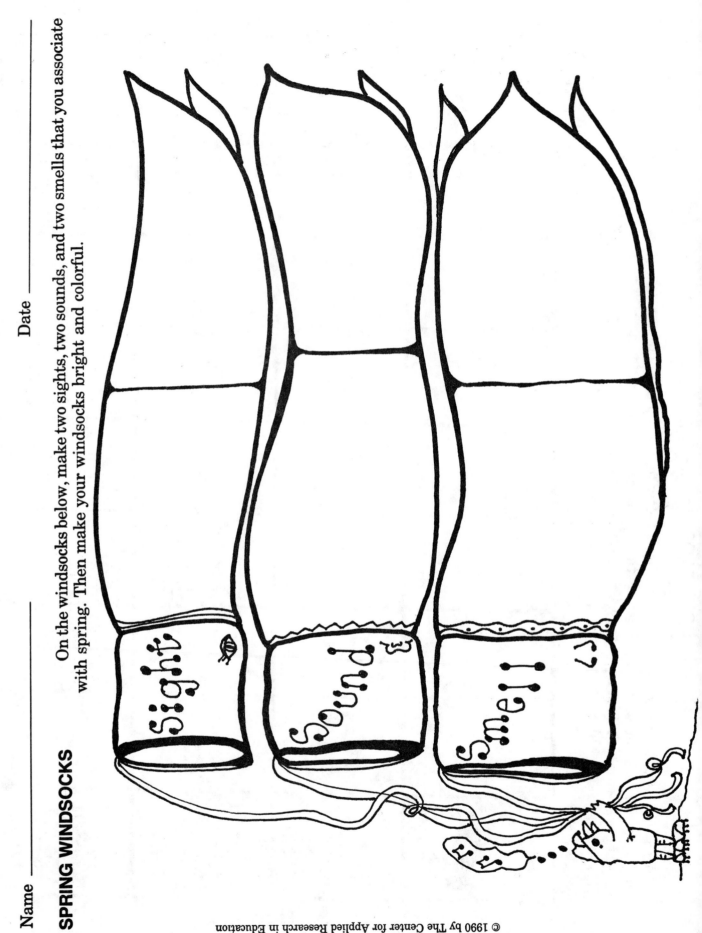

Sight

Sound

Smell

MAKING BEADS

Materials:
4 cups flour
2 cups salt
1 bowl
1 dish of water
waxed paper
toothpicks
heavy thread
needle
brushes
paint   red yellow blue

Procedure:

Mix the flour and salt in the bowl. Add water, a little at a time, to make dough. Put some dough on a piece of waxed paper. Shape the dough into beads. Use the toothpick to gently poke a hole in each bead. Dry. Paint and string them.

POT O'GOLD AWARD

The leprechauns are looking for good helpers, good citizens, good workers, and for those who keep trying. YOU may be singled out by the leprechauns for this award more than once. Keep working!

to _____

for _____

_____

_____

_____

_____

THE LEPRECHAUN LOOK

What do you think a leprechaun looks like? Since no one knows for sure, YOU could be right! Fill in lots of details so that we get a good look at this elf.

Name _____ Date _____

SPRING THINGS

Color the items that tell us that spring is here! Use the back of this sheet to draw more spring things.

April

READING, WRITING, AND RAINDROPS

April brings the Easter bunny, vacation, and a growth spurt for many first graders. Some children seem to suddenly blossom, and make significant academic progress in reading and math. This is a rewarding time for the first grade teacher who needs to continue to provide learning challenges for all students. They're still eager to learn, and your attitude, dedication, and caring are critical ingredients during this time of rapid change.

RECOMMENDED CHILDREN'S BOOKS FOR APRIL

- *The Easter Egg Artists* by Adrienne Adams (New York: Charles Scribner's Sons, 1976). The Abbot rabbits paint the beautiful designs on all Easter eggs. What do rabbits, who love to paint, do the rest of the year? They transform their car, their house, and their surroundings with delightful designs.

- *Humbug Rabbit* by Lorna Balian (Nashville: Abingdon Press, 1974, 1986). This story takes place (visually) above ground and below ground. Above-ground people are preparing for the Easter Bunny and, in the rabbit burrow below ground, Father Rabbit does not want to hear any more of the Easter Bunny talk. "Humbug!" he says. The night before Easter, the cat works a miracle and Father Rabbit becomes a true believer. This delightful tale has a dual story plot that children enjoy following and comparing.

- *The Very Busy Spider* by Eric Carle (New York: Philomel Books, 1984). The spider is busy spinning a web. As you turn each page, a different animal asks the spider if it wants to play, but the spider keeps spinning. The reader watches the development of the spider spinning the web with each turning page. In the end, the spider's hard work pays off. The book contains big colorful illustrations that delight young children.

- *Chickens Aren't the Only Ones* by Ruth Heller (New York: Grosset & Dunlap, 1981). This award-winning book takes one theme—eggs—and, through the use of rhyme and exceptionally bright, beautiful illustrations, gives the reader a wealth of information about the subject and an enriching visual experience. Children go back to this one again and again.

- *Will It Rain?* by Holly Keller (New York: Greenwillow Books, 1984). This is the time of year when you can just "feel it" and so can the animals. It's going to rain. As the black clouds darken the sky, we observe the animals scurrying, wriggling, and disappearing before the thundering crash. Then, when it's over, it feels different again. This book gives us a visual experience of a thunder shower.

- *Better Move On, Frog!* by Ron Maris (New York: Julia MacRae Books, a Division of Franklin Watts, 1982). This book about a little frog looking for a shelter of its own is a visual treat for the reader. It seems that just about every hole is taken by badgers or rabbits or owls or mice. Finally, the thunder shower provides a hole for the frog to move into. Children enjoy reading this and acting out the story.

- *Apple Pigs* by Ruth Orbach (New York: Collins Publishers, Inc., 1979). This delightful tale is told in rhyme. Look for a tree to grow more big, bright, red apples than you can eat, give away, or store under the bed or in the piano. It's time for a spring feast for "man and bird and woolly beast."

- *Never Trust an Ogre* by Gregoire Solotareff (New York: Greenwillow Books, 1987). This man-eating ogre means business. After he's eaten up his family and many animals, he becomes so fat that he tries to entice the animals as they go by. Imagine an ogre practicing his smiles! The animals are perplexed when he sends them an invitation to a "Friendship Dinner." They go, but it's a good thing they're on guard.

- *One Bad Ant* by Chris Van Allsburg (Boston: Houghton Mifflin, 1988). The ants, always busy doing their chores, come in contact with the outside world and one decides not to return to the ant colony. Surely there must be more to life! But the world is not a friendly place for an ant, and there's nothing more soothing than home sweet home when you've had a frightful adventure. The perspective in the illustrations is fascinating to young children because of their size in relation to their own surroundings.

- *Old Hippo's Easter Egg* by Jan Wahl, illustrated by Lorinda Bryan Cauley (New York: Harcourt Brace Jovanovich, 1980). Old Hippo lives alone, except for a little mouse who rents out his vest pocket, and he longs for a little child so that he can paint Easter eggs for him or her. On Easter morning, a surprise basket is left on Hippo's doorstep with an egg in it—and there's something alive and growing inside it. This is a touching story aided by detailed illustrations.

SPOTLIGHT ON READING

"The Love Bug" Award

Love Bug loves good books to look at and to read. He is starting his own award for a favorite book character. The students can help Love Bug by giving the award to their favorite picture book or storybook character (person or animal). Have students become acquainted with award-winning picture books if they have not already been introduced. The Caldecott Medal (gold) is awarded yearly for the book with outstanding illustrations. Ask your librarian for samples so that these works of art can be shared and enjoyed with the students. There are also Honor Books (or runner-ups) that receive a Caldecott Medal (silver) as well.

Have children carefully and thoughtfully take time to select their very own favorite book character. They can give it The Love Bug Award. They can make a brand-new, beautiful book jacket for the book they have chosen, and make an award for it from construction paper. These characters can be outlined and painted on butcher paper, then cut out, and displayed in the room for all to enjoy. Have a Love Bug Book Browsing Time and then read one of the books while the children relax and enjoy a cookie treat.

"The Bear Hug" Award and "The Rooster's Crow" Award

If you are in a literature-based reading program and have been working with many, many picture books throughout the school year, it may be difficult for the children to select their favorite because there are so many beautiful books available today. So, after they give "The Love Bug Award," students can still make more choices—The Bear Hug Award and The Rooster's Crow Award. These books would be worth hugging and crowing about! Children can wear badges to "advertise" their book choices. (See the reproducible activity pages.)

Digraphs—Some April Fool's Day Fun!

While the Alligator and the Ogre were on vacation, the alphabet letters were playing and having some fun. The Unicorn rode through ABC Land daily to deliver mail to the letters, and Love Bug rode along nestled in the Unicorn's ear. He's a marvelous storyteller! He likes to read and then tell the story aloud. (Students can be encouraged to do this as well for sequencing of ideas, voice inflection, memory retention, listening, language development, and so on.)

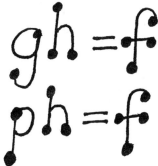

The fun began on April Fool's Day—April 1, and continued throughout the month. Some letters decided to play a trick on the letter F. The trickster was the letter H who persuaded the letters G and P to join the fun.

Review with the students the letter sounds, for example:

"f " as in the word "fish"   "h" as in the word "hello"

"g" as in the word "green"   "p" as in the word "purple"

Explain this concept to students, just as a storyteller would. That is, make it very much an item of interest, with many exclamations of "Well!" "Hmmm!" and "Oh!"

A Tricky Letter Story

The letter F was working in the yard, raking the lawn. Along came GH and said, "Hi! We're rouGH, and touGH, and we've had enouGH!"

When F heard its very own sound, it dropped the rake. F stared at GH and asked, "What did you say?"

They repeated, "We're rouGH, and touGH, and we've had enouGH!"

Then they ran up to F, shook hands, grinned, and shouted "April Fish! We hooked you!"

Well, F was VERY relieved, and went back to working in the yard. As the day went on, more and more letters began to get together and make up other sounds. They called themselves DIGRAPHS. At the stroke of midnight when the gate to ABC Land clinked shut, some of the words and letters did not make it back on time, so these words remain mixed up forever and don't follow the usual rules. They still try to fool people— and often do. People end up saying, "Ugh! That word fooled me again!" THE END.

Remind students that when they see GH and PH together, they are usually trying to trick us by taking on the sound of the letter F. Other letters make digraphs, too. You can use the basal reader to locate more of these tricky April words.

Print these words on the chalkboard to help with the PH digraph. Students can circle the "culprits":

Philip   telephone   elephant
pheasant   telegraph   earphones

Use a beginning dictionary and go on a Digraph Hunt. Be sure to make a list of each digraph pair.

Let's Put on Our Thinking Caps

Critical and creative thinking games foster listening skills, strengthen attention and memory spans, increase classification skills, and promote fluency of ideas. These are all necessary ingredients for the able reader. Here are some games that serve to reinforce the skills being acquired by the beginning reader:

- Play "I'm Thinking of a Holiday." You can lead off the game by giving three key words, without mentioning the holiday name itself. Students must try to make the associations and guess the holiday. Be sure to set up the rule that students are to raise their hand when they have the answer and not shout it out loud. This enables others to still have time to make connections. Here are some starters:

"I'm thinking of a holiday: wreath, Santa, tree"   (Christmas)
"I'm thinking of a holiday: bunny, eggs, basket"   (Easter)
"I'm thinking of a holiday: heart, candy, flowers"   (Valentine's Day)
"I'm thinking of a holiday: dad, love, greetings"   (Father's Day)
"I'm thinking of a holiday: witch, pumpkin, cats"   (Halloween)

- Play "I'm Thinking of a Season." Here are some starters:
snowman, skiing, ice skating   (winter)
pool, swimsuit, baseball   (summer)
puddles, umbrella, wind   (spring)
scarecrow, falling leaves, cool (autumn)

- Play "I'm Thinking of a Sport." Here are some starters:

  helmet, ball, kick   (football)
  racket, net, love   (tennis)
  base, bat, glove   (baseball)
  stick, puck, face mask   (hockey)

- Play "I'm Thinking of a Game." Here are some starters:

  chalk, jump, sidewalk   (hopscotch)
  jump, feet, handles   (jumprope)
  run, touch, find   (hide and seek)

Choral Reading

It is a joyful learning experience when students read in unison (all together). The blending of the voices is of benefit to the students for whom English is a second language. It is also beneficial for the hesitant oral reader or speaker. Divide the total group in half. One half can read a sentence or paragraph, and the other half can read the following line, and so on. This is especially good for poetry, with a **variety of verses.** It is good for nursery rhymes and chants, as well. Don't miss out on the joys of choral reading regularly. Choral reading can be developed to a fine art.

It is especially effective with young students when it is done in question-and-answer form. For example, use color questions:

Group One	*Group Two*
What color is the velvet sky?	It's as blue as berry pie.
What color is the tulip bed?	Some are yellow and some are red.
What color is the grass today?	It is brown, the color of hay.
What color is the pig in the sink?	He looks pink, don't you think?
What color is the great big tree?	All of the colors in the sea.

Does it have to rhyme? No! Remind the students that the answers do not have to rhyme. To reinforce this, ask "What is the color of April?" Answers will vary, such as:

April is the color of . . .

. . . bluejays calling

. . . cardinals building their nest

. . . robin's eggs

. . . kites flying high in the blue sky

. . . a rainbow after a thunderstorm

With choral reading, two students could be assigned to each line. Or, all students can say every other line.

Homophones

These words sound alike, but are spelled differently. Here are some examples:

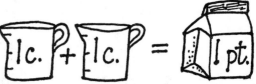

to, two, too	hear, here
no, know	won, one
by, buy	meet, meat

Print a set of homophones on the chalkboard and make up a sentence using one of the words. Call upon a student to come up and circle the correct one. Repeat this with students taking over the sentences and responses. Students enjoy doing this and are learning to construct simple sentences, and strengthen the context clues and visual discrimination skills necessary for determining the correct response.

Make up a set of homophone flash cards on a variety of like shapes. Students who need extra help can gain success with sorting, and can then work on learning the words as well.

SPOTLIGHT ON MATH

A Dry Measure Center

Set up an area for measuring that is apart from the quiet working area. In this area there will be much arm movement (pouring, sifting, lifting, and so on) and many students are still developing fine motor skills, so there are apt to be spills. Use playbox sand or cornmeal or dried beans/peas/lentils in large kettles or plastic containers. You will also need: plastic cups, pint and quart containers, funnel, plastic measuring spoons, and a large plastic pail or two. This center can all be self-contained in a large shallow box for minimum clean-up.

Students can be helped to gain practice with measuring terminology such as teaspoon, tablespoon, full, empty, half full, quart, pint, and so on. They can also be helped to discover relationships and to learn the following:

2 cups equal (will fill) 1 pint
4 cups equal (will fill) 2 pints
2 pints equal (will fill) 1 quart

Later, add a half-gallon and a gallon plastic milk or juice container, and let the students discover more relationships.

From Dry to Wet for Rainy April

A liquid measuring center can be set up in much the same way as the dry measuring center. Use a huge tub to house the materials. Have "Splash Rules" for this area; that is, it is a work area and not a play area. Students may dip but not plunge items into the water, for example. Again, plastic measuring spoons and containers of various sizes will work well. Students learn the relationships between and among these sizes as they manipulate them, feel them, and sense the weight of them (holding with one hand or two hands). This area can be set up on a low table that has been covered with a plastic tablecloth.

Splash Rules
1. Dip- Do not plunge.
2. Work on paper.
3. Clean up spills.

Even though students are working only with water, "recipes" can be printed on 4″ × 6″ file cards to make the measuring go more smoothly, such as:

Friendship Soup Mix

1 cup smiles

1 tsp. winks

2 cups good citizenship

Stir together. Put 5 tbsp. in the red bowl for Teddy Bear. Serve with a happy face. CLEAN-UP: Put all liquid back into the big tub. Place cups upside-down to dry.

Fresh April Showers

½ tsp. love

¼ tbsp. sweet words

3 pints rainbows

Stir together slowly 16 times. Blink both eyes. Stir slowly 12 more times. Put 1 pint in a container for the Unicorn. Serve with a big grin. CLEAN-UP: Put all liquid back into the big tub. Place cups upside-down to dry.

Students can be helped to make up their very own special recipes for storybook characters, cartoon characters, or characters from favorite children's television programs.

Estimation/Prediction

Since April is the month of showers and boots and raincoats and puddles, students can gain practice with weather prediction. This is a good math activity at the end of the day, just before students are getting ready to go home. Review: What was our weather today? What has our weather been all week? Predict: What will the weather be like tomorrow?

This can be done on a felt-board with circular felt cut-outs. Students can take one symbol (yellow circle for the sun, a green circle with a stick as an umbrella for rain, or a dark circle for cloudy) and place it on the felt-board.

At first, students will place them in a scattered pattern. From this, show students how to group the items into sets. Then later in the month, have them do their estimation as a vertical or horizontal bar graph that they build right on the spot. Keep a record of the group's accuracy.

It's Raining Tens and Ones

Hang two real umbrellas high from the ceiling. Label one "Tens" and the other "Ones." From the ones umbrella, hang nine strings. Each day for nine days, attach a raindrop to the umbrella string. After nine, then what? No more strings. So, on the tenth day, all of the raindrops are removed and put together with a paper-clip and hung from a string on the tens umbrella. The next day, begin all over again with the ones umbrella.

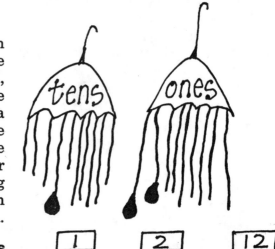

It's Raining Hundreds, Tens, and Ones

Students can gain practice with this concept at the felt-board using felt cut-outs of umbrellas and raindrops. They will have a good start from the actual umbrellas in the room. By adding the hundreds, they will gain practice counting with tens. Use string or yarn to bundle the raindrops of ten.

Using Math for the Lunch Count

Make a sturdy cardboard poster with appropriate pictures and labels for "Milk Only," "Hot Lunch," "No Purchase," and so on. Also, you will need a clip clothespin for each student. Put their names on the clothespins with a felt-tip pen. Each day, when students come to school, they can find their name clothespin and clip it to the appropriate poster picture. This gives the class an immediate picture of what the lunchroom line-up and count will be for each day.

After lunch, appoint students to remove the clips, and clip them around the rim of a shoebox that has been covered with self-stick design paper. Students can get in the habit of doing this each day. You can involve students in the counting procedure to show that math is important to us and that we use it every day.

Beanbag Toss for Column Addition

Cut up a medium-sized cardboard box and use one side to make a math game. Divide the cardboard into four sections. Cover each one with construction paper of a bright color, or have students paint them with different bright colors. Laminate with clear self-stick vinyl. Then make a set of number cards from 0 through 9. Shuffle the number cards and place the first four on the four squares. That becomes the value of each square. Each student can toss a beanbag three times and record, in a column, the three numerals from the squares on which he or she landed. This can be done on the chalkboard or with a calculator or with pencil on vertical sheets of paper. Work in teams or individually. After five tries, the winner is the one with the highest score.

Beanbag Five

Use the same number board previously described. Students can toss the beanbag five times. But, this time they must SUBTRACT the LAST number. For example, they can have a score of 5 + 4 + 5 + 6 + 1 which is equal to 21. Now they must figure out 21 − 1 = _____ ; and that is the score. Several calculators can be used to help check the addition and subtraction facts.

Shape of the Month: Rectangular Solid

Students understand the concept of a square and a cube, a circle and a sphere, a triangle and a cone, and a rectangle and a rectangular solid. Some shapes are flat and some are solid.

Take a good look at boxes. Have a variety of rectangular boxes with lids, and have students guess what could come in each box. Be on the lookout for rectangular solids in the classroom (books, pencil boxes, lunch boxes, game boxes, and so on) and also in magazines.

Be sure to have a rectangular solid snack, such as a brownie, an ice cream sandwich, or a bar cookie.

The Concept of Solid

Take two pieces of bread from a loaf. As students observe, carefully cut around the inside crust of one of the bread pieces and remove the middle so that just the crust remains. Compare it to the solid piece of bread.

Which one can hold jam and peanut butter? Which one would students rather have for snack time? Which one is solid?

- Use a pencil and a straw to further help with this concept. We can "see through" the straw from end to end, but not through the pencil because it is solid.

- Assorted macaroni pieces help with this concept, too. Some pieces are solid and some are tubular, such as rigatoni and elbow macaroni. Students can hold them up and peek through one end. Therefore, it is not solid.

- Remember, something is solid when the space is filled up. If we were to slice the object in half, there would not be just a rim. The inside space would be taken.

Are Pipes Solid?

No, they allow the water to come through the faucet.

Is a hose solid? No, it allows water to come through to sprinkle the lawn.

Is a sprinkling can spout solid? No, it allows water to come through to water the flowers.

Is a dill pickle solid? Yes. When we bite into it, there is not just a rim.

Is an ice cube solid? Yes. If we could cut it in two, it would not be just a rim.

Encourage students to think in terms of what is solid (all space is filled) and what is not solid, but just a rim or outline.

HANDS-ON SCIENCE

Frogs

The frog is an AMPHIBIAN (new vocabulary word), which means that the frog is equally at home in the water or on land. Some frogs have been hibernating all winter in the warm mud under a pond, and they wake up as the weather warms. The female frog lays hundreds of eggs in water. They are in a sticky jelly that helps to protect them. After two weeks, tiny black tadpoles hatch and wiggle free from the jelly. This is what happens next:

5 weeks later, the back legs begin to show

5 weeks after that, the tadpole has lungs and front legs

2 weeks after that, the tadpole has all four legs

4 weeks after that, the young frog is ready to leave the water and visit the land

Let's Examine Tadpoles

If you are fortunate enough to live in an area where tadpoles abound in ponds and streams, some students may bring in a murky, water-filled jar of tadpoles for observation. These are fascinating for the children to observe as they dart about. Keep them in the same water—do not put them in fresh water from the faucet. After the second day, encourage the students to take the tadpoles back and release them in the same stream so that they have a chance for survival.

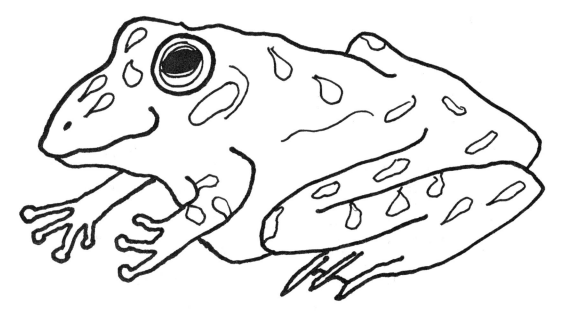

Time to Play Leap Frog

Did you know that the Leopard Frog can leap 13 times its own length? Have students measure their height with a string, having one student holding it taut at the bottom and another holding it at the top. Cut the string and lay it on the playground. Put a "frog marker" there, such as a big stone. Then lay the string out in a straight line 13 more times. Students will be amazed at the length. Put a "frog marker" there, too. How many times their own length can each student jump? Keep practicing.

Invite a Frog to Lunch

Contact the science supervisor in your school district, or the science department at the high school, or a pet store to find out how you can invite a frog to spend the day in your classroom. Be sure that it is in a deep container. Frogs eat live insects, worms, slugs, snails, and spiders. That is the luncheon menu. However, a frog is attracted by movement and prefers to have its meal while the meal is still alive. BE CAREFUL, though, because larger frogs eat smaller frogs and tadpoles—even their own little sisters and brothers!

Students can create an invitation for the frog and produce a menu that gives fancy names to the frog's favorite food, such as: warm, wiggly worms; slithery, sloshy slugs; and so on. Divide them by appetizer, main course, and dessert. What shape will the menu be? Will there be illustrations?

If you don't have access to a real frog, try to locate a film about frogs from your media resource center or the local library. Invite a stuffed toy frog to spend the day, and still create the fancy menu. Students can make the menu items from plasticene of different colors. Label them. Take the frog's order, and serve them on a green plate (lily pad) to the frog. You will be surprised at how much students do learn about frogs and the food they eat!

Would You Kiss a Frog?

In many fairy tales, the princess is supposed to kiss a frog and then the frog turns into a prince. After seeing a real frog, or a movie of a frog, ask the children how they would feel if they were given the order to kiss a frog. (There will be many grunts and groans.) Now we know exactly how the princess felt, don't we?

PLANT A TREE FOR ARBOR DAY

Arbor Day started over 100 years ago in the state of Nebraska. (Locate Nebraska on the map. How close are you to this state?) Nebraska pioneers planted trees on the treeless plains because they recognized that trees do many things for us. They purify the air we breathe; they serve as protection from heat and cold; they "muffle" the sounds of the city; and they serve as homes for birds and squirrels.

Contact a local nursery to find out if it will donate (or sell at a reduced cost) a small tree that can be planted on the school grounds. (Of course, first check with the building principal.) Ask the principal or superintendent of schools or even the mayor to visit and give a speech during the celebration. After they have given their speeches, have children practice giving a speech. The next day, the students can each give their very own Arbor Day Speech.

Make an Arbor Day picture booklet showing the planting ceremony, the tree as it looks now, and the tree as it will look some day. Donate a booklet to the school library, complete with a map showing the tree's location so that the special tree will be on record for the future.

EASTER IS A TRADITION

Easter is always the first Sunday following the full moon on or after the spring equinox (the first day of spring). The earliest date is March 22 and the latest date is April 25.

Why the Easter Bunny?

The hare is a symbol for the moon (Egyptian mythology). The Easter date is associated with the full moon, as stated earlier. Over many, many years, the term "rabbit" has come to be associated with Easter, and today we know this rabbit as the Easter Bunny. Have students make fuzzy-looking Easter bunnies by using small sponges and tempera paint. Encourage them to make their hand "hop like a bunny" with the sponge, as they create their rabbit shape (two circles, a tail, and two long ears). If they do make the sponge hop up and down on the paper, the effect is light and airy, rather than heavy like a thick elephant line.

The Easter Egg

The egg is a symbol of life. At one time, Chinese parents sent a red egg to relatives or friends when a baby was born. This was like an announcement card. Many of our Easter greeting cards are shaped like an egg. Students can have fun making an egg-shaped card for

Easter greetings. The following folk art symbols have been handed down through the ages and are painted on Easter eggs:

 sun (for good luck)

 flower (for love and beauty)

 hen or rooster (for making wishes come true)

 deer (for good health)

In the Ukraine, eggs were popular gifts to exchange at Easter, and young girls rubbed their cheeks with the red-colored eggs when they found them to give their cheeks a rosy glow after a long winter.

The Traditional Easter Parade

There are many Easter parades with people dressed up in new clothes, marching along the street to welcome the spring. In England, it was once considered bad luck to be seen on Easter Sunday wearing old clothes. Today, people wear old and new clothes for Easter, but many still buy a new Easter outfit. In the United States, there is the traditional New York City parade along Fifth Avenue, and another famous one along the boardwalk in Atlantic City, New Jersey. Does your city or town have an Easter parade? Why not have a classroom parade to celebrate spring?

An Easter Nest

In Germany and Switzerland (locate these countries on a map or globe), children make nests of grass in the garden in order that the Easter Bunny may fill them with eggs. Our green "grass" (or purple, yellow, or pink) that we buy for Easter baskets may have been handed down from this custom.

The Chocolate Egg

In England, children receive chocolate eggs wrapped in fancy paper. Make a giant egg shape on butcher paper and have students decorate it with fancy art using colorful felt-tip pens. This can be cut and used as a tablecloth at a gala party, or it can be hung on the door as a decoration.

The Easter Egg Tree

This tradition first started in Germany. Eggs were colored and tied to the branches of a tree to herald the spring season. An Easter egg tree can be made in the classroom—adding a fresh look to the classroom setting!

The Easter Egg Roll or Easter Egg Hunt

In the United States, children gather on the lawn of the White House in Washington, D.C., and take part in rolling Easter eggs on the lawn. In many European countries, eggs are hidden inside and outside in the garden and, at a given signal, children carefully hunt for the eggs. "Finders keepers!"

Hide a colorful hard-boiled egg in the classroom and have students go on a hunt for it. Or, have one student leave the classroom and step out into the hall. Hide the egg so that everyone else knows where it is. When the person is invited back into the room, have children thump on their desk with their forefinger if the student seeking the egg is quite close, and thump thump if he or she is practically on top of it.

The Rabbit Hid Them

In the classroom, students can make Easter baskets from cardboard containers, strawberry baskets, or construction paper. These can be filled with colored paper that has been cut into strips for grass, or commercial grass can be purchased for the baskets. When students go to lunch, have the baskets removed from the classroom (and filled with jelly beans or other treats). Ask the class aide or older students in the building for assistance with this activity. When the class returns to find the baskets missing, it means that the hunt is on at a designated time that afternoon. This can be a part of the Easter parade, with the finding of the baskets as the culmination. Sometimes they end up in the office cupboard or in the library or in the principal's office or in the media center. There is no telling where that rabbit will hide these baskets! Students at this age giggle with glee and get caught up in the excitement of the hunt—and they are engaging in a tradition that is centuries old. This is just one way that the schools transmit the cultural heritage of the people.

PASSOVER

This important Jewish holiday is celebrated about the same time as Easter and lasts for eight days. It is a celebration of freedom. At one time, the Jews were slaves in Egypt until they got their freedom. Today, they remember this important time in history by gathering together and celebrating their freedom. They tell stories and make some of the traditional food for this holiday: horseradishes are eaten at the dinner and represent the bitterness of slavery, roasted eggs symbolize life, and charoses symbolize the sweetness of freedom.

Recipe for Charoses (Harosez)

12 medium-sized apples

1 cup raisins

1 teaspoon cinnamon

½ cup frozen orange juice concentrate

1 cup chopped walnuts

Soak the raisins in orange juice concentrate for one day. Then dice or grate the apples. Mix all of the ingredients together. Refrigerate in a rectangular glass baking dish. Cut and serve.

APRIL IS FOR RUNNERS

The Boston Marathon (26 miles, 385 yards) is held every year on the Monday closest to Patriot's Day to celebrate the famous ride (not run!) of Paul Revere (April 19, 1775). This event creates much excitement, and can be followed via the media. Many cities and towns have their own walks and runs during this time of year for various charities. Is there one in your town?

Have a school race. Measure around the edge of the playground or the gymnasium, using a meter stick. Decide how many laps (times around) are required for your very own marathon race.

APRIL FOOL'S DAY

April 1 is a day set aside for pranks and jokes. It is fun to try to "fool" someone else. It is thought that the idea originated in France, where people refer to the "April Fish," or someone who is easily hooked by a joke. Since the weather plays jokes on us in April, it may have been tied originally to the idea that although spring is just around the corner, when we turn over the calendar to April 1, we are apt to be fooled. Winter may still be in charge.

In order that the day not get out of hand, set aside a certain time in the day for this celebration. If you take a half hour after lunch for riddles, jokes, card tricks, coin tricks, and so on, it will encourage students to practice their "act" in the morning.

- This is a day when some of Aesop's Fables can be introduced because there is a lesson to be learned from these amusing tales. Students can be encouraged to give outrageous answers to such questions as "why do dogs drool?" "why do elephants have a trunk?" "why do zebras have stripes?" and so on.

- Play "What Would Happen If . . ." This is another good starter for allowing imaginations to run wild for a time, to come up with some creative solutions, and also to enjoy a good laugh. Some starters are:
  What would happen if . . .
  . . . the sun was green
  . . . the grass was pink
  . . . shoes had open soles
  . . . trousers had only one leg
  . . . there were no can-openers
  . . . there were no pencil-sharpeners
  . . . bluejays meowed
  . . . robins sang TV commercials all day long
  . . . cats crowed
  . . . alarm clocks refused to ring
  . . . stoves refused to cook

THE RETURN OF THE BIRDS

During April, the birds are setting up housekeeping in our backyard trees. The migration from south to north is just about complete. If you introduced the concept of migration in the autumn, it can be reintroduced now as birds appear and disappear from the immediate environment. Make a note of the birds that are in your area that were not there just a month ago, OR the birds that have disappeared from your area because they have gone north for the summer. Set up a birdwatching area in the classroom by a window. Use binoculars to survey the area. Get many bird books from the library for children to enjoy.

- From your local library, get a record of bird calls and have students listen to them and perhaps learn two or three of them.

- Put fresh paint in bright colors, cans, and brushes at the easel. Encourage students to paint giant bird pictures of their favorites. These beauties can be put on display in the classroom or hallway.

- Have a Bird-Fact-a-Day for students to learn. Here are some suggestions for beginning a big bird-shaped chart. Students can provide the illustrations using felt-tip pens and crayons:
  1. A tiny hummingbird can eat over 100 insects for a meal.
  2. The color "robin's egg blue" was named for the beautiful bluish-green color of the robin's egg.
  3. The name "sparrow" comes from an English word that means to "flutter."
  4. Male birds are brighter and prettier than females. Why? Because the females guard the nest, and the male can fly off and catch the eye of intruders.
  5. Starlings fly in flocks, and are often like an army sent in to attack a field of insects.
  6. The robin's song sounds like "Cheer up! Cheer up!"
  7. The bright red cardinal also sings "Cheer, Cheer-r-r-r."
  8. A pair of doves may have four sets of twins in a season.
  9. Baltimore Orioles eat hairy caterpillars.

More Artistic Designs for Birds

Young children are fascinated with birds, and here are some ways to encourage new art experiences using birds as the theme. For these activities, smocks should be worn.

- *Corrugated rubbings:* Have students make a cut-out of a bird shape from corrugated cardboard. Place the shape underneath a 12″ × 18″ piece of colored construction paper, and use the flat side of a crayon to rub over the bird. Keep changing the position of the bird shape to make a flock of migrating birds.

- *Splatter painting:* Have each student make a huge bird shape on a large sheet of shiny paper. Place the paper in an area protected with layers of newspaper. Use a straw to dip into tempera paint, and splatter the paint onto the bird shape. Blow through the straw to disperse the paint for an artistic splattered look. IMPORTANT: Be sure the students blow out, and do not inhale the paint.

- *Stamp pad designs:* Students can make a bird shape from colored construction paper. Then take round, square, and triangular-shaped objects for use with the stamp pad and print these shapes in an all-over design on the bird.

- *Wet chalk drawings:* Wet a 12″ × 18″ piece of manila paper with water and a sponge. Have students quickly draw their bird with chalk before the paper dries. If the paper begins to dry, dab it with a wet sponge again. This gives a painted effect and cuts down on chalk dust.

- *Cutting a design:* Outline a bird shape on a piece of 12″ × 18″ construction paper. Cut it out. Then outline the same bird shape about 1 inch along the inside of the shape. Cut it out. Place the bird shape on a contrasting color. Cut designs from the remainder of the paper and arrange them inside the bird shape. Glue.

Bird Displays

There are many ways to display these colorful birds in the classroom:

- Make a bulletin board nest from construction paper, twine, and newspaper strips. Stack the birds in the nest in a scattered pattern.

- Make a bulletin board tree from construction paper, and pin the birds in the branches, on the ground, and in the sky.

- Hang the birds by string or yarn from the ceiling. These can be traced onto bright paper, stapled, and stuffed.

- Make a very large outline of Butch the Bird and have students fill him in using colored squares of tissue paper brushed on with watered-down white glue. Then create a "Migration Facts" sheet so that Butch can learn about migration.

CELEBRATE INTERNATIONAL CHILDREN'S BOOK DAY

Hans Christian Andersen was born on April 2, so this is a good month to read *The Ugly Duckling*. What other books do we know that deal with ducks

Wise Old Owl Study Buddy Puppet (creative dramatics)
Butch the Bird Study Buddy Puppet (creative dramatics)
Spin and Practice (working with first-grade skills)
Kites and Eggs Memory Game (a memory game)
A Nesting Station (helping the birds)

Name _____ Date _____

THE BEAR HUG AWARD

In the space below, show a scene from the book that you really enjoy. It's a book that you could just hug!

I ♥ This Book

Name _____   Date _____

THE LOVE BUG AWARD

This award is given to your favorite book character (person or animal). Who gets your vote? Use your crayons to show the character in the big medal. Then color the Love Bug.

You Are My Favorite

CHECK THE "IT" ROCKET

Before the "It" rocket can take off, the letters on the cone have to be placed in ABC order under the rocket. Then you have to complete the connections by printing nine "it" words in the rectangles. The first one has been started to help you launch this rocket!

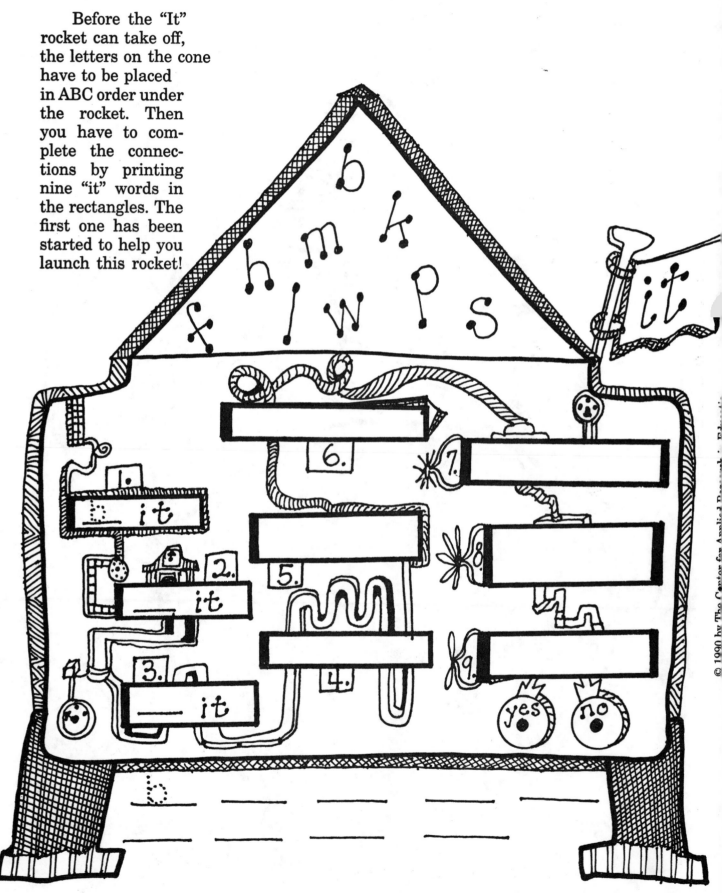

THE VOWEL HATCH

These eggs are almost ready to hatch. You can help crack the egg word code by filling in the vowels that will make a complete BIRD WORD. Remember, the vowels are A, E, I, O, U, and sometimes Y. Learn to say the words. Learn to spell three of them. Then color the bird with happy colors.

ALLIGATOR AND OGRE BOOKMARKS

Name _____ Date _____

THE EASTER BUNNY HELPER

Match the number egg on the left with the number name egg on the right. Then make the matching eggs exactly the same color and design. Use bright colors.

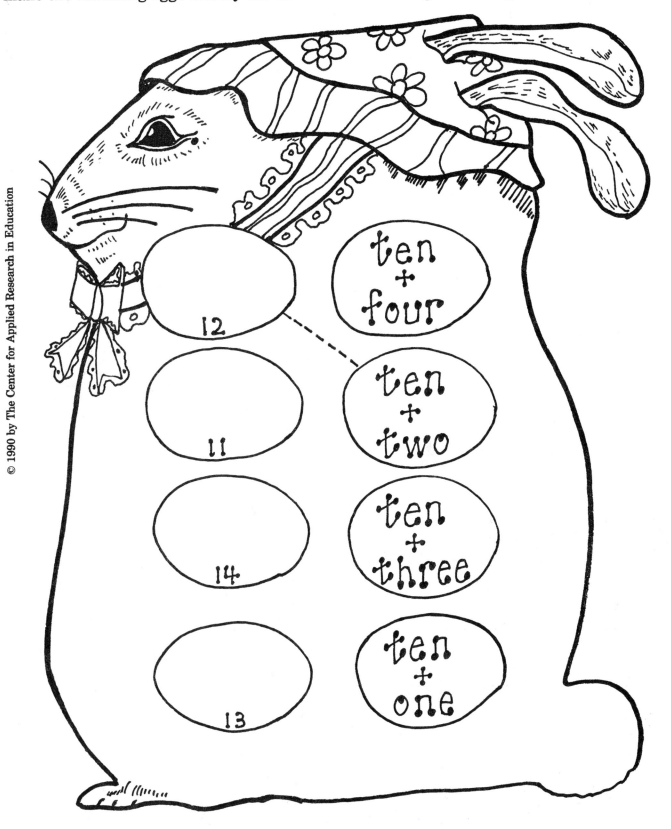

Name _____   Date _____

BUFFY THE BAR-B-Q BUNNY

While Buffy is waiting for the fire to get hot, you can help Buffy practice the subtraction facts. Print the answers on Buffy's apron. Then color PINK all of the EVEN-numbered answers; color GREEN all of the ODD-numbered answers.

On the apron:

10-6   12-7   10-7   12-8

13-8

9-6   9-5   4-1

8-4   11-7

11-6   6-3   5-0

MRS. FROG'S INSECT STEW

Mrs. Frog is getting ready to make supper. She is calling in her order to the market, and YOU can help by drawing the correct number of items in each thought balloon. Make them fat, ripe, colorful, and juicy—and maybe she'll invite you for supper, too! On the back of this sheet, write her recipe for "insect stew."

Name _____ Date _____

A SPRINGTIME TREE GRAPH

Count the number of birds in the tree. Find that symbol at the bottom of the tree trunk. Color in the correct number of squares. Do this for the other items to complete the graph. What is the biggest number? What is the smallest?

LET'S WORK WITH WEIGHT

Find two small rocks and put them on a scale. How much do they weigh? Record the numeral. Then find five items in the room that weigh MORE THAN that numeral and five items that weigh LESS THAN that numeral. Use your crayons to draw them in the boxes below. Compare your items with those of your classmates.

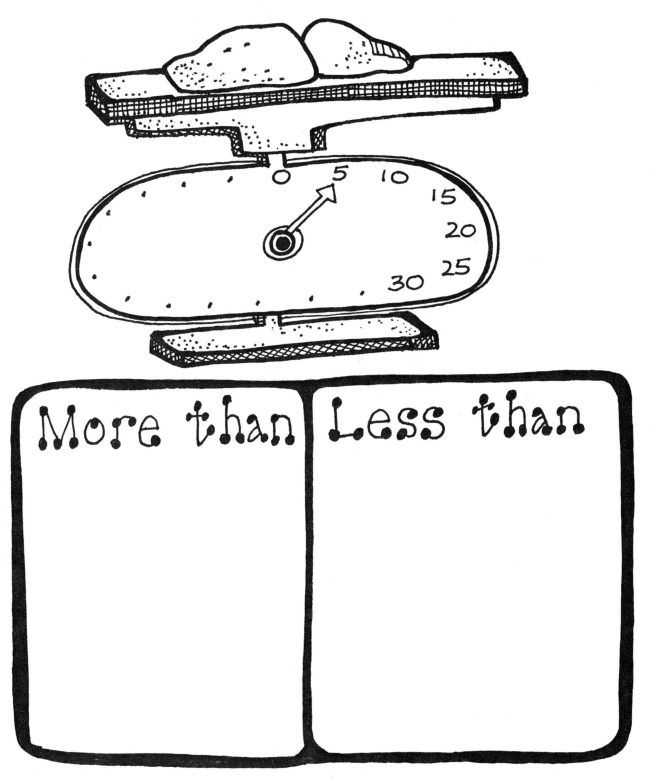

More than	Less than

MY FROG BOOKLET

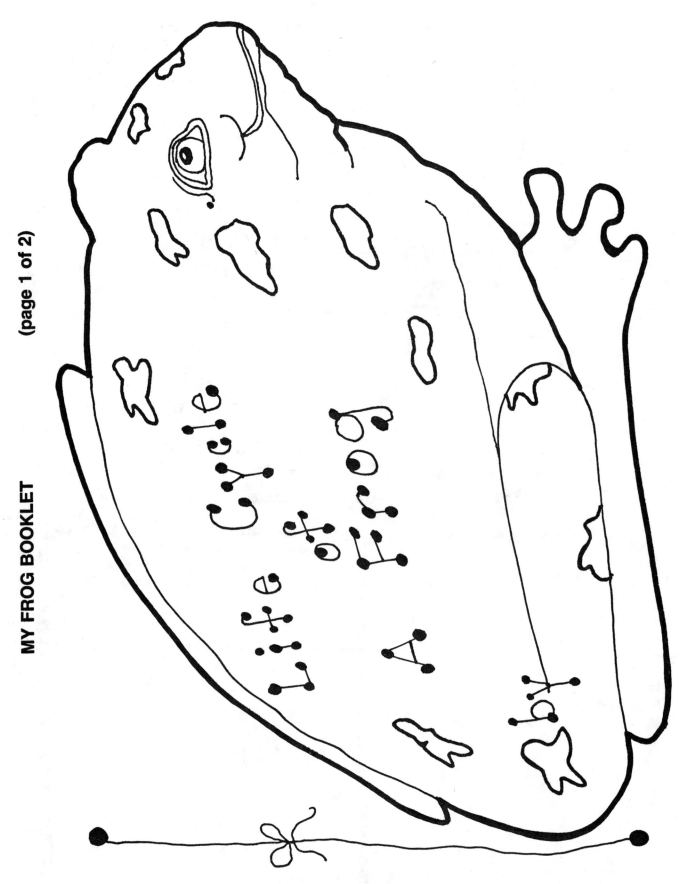

A Frog

Life Cycle of

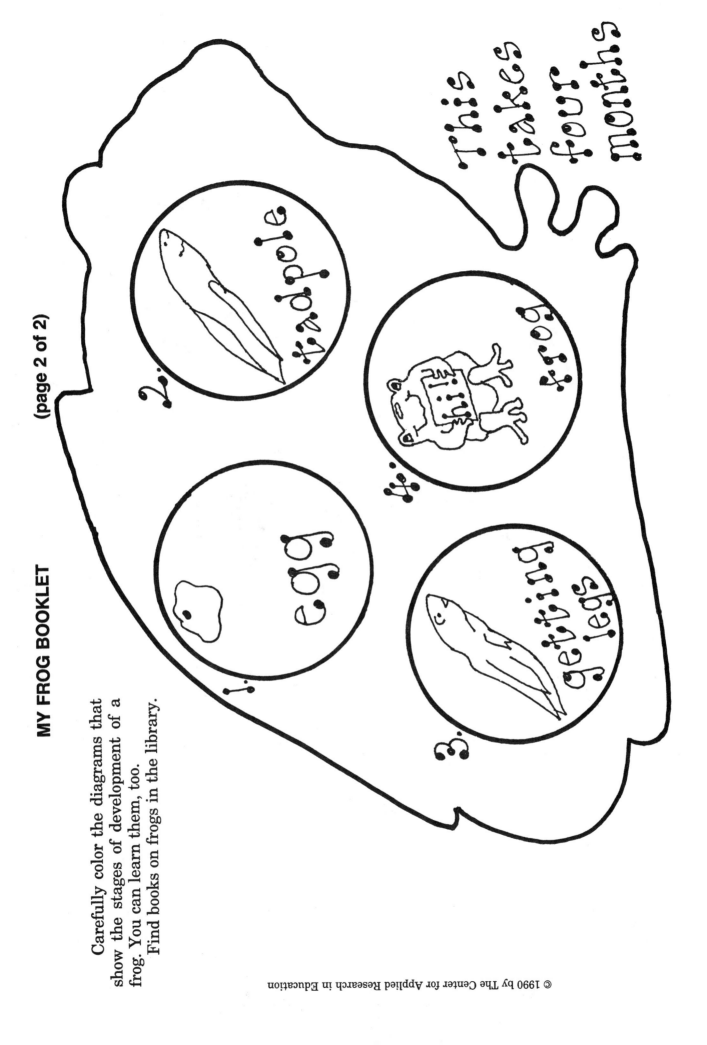

MY FROG BOOKLET

Carefully color the diagrams that show the stages of development of a frog. You can learn them, too. Find books on frogs in the library.

1. egg

2. tadpole

3. getting legs

4. frog

This takes four months

WISE OLD OWL STUDY BUDDY PUPPET

Color the owl. Cut out the shape along the edge. Attach to Butch the Bird. The Wise Old Owl can ask the questions, and you can help Butch with the answers.

BUTCH THE BIRD STUDY BUDDY PUPPET

Color the bird. Cut out the shape along the edge. Attach to Wise Old Owl. The Wise Old Owl can ask the questions, and you can help Butch with the answers.

SPIN AND PRACTICE

Cut out the pointer at the bottom of the page and attach it with a brad to the center of the wheel shape. Spin the pointer and follow the directions. The Wise Old Owl and Butch the Bird can use this to help them study. You can use it with a study buddy, too.

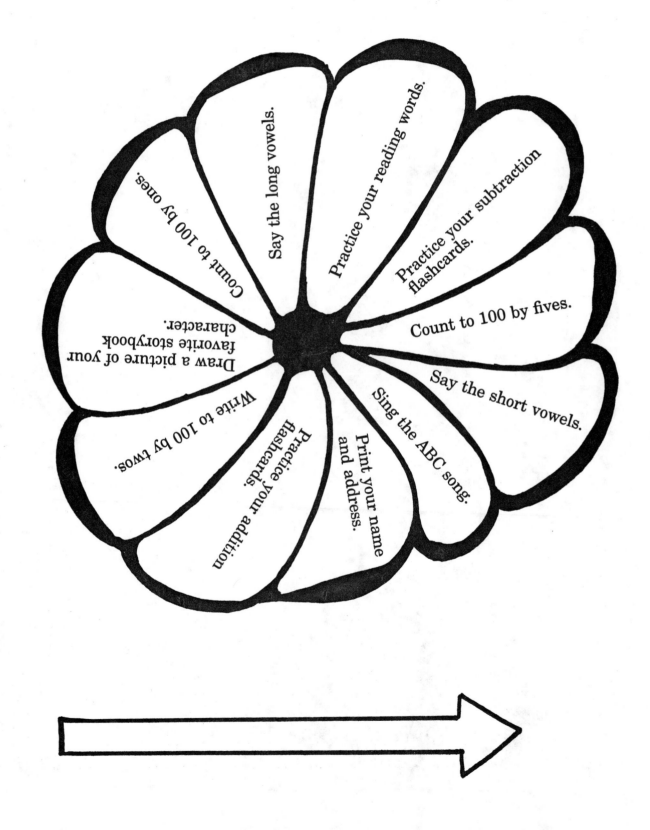

Say the long vowels.

Practice your reading words.

Practice your subtraction flashcards.

Count to 100 by ones.

Count to 100 by fives.

Draw a picture of your favorite storybook character.

Say the short vowels.

Write to 100 by twos.

Sing the ABC song.

Practice your addition flashcards.

Print your name and address.

KITES AND EGGS MEMORY GAME

Find the items that are alike. Color them exactly the same color. Cut out the items along the lines. Place the cards face down on a grid. Turn over two cards. Do they match? If so, keep them. If not, return them and try to remember where they are. Then the next player tries. The winner is the one with the most matching cards. One, two, or three players may play this game. Keep the cards in an envelope when the game is not in use.

Name _____   Date _____

A NESTING STATION

The days are getting longer. That is a signal to birds to start their nests. You can help! Hang up a mesh onion or potato bag, and loosely stuff it with the items shown below. What else can you put in the bag? Draw two more items in the circles provided.

Hang up a mesh bag.
Stuff it with:

cotton

yarn

dryer fluff

feathers

string

thank you

May / June

WE'RE STILL LEARNING, AND WE'LL NEVER STOP

May and June bring the end of the first full academic year. As if by magic, young children are reading, writing, and working math problems among other accomplishments. This metamorphosis happened gradually on a day-to-day basis all through the months, and was nurtured by consistency, planning, organization, and hard work on the part of the sensitive teacher. You are in the enviable position of lighting the lamp and encouraging the glow to get stronger and brighter during this cornerstone year!

RECOMMENDED CHILDREN'S BOOKS FOR MAY/JUNE

- *Cloudy with a Chance of Meatballs* by Judi Barrett, illustrations by Ron Barrett (New York: Atheneum, 1984). Grandfather enjoys spinning tales and, in the town of Chew and Swallow, it never rains real rain or snows real snow. Just imagine what it would be like to live in a place where it rains hamburgers and where the restaurant has no roof so that the food can just drop onto your plate! This story turns out to be a favorite of students and adds zest to your classroom weather reports.

- *The Mother's Day Mice* by Eve Bunting, illustrations by Jan Brett (New York: Clarion Books, 1986). The three little mice awaken early on Mother's Day and venture out into the meadow to find their mother a present. They meet with danger, but eventually they return home with their special gifts from nature selected just for their mother. The beautiful illustrations make this lovely story all the more precious.

- *The Knight and the Dragon* by Tomie dePaola (New York: G. P. Putnam's Sons, 1980). This story about a fire-breathing dragon and a knight who want to fight each other shows that when enemies put their talents together and work as a friendly team, they're happier. At this time of year, with outdoor cooking, these two would be good friends to know.

- *The Pigs' Wedding* by Helme Heine (New York: Margaret K. McElderry Books, 1978). This is the time of year to prepare for the June wedding, and the Pigs are no exception. But how do pigs celebrate a wedding? The guests are treated to the time of their lives, thanks to Porker Pig, who is an innovative thinker. They are bathed, and have new clothes painted right onto their skin with real paint. Even a thunderstorm that washes away their fancy clothes doesn't spoil the celebration. This is a fanciful tale that lights up the faces of the children.

- *Fish Is Fish* by Leo Lionni (New York: Pantheon, 1970). A tadpole and a fish become friends, but the tadpole changes into a frog and soon leaves the pond to see the world. He returns to tell the fish about what he sees. The illustrations are a delight, and make children giggle with glee because the fish has had only a limited experience in his world and makes a literal translation of everything the frog reports.

- *The Mountain That Loved a Bird* by Alice McLerran, pictures by Eric Carle (Natick, MA: Picture Book Studio, 1985). This is a touching tale of a migrating bird named Joy who stops to rest on a desert mountain. The mountain asks the bird to stay, but since there is no way for the bird to live there, it promises to return every year. The mountain, heartsick for the sound of the bird, begins to cry a steady stream of tears. This water creates a new environment and new growth on the barren mountain, and eventually can maintain life. Children like to hear this one again and again.

- *Maggie Doesn't Want to Move* by Elizabeth Lee O'Donnell, illustrated by Amy Schwartz (New York: Four Winds Press, 1987). Simon exclaims, "My sister Maggie doesn't want to move" when he learns that the family has to move to a new house and he has to go to a new school. This is a good time of year to read this story, since many moves are made over the summer. This book may be helpful to the children.

- *The Porcupine Mouse* by Bonnie Pryor, pictures by Maryjane Begin (New York: Morrow Junior Books, 1988). The mouse house is filled to overflowing with mouse children, so Mama sends Louie and Dan, the two oldest, out into the world to make a home of their own. She gives them some good advice and, along the way, the old adage "Mother Knows Best" is demonstrated. The book has delightful text and illustrations.

- *Do Not Disturb* by Nancy Tafuri (New York: Greenwillow Books, 1987). The book begins with the words, "It was the first day of summer . . ."

and the rest is a visual tale with no words. But no words are needed to see that playing ball, going swimming, having a cookout, etc., are disturbing the animals in the surrounding environment. Be on the lookout for a surprise ending!

- *The Little Pigs' First Cookbook* by N. Cameron Watson (Boston: Little, Brown and Company, 1987). The Pig Brothers are just learning how to cook and there are some wonderful recipes, such as Boozled Eggs, Guinea Pig Salad, Grilled Geometric Sandwiches, and Ralph's Bumptious Bananas. Along with the recipes are illustrations and food facts that make this a good teaching tool for beginning cooks.

SPOTLIGHT ON READING

We Like to Write

If you have not already been having the students doing some writing on their own, now is a good time to begin. Students like to name and label things and now they are skilled in locating phrases, and can find sentences that have a complete meaning. Their verbal vocabulary is way ahead of their writing vocabulary, so here are some tools to help make the writing process manageable and enjoyable.

Start from an object, such as something that the student has created from clay, painting, or block construction. The student has experienced the making of this item and, therefore, will have some thoughts about it:

1. *Step One—Prewriting.* Ask students about their clay object or painting. Did it stem from an experience, or a story, or a visit they made recently? Is it their pet? Have them tell about the object in order to generate words and set the stage for writing.

2. *Step Two—The First Draft.* Have students print a complete sentence about the item. Tell something about its shape, size, color, or other characteristics, especially if it is a favored pet.

3. *Step Three—Revision.* Have students read their sentence aloud.

Checklist:
□ Prewriting
□ First Draft
□ Revision
□ Proofreading
□ Publish

Is there anything more to be said? Perhaps another descriptive word might help the reader to understand more about a pet or an event. This is the time to clarify and enrich the sentence.

4. *Step Four—Proofreading*. Have the students read the sentence silently, then aloud. Does it begin with a capital letter and end with a period or an exclamation mark? Are all of the words in order? Does it make sense to the reader?
5. *Step Five—Publishing*. Now is the time to take the sentence and either rewrite it or type it on the computer or have an adult aide or an older student assist with the final printing process. Then this sentence can be put with the object or printed on a sheet of paper. The student supplies the illustration. This is the final product.

Repeat the writing process with its five steps, and you will soon have students writing stories and making books on their own. They can add these books to a classroom library. If you have students who are having much difficulty with the writing process, refer to picture books that have only one or two descriptive words at the bottom, which may help them to begin. There are many excellent books by author/illustrator Nancy Tafuri, such as *Have You Seen My Duckling?; Do Not Disturb; Who's Counting?; Early Morning in the Barn;* and *Rabbit's Morning*. These books may help students form the visual/verbal union that is required to become an author/illustrator.

High Frequency Words

There are many words that fall into this category that are difficult for students. Refer to the Dolch list for a complete listing of the words. Some are: what, when, who, where, why, me, you, I if, then, so, up do, day, that, this, them, then.

Make flash-card strips. Print three high frequency words on very long flashcards. Say one word and ask a student to select the word that is being named by pointing to it. If the student points to the correct word, discuss it—such as beginning and ending sounds and any other clues. If the student points to the incorrect word, discuss it in the same manner and ask for another try.

Allow students to use these strips in their spare time, or during choice time as an activity that will help them to gain experience in word recognition for smoother reading. They need continual exposure to these words on a daily basis.

Word Detectives

Make a list of words and put them on the chalkboard or on a chart. Then say a sentence leaving out one of the words. Have students select the word that is printed on the chalkboard that makes sense in the sentence. Ask students how they discovered the word and let them tell in their own words about the beginning letter/sound or the ending letter/sound, and so on. Other students will learn from this, too.

Phonics Clusters

A "cluster" in this case is two words put together to make a sound, just like peanuts and chocolate go together to make "peanut clusters." What else go together to make a cluster? Have students use their imagination to come up with "cheeseburger cluster" (hamburger and melted cheese), "pizza cluster" (pizza with two toppings), and "caramel corn clusters" (caramel syrup and popcorn).

Students need to understand the meaning of "cluster" before they can grasp the idea that two letters cluster together to make sounds. Some of the high frequency clusters are "st," "sp," "pl," "pr," "tr," and "cl."

Begin by writing ST on the chalkboard or on a chart, and have students come up with words that begin with that sound. Some starters are:

stack	stood	stoop
stand	strange	struck
stick	starling	stop

Soon the chart paper will be covered with words. Do this for the other clusters. Have these clusters available for students to work with in their spare time or during free choice time.

Students can make cluster cards that have the two letters printed at the top and a listing of the word beneath.

Reteaching and Reviewing

Activities of this type need to be done on a daily basis. Students need review with quotation marks, exclamation marks, letter/sound relationships, alphabet review, exceptions to the rule, and so on.

Introduce a brand-new puppet to the classroom. This puppet just joined the group from a land far away and needs to be instructed in the most simple things that many first graders already know. You can begin to lead the instruction using the puppet, and ask students to take over. Workbooks that were used earlier, or a workbook from a different reading series, are an excellent way for students to work with the puppet. Pairing students carefully at this point will be helpful. Put the "teaching students" together with students who would benefit from the review along with the puppet. At this time of year, many students make

magnificent strides in reading. They need to hear the skill-building information all over again, and seem "ready" for it now.

Drop the Final "e" Before Adding "ed" and "ing"

Review this if it has not already been taught, and see if there are any exceptions to the rule for Love Bug's Word Treasure Chest. Some starter words are:

hope—hoping	bake—baking	come—coming
like—liked	place—placed	slice—sliced

Alligator, Ogre, Unicorn, and Love Bug Year-End Roundup

This is the perfect opportunity to let imaginations soar, and have students create members of the family for a year-end party. It can be a reading, writing, creative dramatics, and art festival all in one. You can take the whole language approach, and have fun and learn at the same time.

Alligator

Who is Mrs. Alligator? What will she wear to the festival? She has to go shopping for a new outfit, so we need to make alligator accessories (designer earrings, new shoes, stockings, a purse, rings, bracelets, etc.). Maybe this calls for an alligator catalog of "Gator Goods," complete with illustrations and prices.

What are the Alligators' first names? What is their complete address on Short Vowel Lane? What do they do all summer when school is not in session? Some students might be assigned to visit the Alligators' home and report about it inside and out. Some might be photographers who visit their home. Some might write about their visit with the Alligators. Of course, their home and furnishings and favorite foods and pastimes would be sprinkled with words that have an abundance of short vowel sounds.

The Ogre Is Looking for a Bride

June is the month of weddings, and the Ogre has decided to put an ad in the newspaper for a lovely ogress. Students can decide how to write the ad, what to put in it, and what to leave out. But first, they can use real newspaper ads to look through (and gain experience reading at the same time).

Perhaps students can team together to write ads that could be "placed" in different papers all over the country. Should the Ogre tell about himself? Or, should the Ogre tell what qualities he is looking for in a mate? Students can write the ads from different points of view, depending upon what they decide.

These ads can be hung on a bulletin board for students to read. Teams of students can answer the Ogre's ads, too, telling about themselves. There can be a regular correspondence set up within the classroom. Pictures can be drawn and painted and sent back and forth with the correspondence. Poetry might be written, too. For inspiration, these are two excellent books to read aloud to the students: Zerelda's Ogre by Tomi Ungerer, and *Helga's Dowry, a Troll Love Story* by Tomie dePaola.

This topic affords many opportunities for reading, writing, speaking, listening, visual art, and creative dramatics. Students can be at-the-scene reporters as the Ogre returns from fishing in his Long Vowel Woods. They can give a TV update for the 6 o'clock news.

Will the Ogre find a June bride? Remember, he's fussy. Will the spider that dangles from his hat have anything to do with this decision? Will this pet spider detect the "frauds" who answer the ads? It will be entirely up to the students as to whether or not they come up with a good candidate. Will they have a face-to-face meeting or a telephone conversation? Will there be a class wedding, with announcements and refreshments, and a dress-up day? Only the students (and you) will be able to decide. Remember, all of this can be done and, at the last minute, the wedding called off—but students could celebrate anyway. That leaves the class trying to decide if the Ogre should wait or start his ad campaign all over again!

The Unicorn Is Single

The Unicorn plans to remain single! The Unicorn rides over hill and dale, delivering mail to everyone. There are so many friends, so many activities, so much to do that the Unicorn decided long ago that his life was happy just the way it was. One thing to know, though, is that the Unicorn writes poetry and loves to listen to poetry. Get an assortment of poetry books from the library and read and memorize some for the Unicorn.

Now, that's something that would make the Unicorn very happy! If you have not already done so, read *The Jolly Postman* by Janet and Allan Ahlberg to the class. This will generate many ideas for writing. Each student can choose to be a storybook character, and each student's character can write to another student's character. This will promote much writing activity. (Be sure to refer to the writing process described at the beginning of this section.)

Actually, unicorns are mythical figures. Your class has been fortunate to know a unicorn this year. Unicorns have been immortalized in beautiful artwork, and woven into tapestries over the centuries. Secure art history picture books from the library, and have students search through them for pictures of the unicorn. What will they name theirs?

A Whole Language Approach to Love Bug

Use the opaque projector to make a giant Love Bug shape on butcher paper, paint it, and cut it out. This shape can be doubled and stapled and stuffed for a giant Love Bug to have in the classroom. (It could also be made from real material, with accessories glued onto the fabric and could be in charge of a cozy reading corner.)

Love Bug can listen to students read; he never tires of this. Love Bug can set up an author/illustrator corner for student work, with a special desk and a lamp, and unique writing supplies. Love Bug can write a note home asking for a typewriter to be donated to the classroom to help with the students' writing skills. Love Bug can bring in an author/illustrator-of-the-week book series for students to enjoy. Some excellent ones are:

Eric Carle—*The Grouchy Ladybug; The Very Busy Spider; The Mountain That Loved a Bird* (illustrator); *1, 2, 3 to the Zoo;* and *The Very Hungry Caterpillar*

Donald Crews—*We Read A to Z; Truck; Freight Train; School Bus;* and *Parade*

Ruth Heller—*Chickens Aren't the Only Ones; The Reason for a Flower; Plants That Never Ever Bloom; Animals Born Alive and Well*

Brian Wildsmith—*Python's Party; Goat's Trail; Pelican; Squirrels; The Little Wood Duck;* and others

SPOTLIGHT ON MATH

Problem Solving

Have a "problem of the day" that students need to focus upon. When they think they have the solution, have them put the answer on a slip of paper and insert it into a special place that has been designated, such as a shoebox. The problem can be written on the chalkboard with different colors of chalk for variety. It can be in a picture form, too, such as a rebus. Some suggested problems are:

Write the members of the "8 Family."

Who is wearing an outfit with straight lines?

Who is wearing an outfit with wavy lines?

Can you solve the puzzle in Section D, Page 4 of today's newspaper?

Conduct a survey of ____ and graph it.

Walk the Number Line for Subtraction

Laminate a huge number line, and tape it to the floor across the entire back of the room. For the number sentence "11 − 3 = ____," for example, have students walk the line to the LARGER NUMERAL FIRST, then back-track three spaces (10, 9, 8) in order to land on the correct space. This is a kinesthetic approach to subtraction, and may be helpful for some learners. Have a flash-card set for students to "act out."

Using Numbers Through 99

- Students need to be familiar with numbers from 1 to 100. Make two large floor grids using oilcloth. Tape one grid to the floor. On the other grid, print the numerals from 1 to 100. Then cut them up in groups of four and five, and challenge students to place them on top of the floor grid. This may make it easier for some students to put the grid back together again.

- Use water-base markers and have students fill in the number grid. This can be easily wiped off for the next student.

- Another idea is to work in groups of ten, with one line at a time. On each line, you can put a specific numeral in the beginning square and one or two more on each line. For example:

20 __ __ 23 __ __ __ __ __ __

60 61 __ __ __ __ __ 67 __ __

40 __ __ __ __ __ __ __ 48 49

10 __ __ __ 14 __ __ __ __ __

Students are then really concentrating on the numbers themselves and not relying on rote memory.

Down on the Farm for a Review of "in, out, over, under, up, down"

Have students make a model of a farm using building blocks, and commercial materials for constructing barns, houses, trees, and so on. Students can also bring in their toy animals, or can use plasticene to make animals for the farm. Then they can follow directions that are written on a card (or that someone can read to them). The directions might include the following:

Put the chicken IN the barn.

Put a bird ON the roof.

The cat just came OUT of the house.

The ducks are UNDER the bush.

Students can make up more directions. They can also construct a zoo and mold exotic animals from plasticene and put them in a variety of places.

- For variation, a student can follow directions by taking an animal, molded from plasticene, on a trip through the zoo that has been set up. The student can be given a map of the zoo that follows the construction plan. This is a good way to move the animal through the zoo maze, and also to follow along with pencil and paper at the same time. This is a union of a visual and kinesthetic learning experience, and may help some students make sense of the concepts.

Anytime Is Pizza Time

Pizza has been rated as one of the all-time popular foods with children. If you can plan a pizza lunch (have it delivered), it is a good way to review fractions.

- Another idea is to have students make mini-pizzas, using the following recipe:

  > 1 English muffin cut in half lengthwise.
  > Spread 1 tbsp. pizza sauce on each half.
  > Sprinkle with grated cheese.
  > Put ___ pieces of pepperoni on each half.

  An adult then places the mini-pizzas in a toaster oven (or microwave oven) and warms them. Students can use plastic knives to cut their two halves in half, to make four quarters.

- Suggestion: This "Pizza for Lunch with Teacher" can be used as a bonus at the end of the week for three or four students at a time. It is a good opportunity to share some time with a few students while the others are elsewhere, knowing that their turn will come. It's a special treat that they won't forget—and maybe they'll learn something about fractions, too.

Jump-Counting by Fives

Have students count by five to 100. In order that students can "jump in" at any place and finish the count, do the following:

jump in at 35 and count by fives to 100

jump in at 80 and count by fives to 100

jump in at 55 and count by fives to 100

If students can do this while jumping rope, it seems to make good sense to them. If they cannot, use flash-cards and have them turn the cards over and begin at the number they turned up.

Probability with Marbles

Use two blue marbles (bluejays) and one red marble (cardinal). Put them inside a little drawstring pouch. Have students reach in and, without looking, select one marble. Is it a cardinal or a bluejay? Record it. Return it to the pouch. Shake the pouch. Select again without looking. Do this ten times. How many times did they pick a red one (cardinal)? Add them. The PROBABILITY of selecting the bluejay more times is twice as great, since there are twice as many blue marbles as red ones.

This is an exercise with DISCRETE probability. That is, each time a student reaches into the pouch, that action is unrelated to the time before. Each draw is separate and distinct. In other words, because the blue marble was picked four times in a row, it does not mean that now "it is the red's turn." Each draw is separate and does not depend upon the draw made previously. Some first graders are ready for this concept.

Is Weight Related to Size?

No, it varies. A pound of sugar is in a small box, and a pound of styrofoam peanut packing takes up a great big box. Bring in a great big box and have students fill it with packing material to make the point. Have students be on the lookout for items that are SMALL AND HEAVY and BIG AND LIGHT. For starters, small and heavy can include magnets and a golf ball. Big and light can include a kite and a beach ball. This exercise helps students who are attending only to size when it comes to the concept of weight. Be sure to have a scale available for verification.

Going from Horizontal to Vertical

This is a difficult visual concept for some students. For example, the following two problems look very different:

$$23 + 16 = 39 \qquad \begin{array}{r} 23 \\ +16 \\ \hline 39 \end{array}$$

One way to translate this number statement from horizontal to vertical is to put a ring around all of the ONES, and make sure they are in the same column when written vertically. A square can be placed around all the TENS, and students can make sure they are in the same column. Give students plenty of practice at the chalkboard with this concept because they need to be familiar with both horizontal and vertical representations.

Also, putting these numerals and signs on transparencies for use with the overhead projector enables you to move the numerals from the horizontal to vertical position, thus modeling the process. Students can be given a chance to do this as well.

Make a Game of It

There is an abundance of commercial material that pertains to math games. Have a shelf of math games in your classroom. Parents are often willing to donate the games. Games appeal to students because of the following:

the element of chance (the best doesn't always win)

opportunity to practice or develop skills while having fun

promotes competition with oneself

enables students to develop strategies

they are short

In reading, teachers give 20 minutes for sustained silent reading and note student progress. The same principle applies with math. How about giving 20 minutes, two or three times per week, for Sustained Uninterrupted Math Activities (SUMA), either working singly or with a partner. The same rules apply: keep it quiet, and stay with the game or activity you've chosen. Students benefit from this time, and it gives the student who doesn't finish work on time daily and who never gets to these activities, an opportunity to do so. Students enjoy this self-directed quiet time, and they're learning. If you get a rained-out recess period, turn it into indoor-math-game time and, before you know it, students are engrossed in their activities and don't want to give them up when time is called. (Remind them of this when they "groan" because they probably "groaned" too when they learned that there was no outdoor recess that day!)

Some teachers have solved this by having as a class rule: NO GROANING ALLOWED. In other words, learn to take things in stride. Shaping attitudes is just as much a part of the math instruction time as it is at any other time of day.

A Resource at Your Fingertips

Take advantage of the Teacher's Edition of your math textbook. It's filled with an abundance of ideas for teaching the concepts and skills at this grade level. There are many ideas for enrichment, challenge, reinforcement, reteaching, skill building, and so on. It's right at your fingertips.

Without Math, We're Sunk

Make up a bulletin board with that caption. Make a construction paper cut-out of a fisherman, with a glossy yellow slicker and hat, holding a stick from which a string and magnet are dangling. At the bottom, put cut-outs of items that are "sunk" or not attracted by the magnet.

In the middle of the display, list all of the ways that we use math in our daily lives. Students are amazed when it is pointed out to them that we are extremely dependent upon math. Some starters are:

We use math when . . .

. . . we set our alarm clock

. . . we catch the school bus (time)

. . . we take lunch count

. . . we know when to go to special classes

. . . we know how much food to give a pet

. . . we count out money when we buy a present

. . . we figure out how much groceries will cost

. . . we find out how long it takes to roast a turkey

. . . we look in the newspaper for the time of our favorite TV show

. . . we turn to the numeral on the TV channel or radio dial

. . . we get the right-sized shoes

. . . we get the correct-sized clothes

. . . we buy two boots instead of walking out of the store with just one

. . . we know when to go to bed

. . . we dial the telephone

.. we set the VCR to record a TV program

... we know the month, day, date, and year

... we can say the number that represents how old we are

... we make a cake "from scratch"

... we keep score in a game

This can go on and on. So let it, so that students gain an appreciation of math and that we are doing math now!

- Put up a Number Detective Chart. When students "catch themselves DOING MATH NOW," they can print it on the detective chart. They will be amazed. (They are using math when turning to a page in a book, reading *x* number of pages, finding a room number in school, doing *x* number of math problems, writing spelling words *x* times, and so on.) Make a game of it. But also make students aware that math is an EN-ABLER—it adds organization and order to our world.

Math Is Caught and Taught

Above all, as the first grade teacher, leave children with a sense of wonder and appreciation for math. This is a cornerstone grade, and children need to have a good feeling about their math ability.

Bring in at least ten number books from the library that authors and illustrators have made delightful for students, and let the children enjoy these books and then create their own wonderful number books.

Some book suggestions are: *The Very Hungry Caterpillar* by Eric Carle; *1, 2, 3 to the Zoo* by Eric Carle; *Circles, Triangles and Squares* by Tana Hoban; *Big Ones, Little Ones* by Tana Hoban; *Anno's Counting Book* by Mitsumasa Anno; *An Invitation to the Butterfly Ball, A Counting Rhyme* by Jane Yolen; *Odd One Out* by Rodney Peppe; *1 is One* by Tasha Tudor; *One Was Johnny, A Counting Book* by Maurice Sendak; *Moja Means One, A Swahili Counting Book* by Muriel and Tom Feelings; *Bicycle Race* by Donald Crews; *Pease-Porridge Hot, A Mother Goose Cookbook* by Lorinda Bryan Cauley; and *Numbers* by John Reiss. These are just a few. There are many more delightful number books on the market today. Share them with your students!

Math Shape

For the end of the year, do a variation on the word "shape." You can do the following:

- have the students walk a shape (see the reproducible activity pages)
- identify shape patterns by touch
- form shape patterns in the air
- play "I'm Thinking of a Shape." Examples might be: a shape that rolls, a shape that has three points, a shape with four edges, the same shape as the flag, the same shape as a ball, the same shape as a telephone pole.
- make shape booklets
- go on shape hunts in magazines
- play Shape Bingo

HANDS-ON SCIENCE

Every plant has a name, and there are over hundreds of thousands (350,000) of plants on record. The tree is the biggest plant. People who study plants are called *biologists*. A seed becomes a plant when the seed coating bursts open and the green seedling is visible. Seeds hold a certain fascination for young children.

What's Inside a Seed?

A tiny plant is inside each fertile seed. Plant a variety of seeds (pea, marigolds, lima bean, popcorn, zinnia, pumpkin, hollyhock) in styrofoam cups that you place along the window ledge. Place several seeds inside each cup and label them. Children enjoy assisting in the planting of seeds. They can also take care of the seeds by seeing that the soil does not dry out. It is a joyful occasion when the seeds sprout!

When Seeds Sprout

Have students keep track of the daily growth by using a ruler to measure the seedling. They can make a diagram and use pencils and crayons to show the daily growth.

It is important that students learn that growing things takes time. A rose doesn't become a rose overnight! It is a long process. Some educators, such as Maria Montessori, believed that when young children tend to growing things, it helps them learn patience. They must learn to wait; there is no hurrying a plant.

Seed Classification

Secure a variety of seeds from a garden shop, and also have students bring them in. Classify them in muffin tins and egg cartons. Compare colors, size, and shape of seeds. Students can also remove one of each seed from the muffin tin and classify them from largest to smallest, from darkest to lightest, and so on.

Seeds Contain Stored-Up Food

Let's eat! Rather than plant some seeds in the ground, people eat them. Bread, muffins, and cakes are made from wheat and corn that have been ground or mashed to make flour or meal. This is a good opportunity to bake bread, muffins, cookies, or cake with students. It gives them experience with liquid and dry measures, and time and temperature. They can sprinkle poppy seeds or sesame seeds on top of their muffins, too.

Plant an Herb Garden

The Pilgrims relied upon herbs to give variety to their soups, stews, and salads. Plant some herb seeds (available in packets at garden stores) in cardboard milk containers. Some hardy ones are parsley, sage, winter savory, and basil. Have students note the differences in leaf design. From your local historical society, you may be able to get recipes that use the herbs. Send a container of herbs home, with pretty construction paper wrapped around it, and a pink ribbon for a Mother's Day remembrance. Tuck a recipe that calls for the herb inside the container. Herbs usually flourish indoors on a sunny windowsill.

A Sprouting Garden on a Sponge

Use an aluminum pie plate half filled with water, and place a sponge in the middle. Sprinkle seeds (bird seed, too) on the wet sponge and watch them sprout. Examine the seed parts with a magnifying glass. Can students find the cells? Try looking at a seedling through a microscope. Now can students find the cells?

HELP PROTECT THE ENVIRONMENT

It's not too late for spring cleaning. Go on an Ecology Walk around the playground with a huge plastic bag, and two or three sets of garden gloves. Students can help clean up the environment by taking turns wearing the gloves and placing things in the bag (except for glass) that have been discarded by people. Students will be amazed at the collection of cans, papers, little bags, and so on, that we refer to as "litter." Tie the plastic refuse bag securely, and seek assistance from the custodian regarding its disposal. (Be sure to keep in mind any local recycling regulations in effect.) Perhaps it could be weighed first to determine how many pounds of litter the students collected.

- Have students write an experience story about their Ecology Walk.
- Have students make badges or posters that encourage others to keep their environment clean.
- Encourage students to write letters (get approval from the principal) to a city or town official, asking what measures are being taken to help keep the area clean from litter. (Students will find out that in many cases it is "against the law" to throw items from a moving car, or to throw wrappers into the street, and that they can be fined for doing so.)
- Start a school campaign against clogging up the environment through carelessness. Ask for "air time" on the school public address system so that students can make their opinions known.

The Butterfly

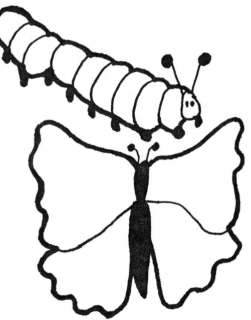

Metamorphosis is a new vocabulary word for students. This is the name given to the process (or stages) of going from egg to butterfly. Explain that there are four stages to becoming a butterfly: egg, caterpillar, pupa, and butterfly.

1. *Egg*—This is laid on the leaf that it will eat. The egg hatches and the caterpillar immediately begins to eat the plant that it lives on and the plants nearby.
2. *Caterpillar*—This creature eats and eats. It gets too big for its skin, and the skin bursts open and the caterpillar keeps on eating until it bursts again. This happens four or five times during the caterpillar cycle. (People are fortunate that as they grow, their skin stretches and doesn't burst open!)

3. *Pupa*—One day the caterpillar stops eating. It attaches itself to a leaf and spins a cocoon around itself. This turns brown and looks very much like a dead plant. But, inside, it is growing wings and six legs.

4. *Butterfly*—The pupa bursts open and the butterfly comes forth, dries its wings to make them strong, and then flies away.

- Do the butterfly dance. Students can use creative dramatics to simulate the egg (curled up into a ball), the caterpillar (crawling and chewing), the pupa (stop chewing and curl up again under cover), the butterfly (burst out of the cocoon cover, dry off wings, and use arms to flutter around the room in a dance). This can be choreographed to music that other students create, using rhythm band instruments.

- Make a booklet of the four stages. Use cut-outs of cloth material that are appropriate for each stage. Also see the reproducible activity pages.

Down on the Farm with Alligator and Ogre

Since we are nearing the end of first grade, the Alligator and Ogre do not want us to forget the long and short vowel sounds, so they got together and wrote a song to the tune of "Old MacDonald Had a Farm." They hope students will learn it with the accompanying motions. (It could go with the wedding celebration that is referred to under this month's reading section.) It goes like this:

"Alligator Farm" (short vowel sounds)

make fingers crawl over body

Alligator had a farm, ah, eh, ih, aah, uh.
And on this farm he had some ants, ah, eh,
   ih, aah, uh.
With an ant, ant here and an ant, ant there
Here an ant, there an ant, everywhere an ant, ant.
Alligator had a farm, ah, eh, ih, aah, uh.

clasp hands together and swing arms as "trunks"

Alligator had a farm, ah, eh, ih, aah, uh.
And on this farm he had some elephants, ah, eh,
   ih, aah, uh.
With an elephant here and an elephant there
Here an elephant, there an elephant, everywhere
   an elephant.
Alligator had a farm, ah, eh, ih, aah, uh.

gently rub eyes, ears, elbows, ankles

Alligator had a farm, ah, eh, ih, aah, uh.
And on this farm he had an itch, ah, eh,
   ih, aah, uh.
With an itch, itch here and an itch, itch there
Here an itch, there an itch, everywhere an itch,
   itch.
Alligator had a farm, ah, eh, ih, aah, uh.

entangle arms around body

Alligator had a farm, ah, eh, ih, aah, uh.
And on this farm he had an octopus, ah, eh, ih,
    aah, uh.
With an octopus here and an octopus there
Here an octopus, there an octopus, everywhere
    an octopus.
Alligator had a farm, ah, eh, ih, aah, uh.

make hand motions going under arms, elbows, feet

Alligator had a farm, ah, eh, ih, aah, uh.
And on this farm he had an underground, ah, eh,
    ih, aah, uh.
With an underground here and an underground
    there
Here an under, there an under, everywhere an
    underground.
Alligator had a farm, ah, eh, ih, aah, uh.

sway body from side to side

Oh . . . we love to visit Alligator, ah, eh, ih,
    aah, uh.
His old farm is one big crater, ah, eh, ih,
    aah, uh.
With an ah, ah here and an eh, eh there
Here an ih, there an aah, everywhere an uh, uh.
Alligator had a farm (slowly) ah, eh, ih, aah, uh!

"Ogre's Farm" *(long vowel sounds)*

pretend to pick acorns from a tree and the ground

Ogre, Ogre had a farm, a, e, i, o, u.
And on this farm he had some acorns, a, e, i, o, u.
With an acorn here and an acorn there
Here an acorn, there an acorn, everywhere an acorn,
    acorn.
Ogre, Ogre had a farm, a, e, i, o, u.

flap arms, and bend and soar as if flying

Ogre, Ogre had a farm, a, e, i, o, u.
And on this farm he had some eagles, a, e, i, o, u.
With an eagle here and an eagle there
Here an eagle, there an eagle, everywhere an
    eagle, eagle.
Ogre, Ogre had a farm, a, e, i, o, u.

begin in crouched position, then grow upward

Ogre, Ogre had a farm, a, e, i, o, u.
And on this farm he had some ivy, a, e, i, o, u.
With an ivy here and an ivy there
Here an ivy, there an ivy, everywhere an ivy,
    ivy.
Ogre, Ogre had a farm, a, e, i, o, u.

rock back and forth as if riding the waves

Ogre, Ogre had a farm, a, e, i, o, u.
And on this farm he had an ocean, a, e, i, o, u.
With an ocean here and an ocean there
Here an ocean, there an ocean, everywhere an
    ocean, ocean.
Ogre, Ogre had a farm, a, e, i, o, u.

gallop in place as if riding the unicorn

Ogre, Ogre had a farm, a, e, i, o, u.
And on this farm he had a unicorn, a, e, i, o, u.
With a unicorn here and a unicorn there
Here a unicorn, there a unicorn, everywhere a
    unicorn, unicorn.
Ogre, Ogre had a farm, a, e, i, o, u.

sway body from side to side

Oh . . . Ogre, Ogre had a farm, a, e, i, o, u.
And on this farm he had some vowels, a, e, i, o, u.
With an a, a here and an e, e there
Here an i, there an o, everywhere a u, u.
Ogre, Ogre had a farm (slowly) a, e, i, o, u.

A variation of the song would be to name creatures or objects that do not begin with the long or short vowel sounds, but have them within the word. For example:

for alligator (short vowel sounds)

> short a—bats, cats, rags, hags, fan, man
>
> short e—jell, hen, pen, pegs
>
> short i—fish, dish, pick, mittens
>
> short o—frog, mom, pompons
>
> short u—slugs, bugs, mugs, mutts, huts

for ogre (long vowel sounds)

long a—cape, tape, paste, rake

long e—peach, seal, treat, leaves, seed, weed

long i—kite, pipe, bike, light

long o—boat, moat, snow, coats

long u—bugle, cucumber, cube, music

A Closer Look at the Teamwork of Ants

Most people do not like to have ants invade their picnic territory. Perhaps, though, as we are having our spring and summer picnics, we are invading the space of the ants! Here are some facts about ants that everyone should be aware of:

- Ants are social insects and live in groups.
- Ants build cities underground, complete with streets and storage areas.
- Ants have special "rooms" in which to live.
- Ants have special jobs in their community, such as being farmers and hunters.

Be sure to read aloud to the students the delightful book *Do Not Disturb* by Nancy Tafuri.

HANDWRITING SAMPLES

Last September, the students wrote (as best they could) their names on a piece of paper. Hopefully, each month they have been writing their name on that same sheet of paper. If not, it's time to take out the sheet that was put away in September. Have students carefully print their name on a new sheet of paper and attach the two sheets. The writing growth that they have made, as they have become better able to control the small muscles of the hand, is amazing. Parents appreciate having this record from school; it can be sent home as a "present."

MAY DAY

The first of May is a traditional spring festival, and it is often celebrated by dancing around a Maypole. Borrow a giant-sized pole that the gym teacher uses to help hold up volleyball nets, and put crepe-paper streamers around the top. Then have students dance around the pole, winding the paper in an under, over, under, over pattern. When finished, have them dance in the other direction and unwind the streamers. Begin again with a second set of student celebrants, while the rest of the students clap in time to the music.

Traditionally, there is a crowning of a May Queen. There can also be a King and other members of the court. Everyone can be "crowned" (make construction paper crowns) and be King and Queen for the day.

FLAG DAY

Flag Day is June 14, and is in celebration of the day when the United States adopted the flag. Students can make American flags by using a 12″ × 18″ sheet of construction paper, red stripes, and a blue field with stars put on with white chalk dipped in water. This can be stapled to a sturdy cardboard strip. Have a parade in the classroom, down the hall, out the door, around the playground, and back inside. Don't forget to make the pointed hats from newspaper.

MOTHER'S DAY AND FATHER'S DAY

Be sure to make special cards for these special days. (Keep in mind that you must be sensitive to students' particular family-life situations, such as single-parent homes.) Students can learn a poem to recite, practice reading a story, or practice doing a magic trick, and then perform it for their parent on the special day. Remember the herb garden plant for the windowsill for mom (or dad).

Use a special coupon that entitles the giver to fill in the blank. Such things as hugs, kisses, helping with the dishes, helping with yard work, cleaning up one's room, and so on, can be filled in by each student. Remind students to be "true to their word" and carry out the promise. (See the reproducible activity pages.)

THE CLASSROOM AUCTION

Instead of disposing of reading charts, math charts, murals, and so on, have students take a number from 1 through 100. The student who gets closest to the number wins the item to take home. It encourages "playing school" during the summer months. Do this daily during the last week of school. Auction off extra packets of reproducible activity pages, too.

HELPING WITH THE INVENTORY

First graders are excellent at helping with the counting of the rulers, scissors, books, workbooks, and other materials that need to be accounted for at the end of the school year.

SPRING AND SUMMER SAFETY

Caution students that drivers of cars, buses, and trucks are not used to seeing little children on the sidewalks and along the street because during the long winter months, many hours were spent indoors.

Safety First

- Make sure that the students understand to look to the LEFT (this way) and to the RIGHT (that way) before crossing the street. Have students practice this in the classroom with chairs lined up to simulate a street. Simulate crossing the street on green or "walk" only; simulate waiting patiently for an EXTRA LONG light instead of darting out into the street; simulate walking to the corner to cross the street rather than going in between parked cars, and so on.

- Review water safety rules with students. Caution them to never go swimming alone; to never jump into a stream of water (either feet first or head first) when they don't know how deep it is; remind students to wear "water wings" when boating or in swimming pools. Other safety rules are usually printed in the newspaper at this time of year. Read them aloud to students, and post them, or make a copy to send home to each parent.

REMEMBER THE PARENT ASSISTANT, THE AIDE, AND OTHER HELPERS

Have students make a booklet for each classroom helper you've had during the school year. Review all of the nice things they (or a parent committee) did for the class. Assign students to draw pictures of certain holiday parties and classroom trips. Have students carefully print a thank-you sentence along the bottom. Compile these into a book and give them to the class helpers at the end of the school year.

A variation of this is to make the booklet using mimeograph paper and black felt-tip pen. Reproduce the pages so that everyone has a copy of this special booklet. The students enjoy coloring the pages, too.

KEEP LEARNING ALIVE ALL SUMMER

Send home summer learning packets with the students so that they will be able to keep learning "alive." These packets can include: writing paper; reproducible activity pages from this book in reading and math; directions for making books; a July Learning List for the refrigerator (see the reproducible activity pages); and an August Learning List for the refrigerator (see the reproducible activity pages).

SHOW TIME

Play back any videotapes made of the class during the year, or have a 35mm slide show that chronicles the events of the year. Invite parents to participate, and serve lemonade and cookies.

NAMES, NUMBERS, ADDRESSES

Check with parents to see if they approve a class list to be distributed among the students. Many of the students will get together during the summer, or write to each other, or telephone each other. This helps to cement friendships, and to keep learning links alive during the summer months.

CELEBRATE SUMMER BIRTHDAYS

Some students do not get the opportunity to celebrate their birthday during the school year, or to hear the entire class singing "Happy Birthday" to them, so set aside an afternoon during the last week of school to celebrate the summer birthdays (and summer holidays). Have a talent show during this time, arranged and directed by students.

Reproducible Activity Pages for May/June

Author Checklist (five steps for writing)

Cluster Bubbles (working with st, pl, sp, fl, cr)

Let's Read Labels (using food cans and boxes for reading)

Write a Want Ad for a Lost Pet (writing; critical thinking)

Who's on the Farm? (reading and following directions)

Walk a Shape (body movement; math)

Merry, Merry Month of Math (calendar of activities)

My Favorite Number (writing a story)

Tens and Ones Grapes (working with tens and ones; odd and even)

Read an Ice Cream Cone Graph (reading information)

Plan Your Own Number Book (designing and making a book)

Special Delivery from Duke the Dog (positive reinforcement)

The Butterfly Story (stages of butterfly development)

The Butterfly Story (butterfly shape)

Red, White, and Bloom (Memorial Day flowers)

Promise Coupons (Mother's Day; Father's Day)

Bev's Blue Ribbon Winner (favorite book award)

Ocean Pollution Patrol (ecology awareness)

The July Activity Frog (25 activities for July)

The August Busy Bear (25 activities for August)

Name _____

Date _____

AUTHOR CHECKLIST

Put an X in each box as you go through this five-step process.

1. [ ] **Prewriting**

What will I write about? A picture I painted, a trip I went on, my pet, or something else? Will I draw pictures to go along with the story?

2. [ ] **First Draft**

This is what I want to let the reader know.

3. [ ] **Revise**

Maybe I should add more information here, and use another word there.

4. [ ] **Proofread**

Did I begin each sentence with a capital letter? Do I need to check any words for spelling? Maybe I will read it to someone else to see if he or she understands what I am trying to say.

5. [ ] **Publish**

It's fine! Now I can carefully print it or type it.

CLUSTER BUBBLES

Today, the fish are blowing cluster bubbles. You can help by printing two words inside each bubble that begin with that cluster of letters.

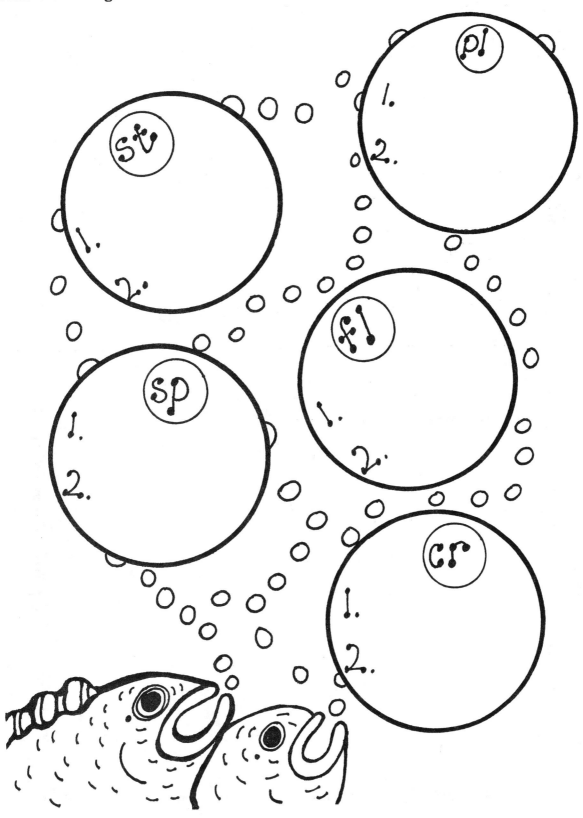

Name ——————

Date ——————

LET'S READ LABELS

    Look at a can of soup. How many words can you read that are printed on the label? Write them on the can. Look at a box of cereal or cake mix. How many words can you read on the label? Write them on the box.

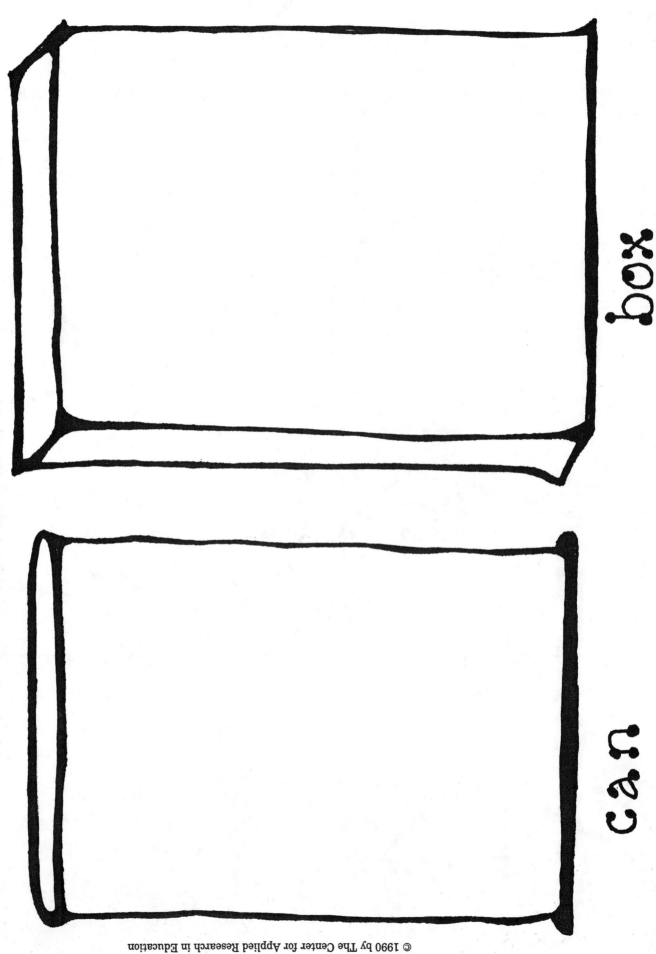

box

can

WRITE A WANT AD FOR A LOST PET

What do you need to include in a Want Ad? What do you need to leave out? Read some real Want Ads in the newspaper. Then write your ad for a lost pet.

HOW MUCH DOES IT COST TO PLACE AN AD IN THE PAPER? For this ad, it is a penny for each letter. Count the letters. How much does your ad cost?

WHO'S ON THE FARM?

How well can you follow directions? Let's find out. Do the following:

Put a bird nest in the tree.
Put a squirrel in the tree hole.
Make a cat at the bottom of the tree.
Put water in the pond.
Draw two ducks swimming in the pond.

Paint the barn red.
Draw a horse looking out the barn door.
Draw five tulips growing by the barn.
Put yourself in the picture.
Make the grass look healthy.

WALK A SHAPE

There are nine different shapes below. Using a crayon, start at the spot marked X and trace the shapes. Then start at the spot marked X in your classroom, or on the playground, and WALK each shape.

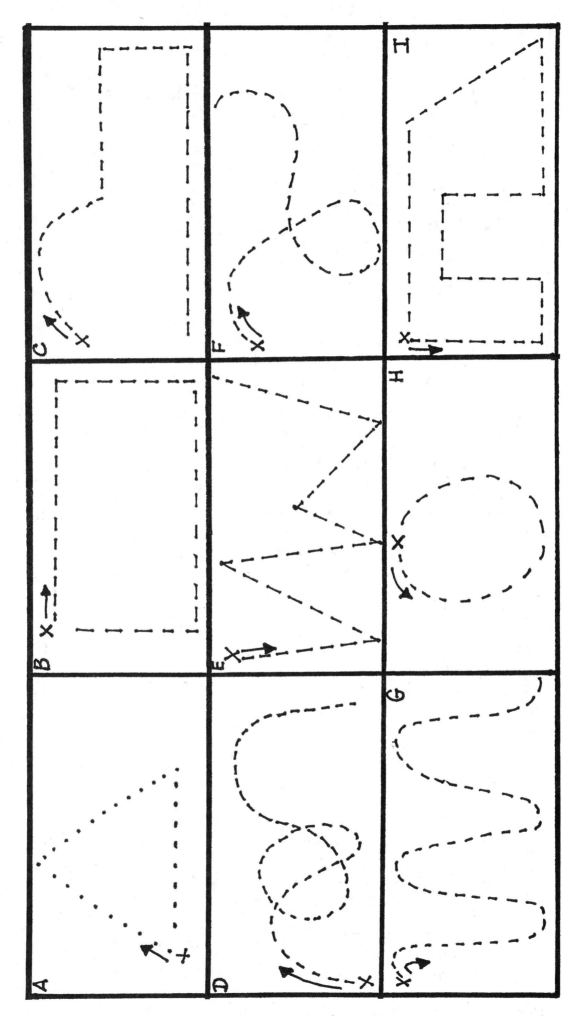

MERRY, MERRY MONTH OF MATH

Use the shapes below to fill in the calendar space on the days when you use that math category:

My Favorite Number
by

The number that I like best is not just any old number. My number is special because...

TENS AND ONES GRAPES

Count the grapes, and match the tens and ones grapes with the correct numeral.
Then, color PURPLE all of the even totals of grapes, and color BRIGHT GREEN all of
the ODD totals of grapes. How many odd and how many even numbers do you have?

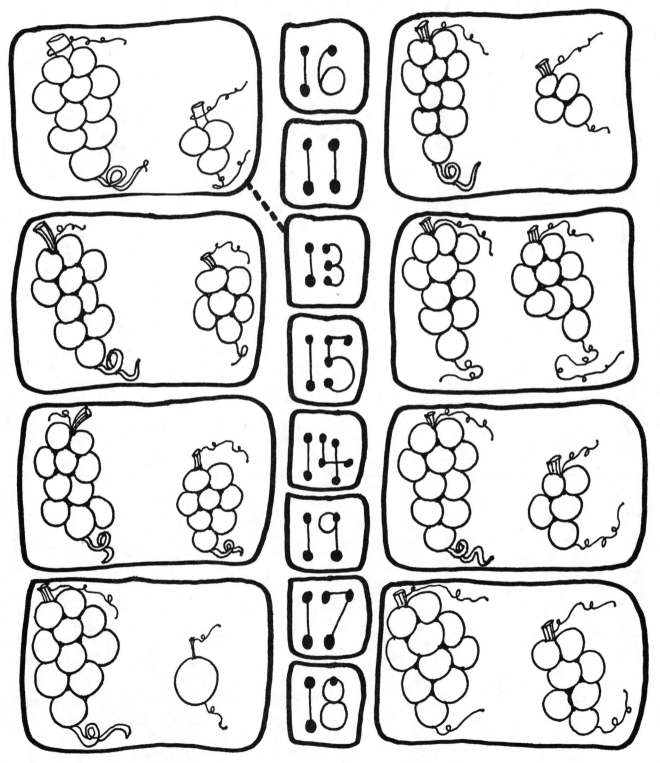

Name _____   Date _____

READ AN ICE CREAM CONE GRAPH

There are three different flavors here. When each person was asked, "Which do you like best—strawberry swirl, chocolate chip, or lemon lime?" their answer was "recorded" by adding another scoop of their favorite flavor. You can read the graph below by counting the following information and writing it in the space provided. Then color the cones and ice cream so they look scrumptious!

1. How many liked strawberry swirl? _____
2. How many liked chocolate chip? _____
3. How many liked lemon lime? _____
4. How many people were asked? _____ + _____ + _____ = _____

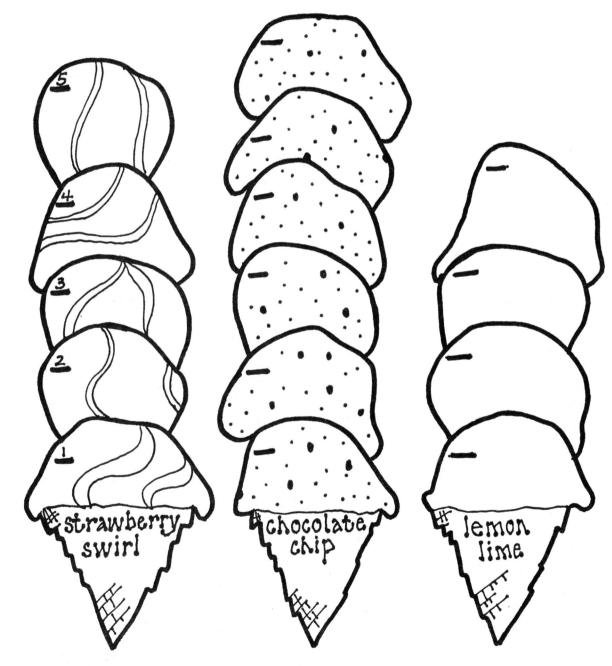

Plan Your Own Number Book

1. Look through many, many number books for ideas before you plan your original book.

2. Where will the numerals appear on each page? Top, bottom, left, right?

3. Will your book have a theme, such as food, sports, flowers?

4. How large will the book be?

5. What media will you use for illustrations?

6. How will you bind the book together?

7. Where will you keep it?

Title:

Author:

Plan for cover design

Plan for Page One

Plan for Page Two

Plan for Page Three

Plan for Page Four

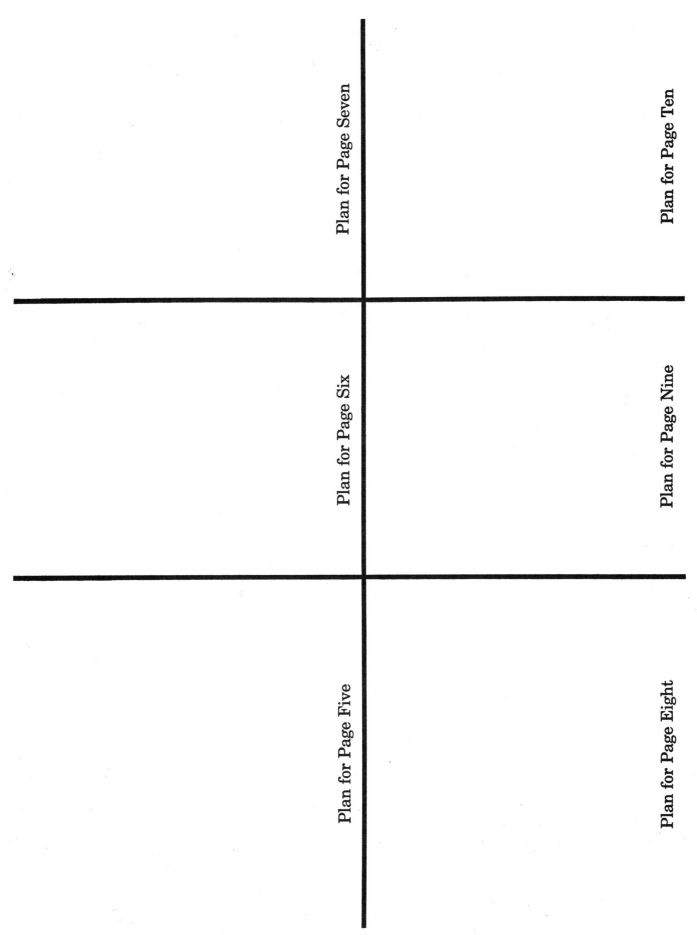

Plan for Page Seven

Plan for Page Ten

Plan for Page Six

Plan for Page Nine

Plan for Page Five

Plan for Page Eight

SPECIAL DELIVERY FROM DUKE THE DOG

Duke grows tulips in the garden. Today, Duke is delivering flowers to YOU and the reason is printed on the card. You can color Duke to show us what he looks like.

Deliver to
_____
_____

For

THE BUTTERFLY STORY

There are four stages to becoming a butterfly. Color the items below. Then, cut out the four circles, and paste them onto the butterfly shape page. Be sure to paste each circle in the correct location, beginning with the eggs. Then, with your crayons, make a beautiful butterfly.

THE BUTTERFLY STORY

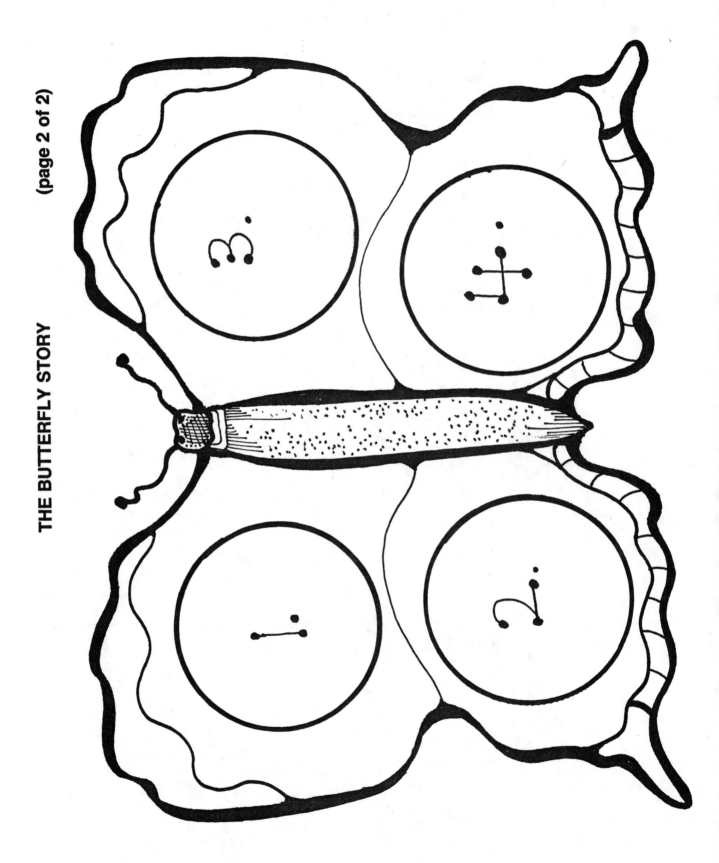

Name _____   Date _____

RED, WHITE, AND BLOOM

Make this vase of flowers look patriotic by coloring the flowers, red, white, and blue. On Memorial Day, give thanks for your freedoms.

I promise...

Happy Mother's Day!

Happy Father's Day

Name _____

Date _____

BEV'S BLUE RIBBON WINNER

Bev is wearing a big blue ribbon for her favorite book. Do you have a favorite book?
Fill in the information below.

TITLE _____

AUTHOR _____

ILLUSTRATOR _____

THIS BOOK IS MY "BLUE RIBBON WINNER"
BECAUSE _____

OCEAN POLLUTION PATROL

"Who wants garbage for lunch?" roared the ocean. "Not me," cried the dolphin. "Not me," cried the turtle. "Not me," cried the crocodile.

"Then we will just send it back where it came from," roared the ocean. So they sent it back to shore.

What can YOU do to fight ocean pollution? Write your story about ocean pollution on the back of this sheet, and illustrate it.

THE JULY ACTIVITY FROG

This frog has 25 activities for you to do during the month of July. Do one a day, Monday through Friday. Color the box when you finish the activity.

Set up a Word Bank Box, for: WORDS I KNOW— WORDS I NEED TO STUDY	Bounce a ball 100 times, as you count from 1 to 100.	Find out if the library has a summer reading program.	Read a picture book today.	Go outside and study the clouds. What shape are they? Draw them.
Count to 100 by fives.	Write a letter to a friend or relative, and mail it.	How many words are in your Word Bank Box? Jeremy has 25.	Keep a journal of your day today.	Look through the newspaper today.
Ask someone to read a story to you.	Make a puppet. Plan a puppet show.	Print the ABCs today.	Read an OLD newspaper and circle all of the vowels.	Make up a poem about summer. Illustrate it.
Make a red, white, and blue picture.	Go outdoors. Look up at a tree. Count 100 leaves. Are there more?	Make a clock. Practice telling time.	Make a set of number addition flash-cards.	Read a story just for pleasure.
Read the cartoon page of the paper.	Get some exercise. Move like zoo animals.	Listen to TV news. Then repeat one story.	Work on your Word Bank. Darcy has 100 words.	Read the labels on food cans in the cupboard.

THE AUGUST BUSY BEAR

Spread out these activities throughout the month of August. Color the box when you finish the activity.

Set up a school with a friend or two.	Count to 100 by 2s.	Write your address and phone number.	Look at the grocery ads. Circle the items under a dollar.	Make a calendar for the month.
Read a story to a friend.	Find 50 stones and make a shape. Fill it in.	Sit outside and read a good book.	Jump 10 times. Skip 20 times. Hop 15 times.	Make a poster for your favorite book.
Take "Litter Walk" with bag and gloves.	Listen to the birds sing. Try to sing their song.	Read a story with a family member.	How is your Word Bank? Claire writes a word each day.	Brushing teeth UP and DOWN? Brush 3 times today.
Watch an educational TV program.	Keep a journal today.	Go on a "Reading Walk." What signs did you read?	Write and illustrate a story.	Practice subtraction facts!
Make a Shape Book.	Make a Color Book.	Work with addition and subtraction facts.	Start smiling! School is almost here!	Memorize a poem. Say it to someone else.